CASE*METHOD^{SM}

Tasks and Deliverables

About the Author

Richard Barker was born in Sheffield, England, in 1946. He went to Edinburgh University where he studied Chemistry, but realized that his interests lay outside the realms of pure science.

He has gained insight into many aspects of information systems through work in manufacturing industry and the Health Service, and the early introduction of database and data dictionary software whilst working with a major hardware company. Subsequently, Richard led a consultancy team specializing in strategic analysis and systems development using structured methods.

He is currently a main board director of ORACLE Corporation UK Limited, and a Vice President of ORACLE Europe, responsible for the Oracle system development method, CASE*Method, and the development of Computer-Aided Systems Engineering (CASE) and Application Package software using the ORACLE RDBMS. He established the UK Training Division to provide education for clients and Oracle staff alike in the use of Oracle products, methods and strategic thinking, and has lectured widely on network and relational database technology, distributed databases, CASE and user involvement in systems development.

Richard is married with three children, and lives in Berkshire, England.

Other Titles in the Series

*CASE*METHOD: Entity Relationship Modelling*   Richard Barker

CASE∗METHOD^{SM}

Tasks and Deliverables

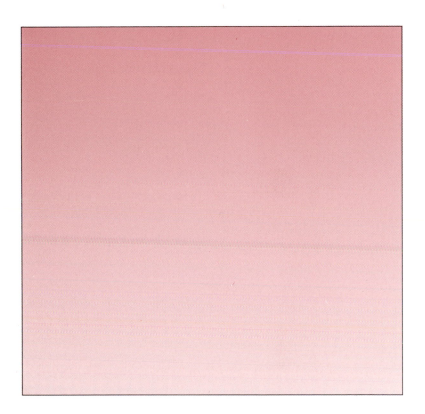

RICHARD BARKER

 Addison-Wesley Publishing Company

Wokingham, England • Reading, Massachusetts • Menlo Park, California
New York • Don Mills, Ontario • Amsterdam • Bonn • Sydney • Singapore
Tokyo • Madrid • San Juan • Milan • Paris • Mexico City • Seoul • Taipei

ORACLE®

The Relational Database Management System

Cover designed by Hybert Design & Type, Maidenhead.

Printed in the U.S.A. by R.R. Donnelley & Sons Company.

First printed in 1989.
Revised edition 1990 (published by Addison-Wesley). Reprinted 1991,
1992 and 1995.

Written by Richard Barker
   with contributions from Barbara Barker, Dai Clegg, Jeremy Davis,
   Chris Ellis, Mary Lomas, Sukhendu Pal and Gill Smith.

British Library Cataloguing in Publication Data
A catalogue record for this book is available from the British Library.

   ISBN 0–201–41697–2

Library of Congress Cataloging in Publication Data
Barker, Richard 1946–
       CASE Method : tasks and deliverables / Richard Barker.
          p.   cm.
       Includes bibliographical references.
       ISBN 0–201–41697–2
       1.   Computer-aided software engineering.   1. Title.
   QA76.758.B37   1990
   005.1--dc20   89-48834
                                                              CIP

When ordering this book through Oracle Corporation please quote the
Part Number 5156. Contact:

Oracle Corporation UK Ltd   Oracle Corporation
Oracle Park, Bittams Lane   20 Davis Drive
Guildford Road, Chertsey   Belmont, CA 94002
Surrey, KT16 9RG, UK   USA

Printed on Warren Recovery Matte, a paper consisting of at least
10% post-consumer waste with a total recycled content of 50%.

FOREWORD

Companies today are faced with daunting tasks. The economic and political barriers are changing rapidly. Market-share pressures on commercial and financial organizations are increasing, and both government and service industries are being forced to become more commercially aware.

One common response to these pressures is a perceived need for larger and more dominant companies. This is typically achieved by acquisition or merger, but the most successful organizations are those able to control rapid growth as they penetrate a market. Such growth is typically associated with rapid geographic market penetration and diversification into complementary products and services.

I do not believe that success in this market can be achieved purely by examining the profit and loss account or looking at the balance sheet. It obviously requires executives with insight and good decision-making capability. Appropriate and flexible organization structures must be put in place with focused incentive schemes and good remuneration packages. But I find the real differentiator these days is when an organization can focus its key information resource alongside its deployment of financial, physical and human resources.

The use of good structured development methods is needed to help management have the confidence that the information systems will be available on time **and** provide the accurate management information needed to make more-informed decisions. This information must therefore reflect the direction in which the business needs to go, as well as the day-to-day operations. At the same time, the method must not be a strait-jacket. It must enable the business to react quickly.

In this book, Richard has very successfully mixed the clear guidance that is necessary along with the cultural attitude that is required. I am always concerned when people religiously follow a prescriptive approach to doing a job without realizing why they are doing it and having the flexibility to modify the approach to meet the objectives and fit into the circumstances.

The second major problem I see in the market today is the technology explosion. Within Oracle we perhaps see the impact of this more than most companies. It is very clear that in the next few years all major users of computer technology will need to make some fundamental decisions as to their use of these new capabilities. In the hardware arena there are the massively-parallel processors, new very-high-density storage devices, sophisticated communication networks and cheap, high-resolution workstations with incredible processing power.

The software explosion will probably have even more effect. Relational database management systems are now accepted as the norm, object-oriented techniques are proliferating, CASE tools and the use of repository systems have been endorsed by all vendors, and there are new breeds of application packages, user interfaces, office systems and so on.

To me, this means that we can expect to be treating hardware more and more as a commodity, aided by the ability to use portable application systems and other software.

However, the companies that will be really successful are those which can take their requirement (from the analysis stage) and design an evolving architecture that can marry the appropriate combination of software technologies. Users do not really care whether they have the very best system that can be evolved. They want good, appropriate systems on time; and if the system happens to be made up of packages from two or three vendors, office systems from another and components built by their IS department, it must still look and behave like a coherent single system.

Many of the tasks covered in the book address these key issues, and it has been my experience that the most important of these is to have a clear and agreed strategic framework within which sound technology decisions can be made. Finally, I would advise you to look at the chapters on project control and quality assurance. These stress the point that assuring success is more about approaching the problem in the right way with the right people than the blind use of control procedures.

Geoff Squire
Chief Executive Officer, Oracle Europe

PREFACE

How do you write a book that usefully tells you what to do to produce a well-engineered solution, without it simply being a set of uninteresting checklists?

Well, I'm not sure anyone knows, but our objective was to distil into a relatively short book as much guidance as possible on **what** to do, with some practical advice and help on **how** to get it right. Other books in this series address a number of the most significant techniques referred to, such as entity relationship modelling, interviewing, presentation techniques and function modelling.

Tasks and Deliverables forms the heart or structure of CASE*Method. It has been derived from many years' collective experience delivering systems to clients and building software products. The primary thrust of the book is for a top-down approach, which reflects our strongly-held belief that any new or revised system must start off within the scope of what the users perceive as their future needs.

We were rather concerned that the book might be used purely as a prescriptive mechanism to set out a project plan. To alleviate that worry we have attempted to add a little of the culture that we have found helps us in the way we approach the work. A good example is when interviewing someone during analysis. Aim to complete the interview with a comprehensive and coherent picture of what the interviewee does, needs and believes in. You will then be able to create various models and requirements based on **understanding** rather than some form of wish list. Given true understanding you can often fill in gaps and make better decisions, thus speeding up the whole process.

Revised Edition

CASE*Method continues to evolve, and *Tasks and Deliverables* has been revised to take account of the latest advances in the field. We have also been very pleased to address feedback from many readers who kindly sent in comments and ideas. Please continue to send in your observations.

Two new chapters have been added to cover quality assurance and its implications in more detail, and to give more guidance on different sizes and types of project. In an ideal world you would be asked to devise a new system from start to finish; without the shackles of integrating with an old and, perhaps, badly-designed system, or trying to sort out the mess left by someone else, or having to cope with a mish-mash of different hardware and software that you personally would not have chosen in the first place. But this is the real world, and you may have to provide a rescue package or coexist with systems that still have some years of life to run.

We have omitted the appendix on data normalization from this edition. It is now dealt with in the *Entity Relationship Modelling* book. Appendices E and F on prototyping and feedback have been expanded from mere skeletons, and Appendix D has increased considerably as the CASE tools themselves have increased in number and scope.

Acknowledgements

Tasks and Deliverables was a team effort, with the leading members acknowledged in the list of writers. We could not, however, list all those colleagues and customers whose contributions have led to the evolution of CASE*Method itself. I would like to thank them for their help over the years. And to our readers, your comments are particularly welcome as a guide to further information you would find helpful.

Richard Barker
January 1990

CONTENTS

Foreword v

Preface vii

Chapter 1   **Introduction** 1-1

What is a System? 1-1

System Development 1-1

Building Systems 1-2

A Staged Approach 1-3

Ease of Estimation 1-3

Top-down Approach 1-4

Cross-checking 1-4

Standard Deliverables 1-4

No Substitution for Thinking 1-4

Generic Models 1-5

Independence from Technical Change 1-6

How to Use This Book 1-6

Chapter 2   **Carrying Out Projects with CASE*Method** 2-1

Overview 2-1

Target Readership 2-2

Role, Possible Job Type, Description 2-3

Use of Computer-Aided Systems Engineering (CASE) Tools . . 2-7

Understanding Your Project 2-9

Quality Assurance 2-12

Ready to Go 2-13

Chapter 3 **Strategy Stage** **3-1**

Aims and Objectives 3-1

Description 3-2

Key Deliverables 3-2

Critical Success Factors 3-3

Approach 3-3

List of Tasks 3-5

Tasks and Deliverables 3-6

Strategy Stage Summary 3-36

Chapter 4 **Analysis Stage** **4-1**

Aims and Objectives 4-1

Description 4-2

Key Deliverables 4-2

Critical Success Factors 4-2

Approach 4-3

List of Tasks 4-5

Tasks and Deliverables 4-6

Analysis Stage Summary 4-32

Chapter 5 **Design Stage** **5-1**

Aims and Objectives 5-1

Description 5-2

Key Deliverables 5-2

Critical Success Factors 5-2

Approach 5-3

List of Tasks 5-5

Tasks and Deliverables 5-6

Design Stage Summary 5-36

Chapter 6   **Build Stage** **6-1**

Aims and Objectives 6-1

Description 6-2

Key Deliverables 6-2

Critical Success Factors 6-2

Approach 6-3

List of Tasks 6-5

Tasks and Deliverables 6-6

Build Stage Summary 6-20

Chapter 7   **User Documentation Stage** **7-1**

Aims and Objectives 7-1

Description 7-2

Key Deliverables 7-2

Critical Success Factors 7-2

Approach 7-2

List of Tasks 7-4

Tasks and Deliverables 7-6

User Documentation Stage Summary 7-14

Chapter 8   **Transition Stage** **8-1**

Aims and Objectives 8-1

Description 8-2

Key Deliverables 8-2

Critical Success Factors 8-2

Approach 8-2

List of Tasks 8-5

Tasks and Deliverables 8-8

Transition Stage Summary 8-30

Chapter 9   **Production Stage** **9-1**

Aims and Objectives 9-1

Description 9-2

Key Deliverables 9-2

Critical Success Factors 9-2

Approach 9-2

List of Tasks 9-4

Tasks and Deliverables 9-6

Production Stage Summary 9-14

Chapter 10   **Project Management and Control** **10-1**

Introduction 10-1

Setting Up Any Project 10-1

Work Breakdown 10-2

Risk Containment 10-4

Categorization 10-4

Interviewing 10-7

Role Playing 10-7

Brainstorm Session 10-8

Cluster Analysis 10-9

Matrix Planning 10-11

Presentation 10-12

Different-sized Projects 10-13

Different Starting Points 10-17

Software Package Integration 10-18

Key Resource Management 10-19

Likely Problems 10-20

Summary 10-20

Chapter 11   **Quality Assurance** **11-1**

Quality 11-1

Quality Assurance 11-1

Quality Approaches 11-3

Quality Plan 11-4

The Audit 11-9

Summary 11-9

Appendices

Appendix A   **Summary of Tasks** **A-1**

Appendix B   **Standard Strategy Report Contents List** **B-1**

            Purpose B-1

            Standard Strategy Report Contents List B-2

Appendix C   **Set of Standard Forms** **C-0**

Appendix D   **Use of Oracle CASE Tools** **D-1**

            CASE*Dictionary D-1

            CASE*Designer D-1

            CASE*Generator D-2

            CASE*Project D-2

            CASE*Bridge D-2

            Overviews D-2

            Screenshots of Diagrammers D-6

            Workstation Use D-14

            Team Orientation D-14

Appendix E   **Prototyping in the Business System Life Cycle** **E-1**

            Use of Prototyping Techniques E-1

            A Word of Warning E-6

Appendix F   **Feedback Structure** **F-1**

Appendix G   **Checklists** **G-1**

            The System as a Whole G-2

            Strategy Study Checklist G-7

            Analysis Checklist G-10

            Design Checklist G-14

            Build Checklist G-17

            Glossary **Gl-1**

            Index **In-1**

1

INTRODUCTION

CASE*Method is a **structured** approach to carrying out the total task of developing systems to meet business needs.

What is a System?

No organization could function without some form of system or systems by which means its objectives are met. A system is often thought of as a named collection of computer processes that satisfy some functional need; for example, payroll, general ledger and order processing systems. The ideal systems, however, are a combination of manual and computer processes that elegantly fit into the way the business needs to run. Such systems will take into account the needs of many functional areas, especially where there would otherwise be duplication of data. They will also take into consideration the day-to-day **and** the management information needs of the organization.

Leading companies have such systems whose goals include:

- supporting the business needs
- supporting management decision making
- integration with other systems
- reacting to business and technology change
- acceptance and exploitation by employees, thus providing
- a competitive edge.

System Development

The development of such systems is far from easy. There are many problems to overcome in terms of the business, technologies, tools, techniques, and the attitude of the users and existing computer development staff.

Business problems vary from industry to industry, but they tend to include:

- the lack of a clear direction
- a rapid rate of change
- no commitment from senior management to systems
- conflicting requirements
- differences in management style
- multiple solutions to the same problem caused by amalgamation, differing levels of responsibility or lack of control.

The rapid evolution of technology has also caused problems with:

- the proliferation of micro-computers
- hardware that has a life-span of only two or three years
- a vast range of non-integrated software
- instant worldwide communication raising expectation levels
- tools emerging only recently to help control development.

But perhaps the most serious problems are those to do with **people**.

- People often do not know what they really want or need.
- They find it difficult to communicate with each other. Many people can talk well, but few are good at listening. Even when **people** apparently share a common language, errors in communication arise when they use the same words with different shades of meaning.
- System builders cannot (or will not) listen to their users and rarely build what is needed.
- System builders are often the last people to accept change in their own domain – the entrenched views of the data processing fraternity.

Building Systems

The task of building systems has a complex life-cycle, analogous to building a new office block. It is about creating and maintaining an architectural model of what is required; following a plan and life-cycle for the system, which goes through stages of understanding, requirement definition, design, construction, implementation, operation and review. The key to success in all of this is coming to terms with the real world, and understanding in detail what is needed for the business **before** selecting design alternatives and technology.

System building is an art.

CASE*Method (in the form of training classes, books, consultancy support and CASE software tools) moves it closer to being a system engineering process. This book, in particular, describes a staged approach to methodically engineer a business system by following a prescribed life-cycle.

A Staged Approach

A large number of tasks have to be carried out in a methodical manner to assure the success of any major system development. The tasks are grouped into major stages, each with clearly defined deliverables that are necessary for subsequent stages. CASE*Method, then, provides a framework for the life-cycle for the business system.

Figure 1-1
The Business System
Life Cycle

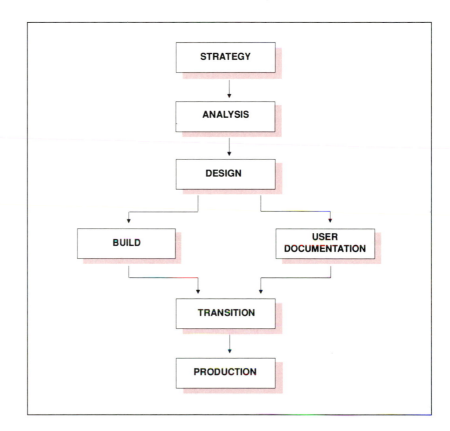

Ease of Estimation

Within each stage the tasks tend to be of short duration and can be estimated easily. Each task in turn is divided into a number of activities. The same task or activity, such as project administration, may be repeated several times for different purposes, as a consequence of which this book helps identify this frequency. During analysis this could be the number of people to be interviewed, whilst during implementation it could be the number of reports required.

Top-down Approach

It is **people** within an organization who collectively know what is actually needed, although they may find it difficult to articulate that need. To be successful, you must get the active participation of these key people throughout the development life-cycle. If the need is incorrectly determined (owing to an inadequate strategy study and poor analysis), no matter how beautifully written the final programs or manual procedures, the system will not satisfy the business requirement.

Cross-checking

The method incorporates many efficient cross-checking techniques to ensure accuracy and completeness. Structured diagrams are used to set out the understanding of the analyst or designer definitively. Standards must be applied to these diagrams to ensure that they can be fully understood by users and other development staff.

The method of presentation of diagrams and any other documentation produced needs to be carefully structured to promote understanding and encourage feedback.

Being definitive is a major virtue as it enables problems to be identified early on and quickly corrected.

Remember people are important. At all points in the development process, good communications between members of the team and other users will facilitate efficient cross-checking and keep the users happy and confident in your work.

Standard Deliverables

For each of the stages there is a set of things that must be produced, the standard deliverables. These **deliverables** must either constitute the final result of the engineering process or must be needed by subsequent stages. In many ways the term **acceptables** would be more pertinent: producing unacceptable deliverables is a waste of time and money. There will be certain key deliverables, which are listed in the overview for each stage, and other deliverables that are specific to your particular project. The deliverables produced during the strategy and analysis stages must be completely independent of any specific implementation technique, to give the designer the maximum opportunity to use the appropriate technology and to design for coexistence with current systems.

No Substitution for Thinking

Although CASE*Method is structured, it is vital not to regard it as a recipe. As a good analyst, or designer, **you** will not be tempted to rely on a mechanistic technique and forget to think for yourself. Lateral thinking, new ideas and innovation all contribute to the quality of the end-product (but avoid going off at a tangent!).

Generic Models

Businesses are often subject to reorganization (Oracle itself is no exception). To a large extent **what** is done will not have changed, although **who** does it and **how** may be different. The models used to define the business requirements must allow for reasonable changes in organization structure.

They must also be independent of all known solutions. The system must continue to function efficiently when, for example, new manufacturing, selling, management or clerical procedures are adopted.

Requirements should be modelled and defined in as generic a manner as possible; function requirements should define **what** is done, not how or by whom. The structure of the data must allow for changes in organization structure, and for current and perceived exceptions and limits.

The diagram below illustrates several of the major modelling techniques and how they overlap. Each of these models of the real world must fit within the context of the overall business direction, which is expressed by its objectives, priorities and critical success factors.

**Figure 1-2
Overlapping Modelling
Techniques**

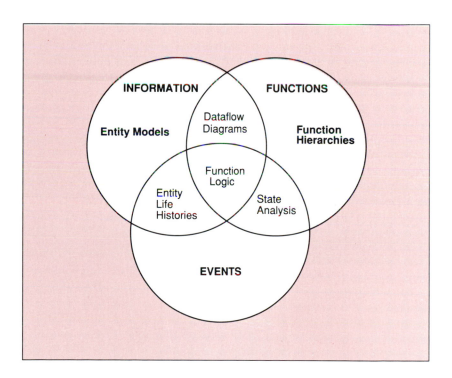

It is worth remembering that policy, both corporate and legislative, changes from time to time, so the definition of business requirement should **not** encompass policy rules. Provision for applying these should be built into the implementation.

Obviously, there are limits to the flexibility of any system. If the business whose system you have developed decides to change from being a provider of banking services to one that also deals in insurance and real estate the same statement of requirement is unlikely to apply.

Independence from Technical Change

It is vital that the deliverables produced during strategy and analysis be completely independent of the implementation techniques envisaged. The solution may embrace a combination of existing computer systems, manual procedures and packages, along with the database management system to integrate the whole.

Independence from both hardware and operating system environments ensures that the business will be able to protect its investment in the project you are developing, should the system be moved to a new, more appropriate or cost-effective hardware environment at a future date.

How to Use This Book

This book has been designed to act as a checklist for development staff carrying out application system development. A separate chapter covers each stage in the development life-cycle. The stage introduction sets out the primary objectives, deliverables and those factors which are critical to its success. An important aspect is the approach to the stage, which is usually illustrated by a diagram to convey the major thrust necessary.

The main body of each chapter is divided into facing pages, each of which covers a task within the stage. On the left the task is described along with its sub-activities. On the right inputs to the task, outcomes, estimating advice, resources and tools required, and applicable techniques are identified. Notes and quality assurance tips should be read before and during the task to help avoid common pitfalls.

It is essential that the project leader decides what needs to be done first, before using the task list to check for things that may be missing and producing a schedule or plan. A network of the tasks is also supplied in the introduction to each stage as guidance to the normal sequence of events. Subsequently, at project reviews the list may be used to check for completeness and quality.

To understand how to carry out these tasks and learn the techniques referenced, it is recommended that development staff are given the appropriate formal training.

Chapter

2

CARRYING OUT PROJECTS WITH CASE*METHOD

Overview

This book is a guide to carrying out a system development project with CASE*Method. It explains the need to understand your project to enable you to select the stages, tasks and activities you require. Each task is then described in some detail so that you can decide whether you need to perform it or not.

*CASE*Method Tasks and Deliverables* has been compiled from the experience of Oracle consultants on real projects, including building Oracle products. But all projects have their own 'features', so the material has been generalized to provide a comprehensive checklist and framework for planning, doing and controlling a 'standard' large project. Chapter 10 contains more information about handling real situations, including different-sized projects, and projects with different starting points.

It is strongly recommended that whatever the type of project you are about to undertake, you think about it carefully **before** this standard is used. You should list all the known or committed tasks, deliverables, timescales and resources available, and other aspects that may turn out to be unique to your project. Then, **and only then**, use this standard as a checklist and to provide a framework for the project.

Areas such as producing terms of reference and plans, performing project control and change control, and liaising with management and steering groups are subjects in their own right and are not covered in detail. You will, however, find them reflected in the tasks, so you can see where they fit in the overall project framework.

To enhance the practicality of this book, summaries and guidance material are included in the appendices. Many techniques are referred to in this book, such as entity relationship modelling, interviewing and normalization. How to carry out these techniques is covered by training classes and a set of further books in the CASE*Method series.

Target Readership

This book is for everyone who has some part to play in making projects successful! Every organization has its own set of job types and descriptions, so the following four pages describe the roles involved in projects, and make suggestions as to the possible job types that will fulfil them.

ROLE	POSSIBLE JOB TYPE	DESCRIPTION
Sponsoring user	Senior grade in the organization (e.g. departmental manager, director, vice-president)	Takes responsibility for quality of user input to the project, for resolving business issues, and for sign-off of each stage. Has to be sufficiently senior in the organization to make decisions and ensure commitment. Can be considered to be the 'user project manager'.
User	Potentially any job type (also known as end user)	A person who will be the eventual user of a new system, or responsible for that system in some way. Users are important as they provide quality input at any stage in the project. This may involve being interviewed, participating in a feedback, working side by side with analysts or designers, participating in the system test, writing the user manual, and so on.
User management	Senior grades in the organization	There is an optional role for a formal steering committee (or informal group of interested parties) to oversee the project in terms of ensuring that it is appropriate, cost-justified and well run. This role may overlap that of the auditor in some respects, but tends to have more of a 'work supervisor' connotation; for example, "Are project progress reports timely, accurate and satisfactory?"
Information Systems management	Any or all of: DP manager, information systems director, project manager, systems manager, technical services manager, operations manager, support manager, development manager	Responsible for approving the project scope and approach from the point of view of technical feasibility, adherence to standards and appropriateness to the overall Information Systems (IS) strategy. Involves checking plans and estimates, making Information Technology resources available, minimizing cross-project contention (e.g. over proposed changes that affect more than one project) and resolving technical or staff issues referred by the project leader.

ROLE	POSSIBLE JOB TYPE	DESCRIPTION
Project leader	Project manager, project leader, senior analyst	Responsible for all application work, project planning and control, putting the plan into action (including getting requisite sign-offs), keeping all parties informed of plans, progress and issues, managing the project team (including users directly involved). The role also includes ensuring the quality of deliverables, via an agreed quality assurance approach and by providing support to the project team (e.g. direct assistance, request for 'expert help', training).
Analyst	Business analyst, senior systems analyst, systems analyst, analyst programmer	Responsible for analyzing the business and identifying the user needs. The analyst will also go on to specify **what** the business requirement is that is to be met by any new or modified system, and to help define **how** a system should be implemented. Following design and build, the analyst is also involved during system testing and support of the user during the documentation and transition stages. There is a tendency to classify analysts either as 'business' or 'detailed/technical/data analysts' depending on whether they are predominantly involved in the early or later stages of the project (i.e. from the detailed specification point in the analysis stage onwards). Where responsibilities are split in this way, it is essential to ensure continuity, and also encourage each class of analyst to 'look beyond' their own involvement and understand the earlier/later stages, so that the work they produce is appropriate to the overall context.
Designer	Analyst programmer, technical analyst, chief programmer, senior programmer, designer, systems designer, system architect	Responsible for identifying and resolving design issues at any stage in the project, and for producing the program specifications and database design, that is, **how** the requirement is to be met. Designers may be involved in the strategy and analysis stages, to review technical constraints and expected performance, and discuss complex functions with the analyst and user. In the design stage, they work closely with the analysts and users to translate the requirement into a design, identifying and assisting trade-off decisions where the requirement can only be met at a price.

ROLE	POSSIBLE JOB TYPE	DESCRIPTION
		The designers will typically start with the production of a system architecture during the strategy stage. Subsequently, they may be involved in prototyping during analysis (to derive ideas), during design (to prove ideas) or during the build stage (to resolve construction issues via an iterative build approach). Analysts and designers should also work together to define what and how clerical and other procedures, training, transition and other aspects are to be implemented.
Implementor	Programmer, senior programmer, analyst programmer, builder	Responsible for program design, coding, unit testing, program documentation, assisting in system and acceptance test (running tests, bug fixing), assisting in operations hand-over (documenting and explaining the system for operations staff).
Auditor	Auditor, person or department responsible for security and control issues	Responsible for setting audit, security and control criteria and ensuring that the system meets them. At a higher level, there is a need to answer the question, "Is this a suitable system for this organization?", which may involve other issues such as legislative requirements, image, efficiency, appropriateness to the business, reliability (including contingency arrangements if the system fails), proven technology, and so on. Although users progress these issues, it is useful to assign an 'assessment' role to a third party.
Data administrator	Data administrator, senior analyst, technical staff member	Responsible for monitoring business models (whether corporate or separate project/system models), advising on data issues (e.g. impact analysis of a data change), defining access security standards and naming conventions, accepting models at the strategy and analysis stages (from the viewpoint of technical standards and applicability to the business). Typically, such a person is senior, with extensive knowledge of the business.

ROLE	POSSIBLE JOB TYPE	DESCRIPTION
Database administrator	Database administrator, systems programmer	Responsible for accepting the database design, agreeing database management system acquisition, performing or checking sizing results, acquiring requisite system software and storage devices, performing data change control, implementing the test and production databases/files. Typically, such a person also maintains a dictionary, or repository, such as CASE*Dictionary.
Technical staff member	Systems programmer, technical support programmer, technical analyst, etc.	Advises on technical issues, installs system hardware and software, provides library control for data and programs, assists cut-over, and helps diagnose and fix bugs where they involve system software or hardware.
Network administrator	Network controller, operations analyst, systems programmer, network analyst, technical analyst	Responsible for identifying required network architecture in terms of nodes, siting of processors, communications between nodes, protocols, and so on. Also runs, monitors and supports the network.
Operations staff	Operator, operations analyst	Responsible for setting up the required operations environment for system test, acceptance test and cut-over, and running the system at these points and thereafter. Provide agreed service levels to the user, recording and expediting faults (e.g. by calling in analysts, programmers), monitoring the system (deriving statistics for usage, performance, problems, machine utilization, etc.).

Use of Computer-Aided Systems Engineering (CASE) Tools

CASE*Method may be followed without any computer assistance, but the full potential of the method is more likely to be realized if many of the complex and error-prone tasks are performed with the support of a computer system developed for the purpose. CASE tools are available from many different vendors.

Figure 2-1
CASE Software
Architecture

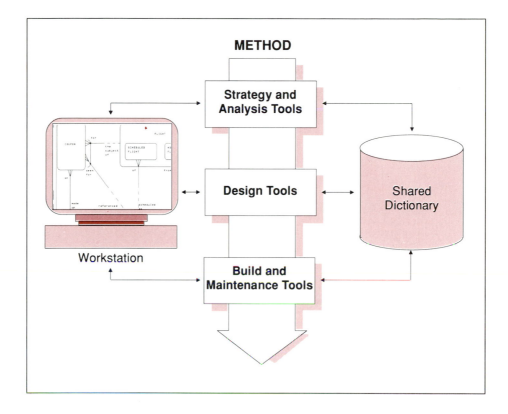

The diagram above illustrates typical architecture for an integrated set of CASE tools. On the left we have a powerful workstation environment through which an analyst, designer or other systems engineer may access information held in a shared dictionary/repository shown on the right. This dictionary is a database for all the information needed during the life-cycle of developing a system. In true database style, each element of information is entered once only and is then cross-referenced as appropriate.

Information may be added to the dictionary by means of either form-based interfaces or through interactive diagrammers. Consistency checking of this data is carried out by referential integrity procedures designed for this complex database.

Different tools are needed during the various stages in the life-cycle. These may be consistency and completeness checking utilities, facilities to take the deliverables from one stage and convert them ready for the next stage, or any other tools required to support the particular techniques being used.

The dictionary forms the nucleus of any CASE tool, acting as a multi-user database for many different users as shown below.

Figure 2-2
Dictionary Users

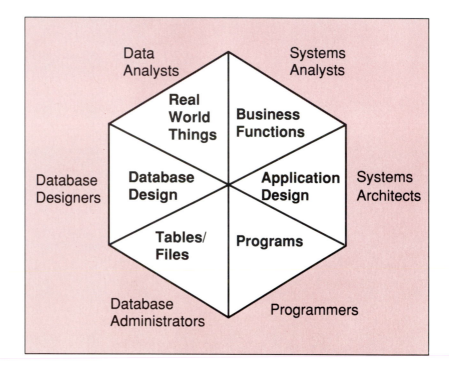

The data analysts may be particularly concerned with defining real world things, such as entities, attributes and relationships. The systems analysts, however, are more interested in recording what is done in the business, as defined by business functions. For complete requirement definition, both types of information must be fully cross-referenced and put into the context of the business organization structure and objectives.

Database engineers and system architects take the statement of requirement and devise new or improved database designs, application programs and systems architectures. The dictionary would then be used to hold the design decisions and assumptions along with the cross-references between data and the applications.

The database administrator then looks after the table and file definitions and ensures their correct implementation on the target database management system. The programs can also be recorded by the programmers and cross-referenced to the data they use and their application design. These program definitions will then be coded or generated to provide the required computer system.

In reality, there are many other people who use the dictionary, such as the users, project leaders and system maintenance staff, and the outcome may well include clerical procedures along with the computer systems.

Understanding Your Project

There is no such thing as a standard project since the starting point, resources and approach can differ very much with circumstances. It is useful, however, to have a standard set of stages, tasks and activities to check against, to help you make informed (and justified!) choices as to what to include, omit or add.

You are aiming to identify the main work content and put it into an overall framework of stages/tasks, such that there is a minimum overhead of control tasks and checkpoints, but sufficient to:

- Estimate the work.
- Split the work so that it can be allocated and supervised.
- Obtain timely information on progress and problems.
- Ensure quality via review of plans and deliverables.
- Keep everyone concerned with the project informed and committed.

A modelling technique will provide something that people can react to, and a good way to model a project is to do a network diagram. This will:

- Highlight stages you propose to omit.
- Show up obvious missing tasks in a sequence.
- Clarify task dependencies for scheduling.
- Enable you to distinguish mainline tasks from control tasks, to check that you have the right balance. You can draw the types of task at different levels (e.g. mainline ones across the middle of the network) and assess whether the checkpoints fall at sensible times. Key checkpoints will become milestones for management control.
- Provide a focus for the team and users, for understanding and motivation.

A simplified network diagram for the strategy stage is shown overleaf, but remember it is only a 'sample' for you to react to.

Figure 2-3
Network Diagram
(Strategy Stage)

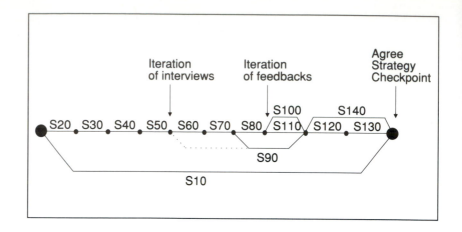

Key

S10	Project administration and management
S20	Scope the study and agree Terms of Reference
S30	Plan a strategy study
S40	Briefings, interviews and other information gathering
S50	Model the business
S60	Prepare for feedback session
S70	Conduct feedback session
S80	Consolidate results of feedback session
S90	Complete documentation of the business model
S100	Evolve information system architecture and make other recommendations
S110	Determine forward system development plan
S120	Prepare verbal report
S130	Report to senior management
S140	Prepare and deliver written report

Note: line length is not proportional to time.

Like all models, this model of your project must change when circumstances dictate: this is the reason for the checkpoint shown on the diagram above – to confirm approach and review the plan.

You should now have a pretty good picture of your project, having gone through a 'mental process' such as the one shown below. This is a mind map, which is just one technique for structuring thoughts quickly to help determine what to do next.

**Figure 2-4
Mind Map**

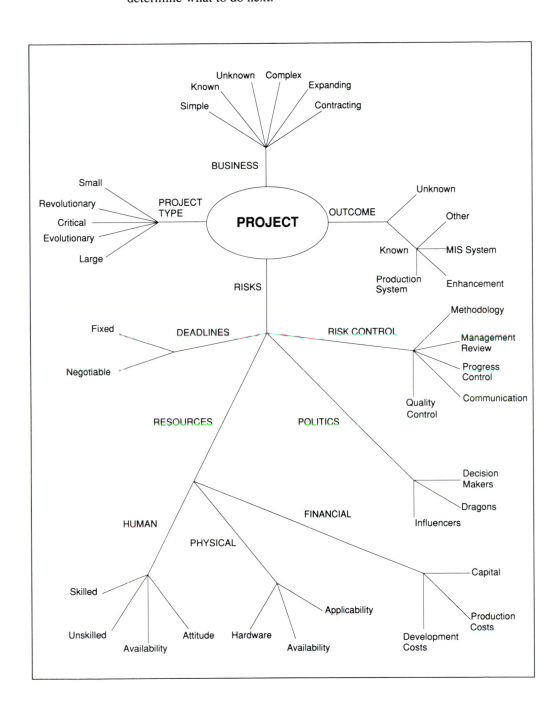

Quality Assurance

Projects should be subjected to stringent quality checks at all stages of the life-cycle. These should not be merely spot checks when and where the project manager has time: they should be planned in advance and resourced adequately. The project plan at each stage should include a Quality Plan, which indicates the points where quality checks will take place and the actions that are dependent on these checks. The details of the tasks at each stage of the life-cycle include hints on quality assurance. Some quality checks may carry the status of project sign-off, for example, the full detailed design specification. Each quality check should be scheduled before the intended end of a task, when there is still time to incorporate suggestions and corrections.

For major tasks (e.g. design and build database) and all tasks that involve frequent repetitions of the same core task (e.g. produce programs) quality checks should be carried out near the beginning and again near the end of the task. This helps to ensure that appropriate standards and a sound approach have been adopted from the beginning, as well as providing an opportunity later to inspect the work actually done. It is much simpler to correct a misunderstanding when twenty percent of the work is done than when eighty percent of the work is done.

The essence of effective quality assurance in software development is prevention rather than cure, hence the need for the Quality Plan. In addition, it is necessary to have the appropriate resources to conduct quality checks. The skills needed include:

- Full command of the technology and tools.

- The ability to grasp an alternative solution rapidly – and to distinguish between a poor solution and what is merely a different solution to a problem.

- The ability to identify, document and communicate weaknesses in the work under review succinctly and diplomatically!

- The ability to identify, document and communicate appropriate responses to these weaknesses.

Obviously people possessing all these skills are rare. In a department or company running many projects, it may be appropriate to dedicate a small number of people to these activities across all projects. However, even where such a service has been established, project leaders should participate in the quality checking process or they risk becoming isolated from the work of their team.

In the end, **real quality** comes from a thorough understanding of what is required, what types of solution can be implemented and the skill, professionalism and experience of the systems engineers involved.

Ready to Go

You know the work content, control structure and how to control quality; and whenever you have departed from the standard task list, you know why (and can justify it!). You have done a risk analysis, and you are prepared for **anything ...**

Chapter

3 STRATEGY STAGE

Aims and Objectives

The success of business systems design depends on achieving a clear understanding of the needs of the client organization, and the environment in which it operates. An understanding of the needs can only be acquired by a distinct separation of analysis ('what is to be done') from design ('how it is to be done').

Figure 3-1
The Strategy Stage in the Life Cycle

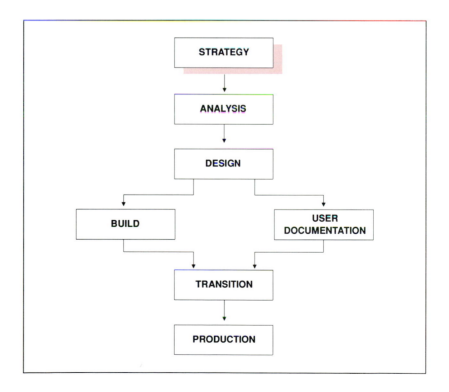

The objective of the strategy stage is to produce, with user management, a set of business models, a set of recommendations and an agreed plan for information systems development, which will serve the organization's current and future needs, while taking account of organizational, financial and technical constraints.

This objective cannot be achieved without first creating a good working relationship with all participants and subsequently gaining consensus on what forward direction is required.

This initial work must also provide an agreed, stable framework that can be used to focus the work of possibly several implementation phases, as they each progress through the stages of analysis, design, build, user documentation, transition and production.

Description

A complete, detailed analysis of an organization would be an excellent basis for evolving a plan for information systems development, but would be uneconomic to prepare. Instead, a strategy is derived by doing complete, but not detailed, analysis from which a broadly-based business model is built. Timescales are kept short, to maintain momentum and avoid results becoming out of date.

The deliverables of the strategy stage must be mutually agreed and sufficiently explicit for the client to recognize how the strategy relates to the business objectives and the circumstances under which it was derived, and to know when further reviews of the strategy are appropriate.

Key Deliverables

- *Statement of business direction*
  e.g. business objectives, priorities, constraints,
      critical success factors

- *Entity Relationship Diagram*

- *Function Hierarchy*

- *Recommendations*

- *Organizational, technology or other issues*

- *System boundary definition*

- *Possible system architecture*

- *Phased development plan*

- *Resource statement*

Critical Success Factors

In the short timescale recommended for a strategy study, it is vital to use every means possible to gain understanding of the business. These include:

- Active participation of key executives, opinion leaders, representative 'doers' and others who collectively understand what is needed.

- Early correction of opinions, ideas and the business model.

- A highly successful, thorough feedback session.

Any previous work and existing systems must be taken into account, since duplication of effort damages credibility.

Approach

The approach to carrying out a strategy study is to work very closely with key people to derive a common understanding of the functions and information needs of the organization. The approach is 'top down' and should start with the overall objectives of the organization.

The approach is methodical but not mechanistic. This means combining the discipline of a step-by-step approach with the flexibility to retrace the steps at any time to correct misunderstandings. Interviews, both in-depth and directional, are used to obtain information directly from those people who are concerned with the achievement of the organization's objectives.

Figure 3-2
The Approach to the
Strategy Study

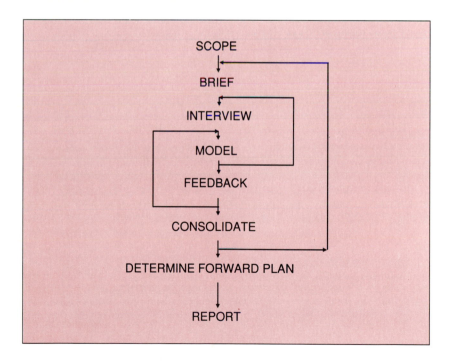

The modelling approach is to create three different perceptions of the business:

- corporate direction
- business functions
- information requirements.

These models must be understandable to all concerned, and group feedback sessions are used to gain complete agreement on the understanding of the business and the possible forward direction.

Figure 3-3
Evolving a Strategy

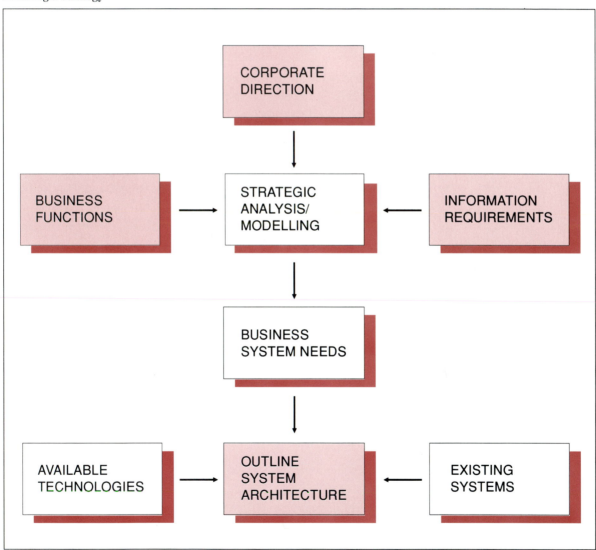

Strategies evolve, and circumstances and objectives may change with time. It is, therefore, not possible to define a prescriptive method for evolving strategy. Hence, it is essential to combine an open mind with the ability to investigate alternative means of achieving the business objectives within the given constraints, priorities and possible types of solution.

List of Tasks

Figure 3-4
Network Diagram of the
Tasks in the Strategy Stage

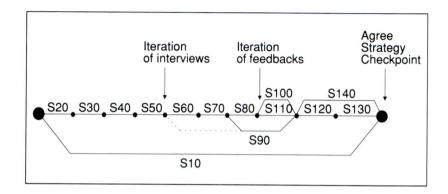

Key

S10	Project administration and management
S20	Scope the study and agree Terms of Reference
S30	Plan a strategy study
S40	Briefings, interviews and other information gathering
S50	Model the business
S60	Prepare for feedback session
S70	Conduct feedback session
S80	Consolidate results of feedback session
S90	Complete documentation of the business model
S100	Evolve information system architecture and make other recommendations
S110	Determine forward system development plan
S120	Prepare verbal report
S130	Report to senior management
S140	Prepare and deliver written report

Note: line length is not proportional to time.

Like all models, this model of your project must change when circumstances dictate: this is the reason for the checkpoint shown on the diagram above – to confirm approach and review the plan.

TASK 10
Project administration and management

DESCRIPTION

This is an ongoing task throughout the entire stage. It comprises control, reporting, quality assurance and administrative activities performed by the team against the terms of reference and plan that are produced in Tasks 20 and 30.

Activity 10 Monitor progress against plan and revise the plan if required.

20 Monitor the quality assurance results.

30 Liaise with other groups (auditors, technical staff, operations staff, data administrator and/or database administrator, other user groups, suppliers, etc.).

40 Monitor staff performance, give guidance, and so on.

50 Report progress.

60 Hold periodic progress meetings with user management and/or the steering group (e.g. monthly).

70 Answer queries; file any material including that for use in subsequent stages.

80 Ensure that strategists and the project leader have appropriate CASE and other tools.

90 Provide general administrative support (booking rooms, scheduling meetings, etc.). Reconfirm meetings and interviews, and thank attendees after the event.

QUALITY ASSURANCE

This is not a glamorous task, but contributes greatly to the success of the stage.

It is the project leader's responsibility to ensure that this task is performed well, which requires the ability to motivate all participants. A key role is ensuring that the strategists have the tools for their trade in a timely manner.

Deliverables

INPUTS
- plans
- minutes of meetings

OUTCOMES
System Deliverables
- *revised plans*

Control Information
- *progress reports*
- *plans*
- *minutes of meetings*

Other Outcomes
- *orderly documentation*
- *awareness of staff strengths/ weaknesses*
- *good liaison with other parties to the project*
- *filed notes for subsequent stages*
- *basis for future estimates*
- *a smooth, well-run project*

ESTIMATES
These activities may occupy 50% of the project leader's time for a team size of up to 5, especially in large institutional organizations.

RESOURCES
- project leader
- team members
- secretary

TECHNIQUES
- progress reporting
- project control
- man management
- patience and persistence

TOOLS
- quality assurance checklist
- timesheet forms
- progress reporting forms
- change control forms

CASE tools
- estimating and progress monitoring tools

NOTES and COMMENTS

Since there is often no formal regular progress meeting in this stage, it is important to ensure that people are kept informed and work closely with each other to produce consistently integrated results. The project leader needs to assert strong leadership, since this is a short but intensive stage.

Ensuring that senior people **actually** attend interviews and meetings can be very difficult; the support of top management is essential.

TASK 20
*Scope the study
and agree Terms
of Reference*

DESCRIPTION

This task encompasses agreeing the basis and scope of the strategy study.

Activity 10 Define the scope of the study in terms of current organization, constraints and company culture.

20 Define and agree the project objectives, constraints and deliverables; in particular, the contents of the strategy report.

30 Estimate the numbers of in-depth interviews, directional interviews, feedback sessions and agree target dates.

40 Define staffing requirements, project management and control responsibilities.

**Figure 3-5
Scoping a Study**

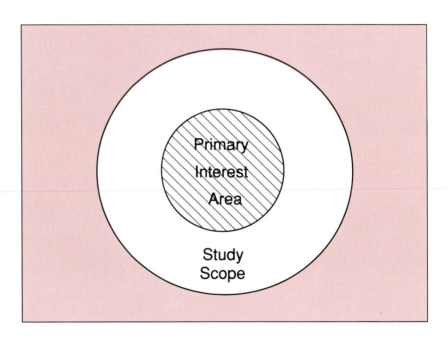

QUALITY ASSURANCE

The Terms of Reference will be checked for feasibility by Information Systems management and for acceptability by users.

Deliverables

INPUTS
– direction and ideas from sponsoring user
– indications of budget and timescale
– organization charts

OUTCOMES
System Deliverables
– *none*

Control Information
– *Terms of Reference for strategy study*

Other Outcomes
– *initial views on timescales*

ESTIMATES
Allow time to acquire sufficient business awareness to judge feasibility of the scope/timescales given the likely problems for this type of business (area).

Typical effort varies between 4-10 man days, dependent on the level of management commitment, understanding of the issues and factors to be considered.

RESOURCES
– project leader
– analysts
– sponsoring user

TECHNIQUES
– meetings

TOOLS
– previous example of Terms of Reference to use as a guide
– estimates for this stage

NOTES and COMMENTS

The scope must be reviewed to ensure that it is wide enough to make the study meaningful: if major interface areas are omitted the strategy may be so constrained that it has to be redone later with a wider scope (see diagram opposite).

Ensure that you have identified the key people and opinion leaders, and any other groups with an interest in the business (area), for example, auditors. The number of in-depth interviewees varies, dependent upon the scale of the study, from around six for a small study, twelve for a medium and eighteen for a large project. Laws of diminishing returns set in above these numbers. Other users are covered by directional interviews, with similar numbers interviewed according to the size of the project.

Staff skills should also be assessed and an appropriate judgement made on timescales.

Tasks

TASK 30

Plan a strategy study

DESCRIPTION

This task encompasses preparation for the study (background reading, scheduling, briefing).

Activity 10 Carry out background reading and identify areas of investigation.

20 Identify with the sponsoring user the interviewees for in-depth interviews (2-4 hours each) and obtain profiles.

30 Identify the interviewees for directional interviews (0.5-1 hour each).

40 Schedule briefing session(s), interviews and feedback session(s), quality assurance sessions and the final report meeting, and then lock down the diaries of the participants. Note: this is repeated for each group of 5-8 interviewees.

50 Identify and schedule any industry or other specialists to help in checking detail and evolving appropriate strategy.

60 Set up a project framework book or dictionary with sections for each strategy deliverable and for good ideas.

70 Brief staff.

QUALITY ASSURANCE

The interviewees must represent the minimum number of people to encompass the entire scope, with a degree of overlap for 'check and balance'. A subset of this group must also be in a position to make and/or approve a subsequent forward strategy.

Information Systems management must approve feasibility of the plan. Users must approve acceptability.

Deliverables

INPUTS
- annual report
- brochures
- business plans
- overviews of existing systems
- organization charts
- interviewee profiles

OUTCOMES
System Deliverables
- *none*

Control Information
- *phased, costed study plan with identified resources*
- *project control and quality control plans*
- *list of interviewees and specialists*

Other Outcomes
- *awareness of user profiles, staff skills*
- *project book and/or dictionary*

ESTIMATES
Allow time for team briefing, which may include a review of methods and approach, and some initial 'internal' interviews (e.g. of users assigned to the project – see Notes). Allocate time for a spare interview for each 6 planned.

RESOURCES
- project leader
- sponsoring user
- analysts
- budget

TECHNIQUES
- project planning

TOOLS
- CASE*Method task list

CASE tools
- application system definition screen

NOTES and COMMENTS

'Staff' should include users assigned to the study, for example, a user representative. Background reading may include other studies done, questionnaires, current systems, and so on. The amount of emphasis to be placed on this must be agreed.

Directional interviews are a useful source of information from interviewees who have very little time, are in line management positions and are in a position to influence the business, but who would not otherwise be a primary source for detailed information gathering.

The intention is to involve the minimum number of people who collectively know what is done now and what needs to be done in the future.

TASK 40
*Briefings,
interviews and
other information
gathering*

DESCRIPTION
This task covers interviews and processing of the information obtained.

Activity 10   Brief the interviewee(s) and confirm the interview and feedback session dates.

20   Prepare for an interview by reading around the subject, preparing open and checklist questions, and preparing the interview environment.

30   Carry out an interview and collect any useful documents suggested by interviewees.

40   Consolidate the results of an interview and read relevant suggested documents: summarize; prepare initial business model including aims, objectives, management statements, performance measures, and so on; check the current situation where possible.

50   Prepare a rough Function Hierarchy and Entity Relationship Diagram.

60   Record entities, their synonyms and statements of significance, terms and their definitions in a dictionary, and file any good ideas or suggestions bearing on strategy or on subsequent stages. Record a few relevant examples for use in subsequent feedback sessions. Define domains for attributes that are mentioned frequently and are of key importance to running the business.

QUALITY ASSURANCE

Briefing should have engendered interest, removed fears and confirmed timescales. Avoid the use of jargon.

Interviews should have demonstrated competence and, in a single process, gained in-depth knowledge.

The project leader must ensure that interviews are thorough by checking notes for scope/content. If the quality of information given seems inadequate, the sponsoring user should be consulted. It may be necessary to substitute interviewees or do extra interviews.

Deliverables

INPUTS
- the knowledge of the interviewees
- documents provided by interviewees

OUTCOMES
System Deliverables
- *consolidated interview notes*
- *initial business model and definitions*
- *rough Function Hierarchy*
- *rough Entity Relationship Diagram*
- *useful examples from the business*

Control Information
- *better knowledge of scope, which may indicate a need to schedule more interviews*

Other Outcomes
- *interview question checklists (from interview preparation)*

ESTIMATES
Using 2 staff for each in-depth interview, preparation takes one man day, the interview takes one man day and consolidation takes 1-2 man days each.

Directional interviews only require one member of staff, and typically take 0.5 man days in total to carry out and consolidate.

RESOURCES
- analysts
- users

TECHNIQUES
- interviewing
- consolidation
- modelling

TOOLS
- interview question checklists

CASE tools
- terminology definition screen
- entity/attribute definition screens or entity relationship diagrammer
- function hierarchy definition screen or diagrammer
- domain definition screen

NOTES and COMMENTS

Ensure that the interviewees remain interested and that interviews are not interrupted.

Don't forget to slay dragons! People who could politically or technically undermine any future strategy need to be (or feel) involved.

Consolidation is very important, and can be done as a group exercise to ensure that everyone is aware of the implications of the information obtained and to spark off ideas and generic modelling.

TASK 50
Model the business

DESCRIPTION

This task prepares a consolidated model of the business and checks for accuracy.

Activity 10 Develop the business direction in terms of business objectives, aims, priorities, constraints, business strengths, weaknesses, threats, opportunities and any identifiable performance indicators or critical success factors.

20 Develop the function model in terms of a Function Hierarchy.

30 Develop the entity model in the form of an Entity Relationship Diagram, and complete the entry of entities, their synonyms, descriptive attributes and statements of significance in the dictionary.

40 For large organizations, identify key business locations and business units. Subsequently, business unit matrices may need to be drawn up for:

- business function: business unit

- entity: business unit

- business unit: business/geographic location.

50 Summarize any ideas for future system direction in terms of system aims, objectives, priorities, technical and resource constraints.

60 Initiate a peer-group quality check of the business model and discuss with industry or other specialists if appropriate.

QUALITY ASSURANCE

The project leader must ensure that the models represent understanding of the business and conform to standards. External quality assurance by a peer is highly desirable.

Cross-check that each element of business direction is supported by business functions and information needs. Cross-check entities to functions. Identify and resolve common functions and information needs for twenty or thirty really important functions and check them in more detail.

Detail function logic is rarely used during the strategy stage, unless a particular complex function is fundamental to the business and needs full definition before a strategy can be evolved.

Deliverables

INPUTS
- interview notes
- rough Function Hierarchy and Entity Relationship Diagram
- brain power!

OUTCOMES
System Deliverables
- *business direction, e.g. objectives*
- *function model: Function Hierarchy, other diagramming types (as required)*
- *information model: Entity Relationship Diagram, entity significance, synonyms, key domains, a few attributes*
- *business locations, business units and matrices*
- *glossary of other terms*

Control Information
- *statement of quality of the business model*

Other Outcomes
- *ideas to develop for strategy recommendations*
- *ideas for possible system components*

ESTIMATES
Allow time to draw, discuss, review, redraw ... several iterations of Activities 10-40.

Schedule the time of a very skilled modeller to help for a couple of days during this period.

Typical effort for the whole task varies between 4-12 man days.

RESOURCES
- analysts
- computerized workbench
- industry specialist

TECHNIQUES
- function decomposition
- other function diagramming techniques if particularly relevant, e.g. event modelling or dataflows
- entity modelling
- matrix modelling
- generic modelling
- cluster analysis

TOOLS
- paper and template
- white board and dry markers
- entity and function diagramming rules and conventions

CASE tools
- screens or diagrammers for functions, entities, business locations, business units, matrices, terminology
- function logic or action diagrams

NOTES and COMMENTS

The purpose of a function model is to show clearly what the organization does, or needs to do, independently of how it can be done or by whom. The model is grouped in the form of a hierarchy, reducing the number of common functions to a minimum. Cluster analysis can also help in this process (see Chapter 10). During the strategy phase only three or four levels of the function decomposition are normally required. But no lower level information is discarded: it is kept for use in the detailed phases of analysis and design. Additional diagram types may be needed to explore complex function dependency or the detail of a function.

Tasks

TASK 60
Prepare for feedback session

DESCRIPTION
This task provides everything needed for the feedback.

Activity 10 Decide the issues to be resolved and how to introduce them.

20 Decide the objectives and structure of the session, including the breakdown into subject areas for presentation (see Appendix F).

30 Prepare visual aids. These will normally cover a combination of functions, entity relationship build-up slides and business examples, each of which contributes towards defining a subject area in detail. Other areas include introductions, business objectives and issues to be resolved.

40 Prepare the printed handout of the Function Hierarchy.

50 Prepare an agenda to sustain interest through the session.

QUALITY ASSURANCE
Does the feedback session have scheduled 'high spots' to keep the interest going and to illustrate relevance to the **users'** needs?

The project leader must ensure that this session is valuable, that it is well prepared, appropriate to the audience, and has achievable objectives.

Deliverables

INPUTS
- examples from the business
- Entity Relationship Diagram
- Function Hierarchy
- business direction statements

OUTCOMES
System Deliverables
- *none*

Control Information
- *issues to be resolved at feedback*

Other Outcomes
- *visual aids,
  e.g. entity 'build-up' slides*
- *questions and issues to be resolved during the session*
- *function decomposition handout*
- *feedback agenda and arrangements*

ESTIMATES
Typical effort varies from between 4-10 man days, dependent on complexity and skill levels.

RESOURCES
- project leader
- analysts

TECHNIQUES
- presentation structuring

TOOLS
- photocopier and transparencies
- see Appendix F for possible structure of feedback session

CASE tools
- diagrammers
- function reports

NOTES and COMMENTS

The feedback session is a most important part of the study, and it is important for all participants to realize that it is a step in the method and not a final presentation of results.

The models are presented for criticism and amendment, and, if necessary, the interview/model/feedback loop must be repeated several times until agreement is reached. It is important to reinforce the objectives of the feedback. It may not be possible to achieve consensus in one go, but the session should result in understanding and agreed actions (e.g. to do further modelling/feedback).

It has been found to be counter-productive to issue copies of the Entity Relationship Diagrams or build-up slides prior to or during the feedback sessions. Ideally they should be sent out **after** the event to confirm the understanding that has been gained.

TASK 70
*Conduct
feedback session*

DESCRIPTION
This task results in rigorous checking of the work to date and provides the basis of the recommendations (to be developed in Task 100).

Activity 10 Set the scene with the objectives of the meeting so that everyone understands what has to be achieved.

20 Present a summary of the study, progress to date and the approach adopted.

30 Present the management aims and objectives, performance measures and pertinent issues.

40 Present the business model, one subject area at a time. The presentation for each area should cover the business objectives, Function Hierarchy (top levels), Entity Relationship Diagram for the area and relevant examples.

50 Present potential recommendations to test the reactions of the participants. (Often done during Activity 40.)

60 Record the accepted alterations and outstanding issues; agree the overall business information needs and the substance of the recommendations.

QUALITY ASSURANCE

One person should be allocated to ensure that group dynamics are catered for, thinking in terms of questions such as:

"Is everyone involved?"
"Does everyone understand?"
"Do we need a break?"
"Would an example help here?"

The project leader must ensure that the time is used to generate maximum information and motivation of users, and to test ideas and relevance of the business model.

Quality will be seriously affected if more than eight to ten users are in the group, and if more than one or two attend who have not been the subject of an in-depth interview.

Deliverables

INPUTS
– feedback agenda
– slides
– control copy of visual aids

OUTCOMES
System Deliverables
– *required changes to models*

Control Information
– *awareness of how near to completion/acceptance the findings are*

Other Outcomes
– *amended visual aids*
– *feedback notes*
– *management consensus*

ESTIMATES
Each participant needs to schedule a full day.

Activity 10	<20 minutes
Activity 20	<10 minutes
Activity 30	<45 minutes

Activity 40   typically takes between 30-90 minutes per major subject area.

The total session will thus tend to take between 4-6 hours, excluding breaks.

RESOURCES
– project leader
– analysts
– users
– copious refreshments
– sense of humour

TECHNIQUES
– group interview techniques
– presentation techniques

TOOLS
– flipchart
– overhead projector, pens, etc.

NOTES and COMMENTS

A good feedback session is the high point of a strategy study. To achieve this end, it is therefore vital to strive for consensus, leave few issues unresolved and keep the relevance and interest high.

During this activity 'business level prototyping' may occur, when the business requirement may be remodelled interactively by competent analysts.

Remember the session is to give feedback of **your** understanding and **also** to **gain** feedback of any changes necessary. **You** must be receptive to and indeed encourage criticism and changes from all participants.

TASK 80
Consolidate results of feedback session

DESCRIPTION

This task ensures that all results of the feedback are incorporated in the strategy.

Activity 10 Correct the master copies of the visual aids, and distribute copies to feedback attendees and other interested and informed parties, such as previous feedback attendees.

20 Request, chase and incorporate further comments, based on revised feedback copies.

30 Revise the records of management aims and objectives, performance measures and record the resolutions of issues, and the reactions to the substance of recommendations.

40 Revise the full Entity Relationship Diagram and the records of entities, terms and functions held in the dictionary.

QUALITY ASSURANCE

The project leader must ensure that all information gained at the feedback is used and all user points followed up to their satisfaction.

Deliverables

INPUTS
– marked-up control copy from feedback
– annotated feedback slides

OUTCOMES
System Deliverables
– *amended business model*
– *amended Entity Relationship Diagram*
– *amended Function Hierarchy*

Control Information
– *none*

Other Outcomes
– *distributed, corrected feedback copies*

ESTIMATES
Allow enough time to revise models, typically 2-4 man days. This is not a trivial task.

RESOURCES
– project leader
– analysts

TECHNIQUES
– modelling

TOOLS
CASE tools
– entity relationship diagrammer
– function hierarchy diagrammer
– terminology definition screen

NOTES and COMMENTS

This may include further working sessions with the users.

Until this point you must maintain an open mind. From this point onwards, you may start to firm up on ideas based on the consensus gained from the feedback.

TASK 90
*Complete
documentation of
the business model*

DESCRIPTION
This task ensures that all information is complete and in a form that allows it to be used subsequently.

Activity 10 Enter synonyms for entity names, relationships and important attributes in the dictionary. Set up cross-references between functions and the entities they use.

20 Print reports required from the dictionary, collate and edit to produce a business model report if required.

30 Collate any other useful material gained during the course of the study (e.g. good ideas filed as input to subsequent stages).

QUALITY ASSURANCE

Relevance, completeness and accuracy are the keys to the success of this activity.

The project leader must ensure that documentation is completed to standards. A participating user may help to ensure the relevance of the information, for example, by checking printed reports. Remember, the only tangible result of this stage is good documentation.

Deliverables

INPUTS
– draft business models
– dictionary reports and screens
– rugged determination to get it right!

OUTCOMES
System Deliverables
– *standard documentation set*

Control Information
– *statement on completeness and consistency*

Other Outcomes
– *ideas filed for subsequent stages*

ESTIMATES
Allow time to complete and check documentation, which typically can take from 1-4 man days.

RESOURCES
– project leader
– analysts
– typists

TECHNIQUES
– quality assurance

TOOLS
– client installation IS documentation standards
– Standard Strategy Report Contents List (Appendix B)

CASE tools
– entity relationship diagrammer
– function hierarchy diagrammer
– attribute definition screen
– lexical analyzer
– diagram print/plot facilities
– reports for entities, functions and their interrelationships

NOTES and COMMENTS

Make every effort to ensure good grammar, correct spelling and a high level of readability. A session can be ruined by mis-spelling the name of the most senior attendee! Try to eliminate jargon and ambiguity.

Use a CASE lexical analyzer to scan function descriptions and automatically set up cross-references to entities directly by name, or indirectly by any synonyms you have set up.

TASK 100

*Evolve
information
system architecture
and make other
recommendations*

DESCRIPTION

This task uses the information gained to produce a system architecture, which is normally the primary recommendation of the study. (See the diagram opposite.) Other recommendations are prepared.

Activity 10 Identify the business needs and priorities, and logical dependencies.

20 Select application areas and system boundaries in terms of the function model.

30 Examine existing systems to determine their future applicability, coexistence and transition issues, and acquire information on volumes and frequencies. For unavailable volumetrics, work with the users to determine likely numbers for all key functions and high volume entities.

40 Identify possible technologies, for example, hardware, packages and other software.

50 Identify possible alternative solutions for each application area, examine the feasibility of each and reject or defer those which are technically or economically unfeasible. If necessary, write separate, fully-costed feasibility reports for alternative solutions or tender for proposals from third-party organizations.

60 Present, discuss and amend the system architecture in the light of feasibility studies and discussions.

70 Make recommendations for the current or future system, the business, the organization or any other areas, as requested in the Terms of Reference or during the feedback session.

continues

Figure 3-6
Evolving an Information
System Architecture

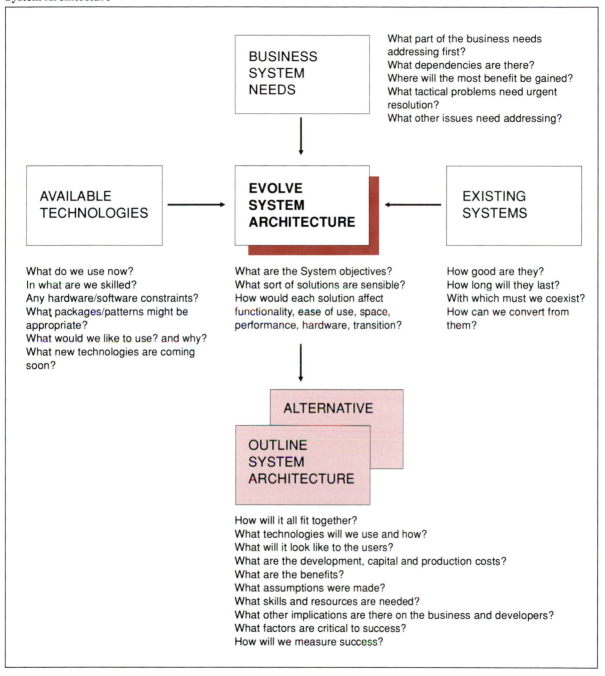

BUSINESS
SYSTEM
NEEDS

What part of the business needs
addressing first?
What dependencies are there?
Where will the most benefit be gained?
What tactical problems need urgent
resolution?
What other issues need addressing?

AVAILABLE
TECHNOLOGIES

**EVOLVE
SYSTEM
ARCHITECTURE**

EXISTING
SYSTEMS

What do we use now?
In what are we skilled?
Any hardware/software constraints?
What packages/patterns might be
appropriate?
What would we like to use? and why?
What new technologies are coming
soon?

What are the System objectives?
What sort of solutions are sensible?
How would each solution affect
functionality, ease of use, space,
performance, hardware, transition?

How good are they?
How long will they last?
With which must we coexist?
How can we convert from
them?

ALTERNATIVE

OUTLINE
SYSTEM
ARCHITECTURE

How will it all fit together?
What technologies will we use and how?
What will it look like to the users?
What are the development, capital and production costs?
What are the benefits?
What assumptions were made?
What skills and resources are needed?
What other implications are there on the business and developers?
What factors are critical to success?
How will we measure success?

For Deliverables for Task 100, see page 3-27.

continued
TASK 100
Evolve
information
system architecture
and make other
recommendations

DESCRIPTION

This task uses the information gained to produce a system architecture, which is normally the primary recommendation of the study. Other recommendations are prepared.

QUALITY ASSURANCE

Volumetric information must be rigorously checked for consistency against existing systems, and understanding gained by questionnaires and the gut feeling of those involved.

It is **vital** at this strategic stage that there is at least **one** feasible means of implementing any recommendations or strategy. The expectations of users and management need to be contained within that viable boundary.

Predicted performance and sizings must be compared with other comparable systems, and factors added for growth and development.

The project leader must ensure that the strategy is reviewed extensively, using peer-group checks, external quality assurance (if required) and test marketing of ideas to the management concerned. Industry specialists, organizational experts or management consultants may be useful at this stage to ensure that any recommendations fit the business, and that the infrastructures are in place to enable them to be put into practice. Check the ideas from the viewpoint of different users, operational consequences, transition from existing systems, examination of possible bottlenecks, acceptability, flexibility to change, integrity, security and any other relevant aspect. There should be no shocks!

Deliverables

INPUTS
- consolidated business models and business direction
- existing system documentation
- existing technology
- strategy statements
- ideas from potential vendors
- Terms of Reference

OUTCOMES
System Deliverables
- *recommended and alternative system architectures, by application system area, with priorities, dependencies, assumptions, etc.*
- *other recommendations*
- *system boundaries between different application systems*
- *optional feasibility reports and vendor proposals*

Control Information
- *list of unresolved issues*

Other Outcomes
- *none*

ESTIMATES
Allow time to draft, review, revise and check the architecture.

The involvement of 2 or 3 highly experienced and objective system architects is recommended. This task is not easy and the effects can be wide reaching.

RESOURCES
- project leader
- business analysts
- system architects
- industry specialist

TECHNIQUES
- feasibility study techniques
- systems sizing
- peer-group checking

TOOLS
CASE tools
- default database design, sizing and index utilities

NOTES and COMMENTS

There are a number of techniques available to help thinking:
- S.W.O.T. analysis (of strengths, weaknesses, opportunities and threats)
- Critical success factors (and related concepts such as key performance factors) which lead to performance indicators, and hence to information needs.

The organizational, financial and technical constraints must be considered, and stated. Evolution of the system architecture is strongly guided by management opinion: sound methods and tools act as catalysts to the process and, if necessary, the end-product is presented in a formal report. Where the constraints affect the implementation plan, the proposed architecture or any other recommendation, they should be highlighted in the strategy report.

Recommendations may cover a wide range of topics, which might include:
- a suggested new organization for Information Systems
- new jobs to be set up, for example, data administrator
- training required for Information Systems staff and users
- when existing systems should be reviewed or phased out
- the sequence of implementation around a geographically-distributed organization.

It is impossible to give guidelines for other recommendations that cover business issues.

Tasks

TASK 110
Determine forward system development plan

DESCRIPTION
This task translates the recommendations into a development plan.

Activity 10 Define the scope of the system development plan and of each application area to be included, and the Terms of Reference for the subsequent development phases.

20 Subdivide each application area into units of work at successive levels, resulting in activities with dependencies identified.

30 Estimate the resources required to complete each activity.

40 Produce an activity time schedule and resource aggregation against it.

50 Set/reset the levels of resource availability and produce a forward schedule to finite capacity; repeat until an acceptable schedule is achieved.

60 Present, discuss and amend the system development plan and provide costings.

Figure 3-7
Typical Phased Implementation Plan

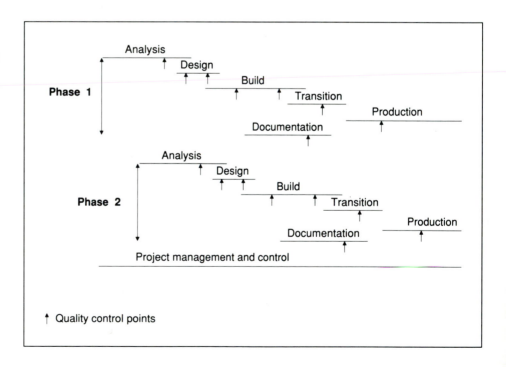

↑ Quality control points

Deliverables

INPUTS
- outline system architecture
- estimates from similar projects
- other recommendations

OUTCOMES
System Deliverables
- *phased development plans for each application area*
- *resource statement*

Control Information
- *project control and quality assurance framework*
- *Terms of Reference for subsequent development phases*

Other Outcomes
- *none*

ESTIMATES
Allow time to draw, discuss and revise plans. Depending on complexity, this task can vary from 4 or 5 man days to 20 or more.

RESOURCES
- project leader
- analysts

TECHNIQUES
- project planning
- time scheduling
- resource aggregation
- forward scheduling to finite capacity

TOOLS
- Tasks and Deliverables: Analysis Stage (Chapter 4) Design Stage onwards (Chapters 5-9)
- project control standards

CASE tools
- project planning tools

NOTES and COMMENTS

The plan will be detailed for the next stage and outline for subsequent stages. Cost analysis must be done to the level required by the user, but all figures are provisional at this stage. If the user requires to examine the investment aspects of the project (rate of return etc.), it is best to involve financial management staff.

The plan must conform to the standards within the installation.

TASK 120
Prepare verbal report

DESCRIPTION

This task reports the combined, recommended system architecture and the development plan, which together comprise the strategy, for management appraisal.

Activity 10 Obtain copies of all material and results gathered during the stage, including models, dictionary reports, feedback results, system architecture, development plans, and so on.

20 Ensure that all documents are complete and up to date.

30 Prepare a draft strategy report as a control copy.

40 Develop a structure for formal verbal presentation, noting the source of material covering all relevant aspects of the study.

50 Prepare slides and handouts, particularly identifying the relevance of the proposed strategy to the business. High-level function dependency diagrams and/or dataflow diagrams are useful to aid communication with senior management.

60 'Dry run' the presentation with members of your own senior management, asking them to be objective in their criticism, ideally acting in the role of user management.

QUALITY ASSURANCE

The verbal report is a formal presentation of findings. Ensure that the material is logically structured and will provide the sponsoring users with everything they need to know to allow decisions about further action to be taken.

Carry out a final cross-check to ensure that all the requirements in the strategy Terms of Reference have been correctly catered for.

Deliverables

INPUTS
- all the material collected during the stage
- material from feedback sessions

OUTCOMES
System Deliverables
- *none*

Control Information
- *issues to be resolved for development to commence*
- *draft strategy report as a control copy*
- *business issues to be addressed by the strategy*

Other Outcomes
- *visual aids*
- *presentation agenda*
- *handouts*

ESTIMATES
Preparation will take at least one day per staff member participating in the report. The total effort is dependent on scope, complexity and skill levels.

RESOURCES
- project leader
- analysts
- your own senior management

TECHNIQUES
- use of visual aids
- presentation structuring
- function dependency diagramming
- dataflow diagramming

TOOLS
- Standard Strategy Report Contents List (Appendix B)
- photocopiers and transparencies

CASE tools
- diagrammers and laser printer/ plotter output
- reports as appropriate

NOTES and COMMENTS

The draft strategy report is constructed by preparing a structure that is known to cover all the points required in the Terms of Reference for the strategy study in a manner that will best be accepted by its target readership. The Standard Strategy Report Contents List may be used as a checklist. Ideas for contents and detail in each section are collated, checked and refined, and then used as input to the verbal report presentation.

The verbal report is presented formally, with time allowed for questions at the end. At this point, any areas where consensus has not been achieved must be raised for management decision. At least some of the decision makers should be familiar with each idea incorporated in the recommended strategy. This task is a last check before the strategy is finalized.

An overview diagram of the top two function levels, in the form of a dataflow diagram or function dependency diagram, can be very useful to convey concepts to senior management. These techniques are not normally found to be useful analytical tools during this stage.

Tasks

TASK 130
Report to senior management

DESCRIPTION

This task allows the opportunity to describe and explain the recommended strategy in a formal, verbal presentation.

Activity 10 Set the scene for the presentation, explaining that it is not an interactive feedback session; the objective being to convey the content of the strategy report and seek approval for the recommendations.

20 Summarize the aims and objectives of the study.

30 Present the findings of the business analysis in terms of the business aims, objectives, constraints and other issues.

40 Present the high-level entity model indicating the main entities, subject areas and interfaces.

50 Present the top-level function from the Function Hierarchy and one level of decomposition identifying subject areas for further development.

60 Present the System Architecture, showing outline solution, implications on end users, organizational issues and computer aspects. Explain alternative solutions that were evaluated but not recommended.

70 Explain the proposed development plan, showing phasing, milestones, resourcing and the transition path.

80 Present the costs and benefits associated with the proposed strategy.

90 Summarize the presentation, highlighting the key points of the proposed strategy.

100 Respond to any questions or points raised and note any alterations requested to the material.

QUALITY ASSURANCE

Strict control of time must be kept during the formal report, which should last approximately two hours.

The use of well-thought-out, non-definitive but explanatory diagrams (see 'fuzzy models') is very useful during this task.

Deliverables

INPUTS
- presentation agenda
- slides
- control copy of draft strategy report

OUTCOMES
System Deliverables
- *there should be no changes to the model*

Control Information
- *comments and other indications that signify consensus and confidence in the recommendations*
- *updated control copy of draft strategy report*

Other Outcomes
- *none, if you have done a good strategy study*

ESTIMATES
The presentation should last approximately 2 hours. However, a day of each participant's time should be scheduled for preparing the room, holding the presentation, consolidating the session (and recovering from the exercise).

RESOURCES
- project leader
- business analysts
- a serious disposition during the meeting

TECHNIQUES
- use of visual aids
- presentation

TOOLS
- flip chart
- overhead projector, pens, etc.

NOTES and COMMENTS

Look for concern in the eyes of the users. This is the last opportunity to clarify any points on the future direction and rationale.

The control copy of the draft strategy report is updated during the presentation to reflect any agreed changes.

TASK 140
*Prepare and
deliver written
report*

DESCRIPTION
This task documents the strategy that has been evolved through the study and was presented during the verbal report.

Activity 10 Review material available, including the slides and notes from the verbal report. Structure in a logical manner. (See Standard Strategy Report Contents List, Appendix B.)

20 Develop/complete the material.

30 Check for consistency, style, grammar, readability, and so on.

40 Issue the report.

QUALITY ASSURANCE

The final report is the only tangible deliverable from the study. It should be a reflection of the quality of the work throughout the project. The project leader must ensure that the material is thoroughly checked and proof-read, and that the final 'copy' is of a high standard.

No surprises in this final deliverable! Everything should have been covered in previous meetings and potentially contentious issues aired at the verbal presentation.

Deliverables

INPUTS
- control copy of draft strategy report
- presentation material
- all other material from the study

OUTCOMES
System Deliverables
- *strategy report*

Control Information
- *none*

Other Outcomes
- *other sensitive issues not covered in the strategy report*

ESTIMATES
Between 5-10 days' effort should be allowed to compile and produce the report, plus secretarial support for the typing, etc.

RESOURCES
- project leader
- business analysts
- secretarial support

TECHNIQUES
- report writing

TOOLS
- Standard Strategy Report Contents List (Appendix B)
- desktop publishing software

CASE tools
- diagrammer output to laser printer/plotter
- graphics software for other diagrams

NOTES and COMMENTS

The main body of the report may be between thirty and sixty pages, depending on complexity, size of study area, and so on. Any additional supporting material, for example, full Function Hierarchy, should be held in an appendix.

Sometimes there are a few sensitive issues that need to be mentioned privately to senior management, rather than presented formally; for example, a statement of capability of someone in a key position who might jeopardize the success of the system development.

The report may cover some very long lead items that may require initial management action. A good example is any change of computer hardware or software, which may require a six-month negotiation with potential suppliers for both development and production requirements. Bring these to the attention of the relevant management.

Strategy Stage Summary

It has been ...

a short, intensive period of gathering and filtering information and drawing conclusions. High-level users have given a lot of time in interviews and feedback, and this represents a commitment to the subsequent stages – an investment for the future.

We have produced ...

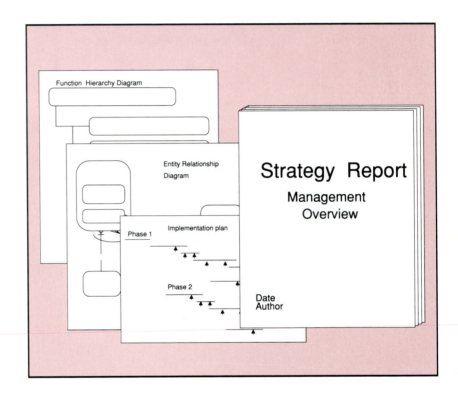

And now for ...

the analysis stage, where users and analysts will work side by side to develop detail from the models, according to the project plan.

Chapter

4

ANALYSIS STAGE

Aims and Objectives

The analysis stage will take and verify the findings from the strategy stage and expand these into sufficient detail to ensure business accuracy, feasibility and a sound foundation for design, within the scope of the organization and bearing in mind existing systems.

Figure 4-1
The Analysis Stage in the Life Cycle

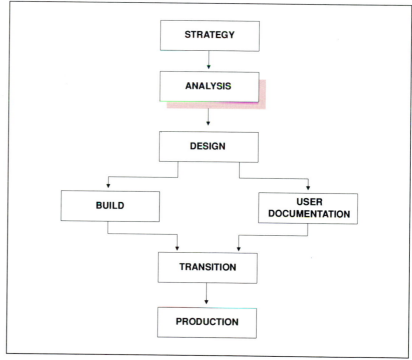

Description

Analysis of the data includes documenting all attributes. Analysis of the functions may involve further diagramming techniques to explore dependencies, data usage, conditions, data states or detailed logic.

Audit/control and back-up/recovery needs are investigated. In addition, detailed analysis must be made of existing systems and other factors affecting transition. Any constraints and assumptions that would affect design, resource utilization or timescales must be identified.

Key Deliverables

- *Agreed Entity Relationship Diagram*
- *Agreed function detail to appropriate level*
- *Function/entity, function/business unit and entity/business unit matrices*
- *Models for dataflow, function dependency and state transition*
- *Data volumes, function frequencies and user performance expectations*
- *Working style definition*
- *Initial transition strategy*
- *Audit/control and back-up/recovery needs*
- *Outline of manual procedures*
- *User acceptance criteria*
- *Preliminary sizing*
- *Constraints and assumptions*
- *Agreed approach to design and build stages*
- *Revised system development plan*

Critical Success Factors

The critical success factors include:

- Committed user involvement.
- Accurate checking of completeness and quality.
- Identification of all key issues and assumptions for design and transition.
- Accurate volumetric information for key functions and data.
- Tight control to maintain momentum during this stage of detailed working, to keep the project team focused on the Terms of Reference and to achieve the planned timescales.
- Agreed definition of the word 'adequate'.

Approach

Analysts work side by side with users during this stage, establishing and checking detailed requirements. Between them, they must make certain that everything is questioned and sifted to determine the real needs and business benefits.

Figure 4-2
Analysis Viewpoints

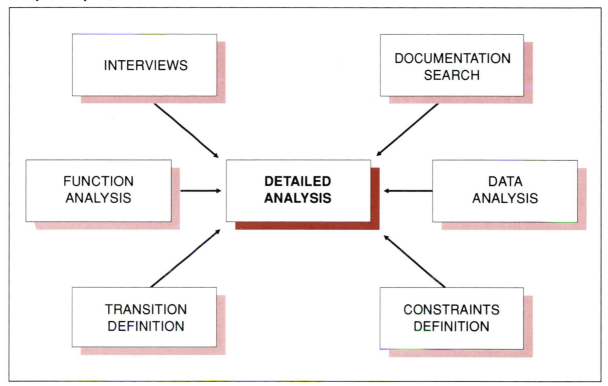

To complete a requirement definition accurately and quickly it is useful to find as many alternative or orthogonal ways of looking at the area of interest as possible. As the diagram above indicates, the current perspective of what is required (gained from interviews) needs to be balanced with what happens in current systems (defined by their documentation). The problem must also be attacked from the viewpoint of business functions and then checked again from the viewpoint of the data. Role playing current and future users, and examining the transition process between the old and the new help to identify further changes. Constraints of budget, human resources, working methods, legislation, policy and so on should be checked to ensure that any requirement can be met within these constraints.

The following more detailed diagram reminds us that analysis is an iterative process and goes through levels of detail. The first level balances the views of users and existing systems within the defined strategy to give us detailed definitions of data, functions and style within revised business objectives.

Figure 4-3
The Analysis Process

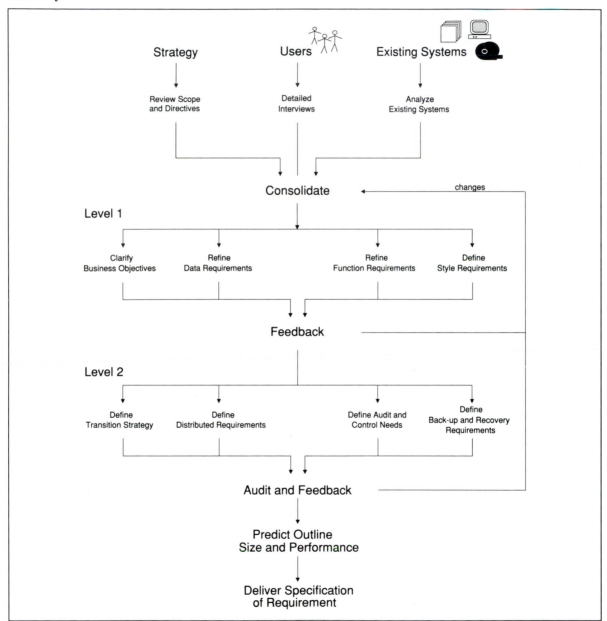

Once agreed following feedback, the second more detailed level can be completed when considerations of transition, distributed requirement, control, security and others issues that might affect the success of any system are defined. Finally, some indication is needed of whether these requirements can be met within the constraints – this is normally an issue of whether the system being envisaged can perform in a satisfactory manner.

The final thing to remember is that although much of the analysis stage is a dissection process, taking apart the information supplied and breaking it down into fine detail to find its fundamental components, the later parts of the stage are concerned with the highly-skilled act of synthesis. Synthesis is the act of creation from component parts; in this case it is the synthesis of a new statement of what is needed in the future.

List of Tasks

Figure 4-4
Network Diagram of the
Tasks in the Analysis Stage

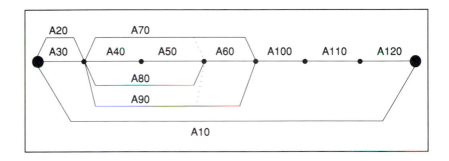

Key

A10	Project administration and management
A20	Plan detailed analysis
A30	Review standards, constraints and potential design issues
A40	Investigate detailed requirement
A50	Review findings against Terms of Reference to confirm approach
A60	Provide detailed specification
A70	Provide initial transition strategy
A80	Define audit/control needs
A90	Define back-up/recovery requirements
A100	Perform outline sizing and predict performance
A110	Review results of detailed analysis
A120	Obtain stage-end commitment

TASK 10
*Project
administration
and management*

DESCRIPTION
This task comprises control, reporting, quality assurance and administrative activities performed by the team.

Activity 10   Review plan, monitor progress against plan and revise the plan if required.

    20   Monitor quality assurance results.

    30   Liaise with other groups (auditors, technical staff, operations staff, data administrator and/or database administrator, other user groups, suppliers, etc.).

    40   Monitor staff performance, give guidance, and so on.

    50   Report progress.

    60   Hold periodic progress meetings with user management and/or the steering group (e.g. monthly).

    70   Attend regular team meetings to provide status reports and to gather/disseminate information (e.g. weekly).

    80   Maintain files, answer queries, and so on.
Note: includes filing any material for use in subsequent stages.

    90   Participate in quality assurance reviews.

    100   Ensure that analysts and the project leader have appropriate CASE and other tools.

    110   Provide general administrative support (booking rooms, scheduling meetings, etc.).

QUALITY ASSURANCE

It is the project leader's responsibility to ensure that this task is performed well, as it contributes greatly to management confidence.

Deliverables

INPUTS
- system development plan
- Terms of Reference
- timesheets
- unresolved issues
- all deliverables from the previous stage
- deliverables to be quality assured
- resources statement
- minutes of meetings

OUTCOMES
System Deliverables
- *revised deliverables*

Control Information
- *progress reports*
- *quality assurance results*
- *change control log*
- *revised plans*
- *minutes of meetings*

Other Outcomes
- *orderly documentation*
- *awareness of staff strengths/weaknesses*
- *good liaison with other parties to the project*
- *filed notes for further stages*

ESTIMATES
Activities 10-50 will occupy most of the project leader's time for a team size of 5 or more. (For team sizes in excess of 7 the leader may need assistance.)

Activities 60-90 will take up to one day per week for each team member.

Activity 100 is ideally delegated (e.g. to the sponsoring user's secretary).

RESOURCES
- project leader
- analysts
- secretary
- users
- sponsoring user

TECHNIQUES
- quality assurance
- progress reporting
- project control
- man management

TOOLS
- quality assurance checklist
- timesheet forms
- progress reporting forms
- change control forms
- CASE*Method task list

CASE tools
- estimating and progress monitoring tools

NOTES and COMMENTS

A regular team meeting is vital for keeping staff up to date and addressing required changes. Changes must be well documented in terms of need, impact analysis and required actions. The project team review feasibility, but it is a user decision (based on cost/benefit, or good understanding of the business) whether to adopt the change. It is, therefore, helpful to have a user attending the meeting. At some point, change control will be done more formally (probably by the end of the analysis stage), because the decisions and timing become more critical.

TASK 20
Plan detailed analysis

DESCRIPTION

This task determines the approach, structure and timescale for the analysis stage.

Activity 10 Confirm/write Terms of Reference (based on the findings of the strategy stage). Typically this will include the scope of this phase of work, defined by a list of business functions and associated information needs.

20 Ensure that business issues raised by the strategy stage are being resolved by users and/or management.

30 Identify interviewees and schedule interviews; sufficient to cover scope, including interfaces to existing systems, and at a level of organization to encompass awareness of business objectives **and** knowledge of day-to-day procedures and problems.

Ideally at least two interviewees should be included for each area of interest. A useful technique is to prepare a matrix of all the functional areas that need to be covered against a list of candidate interviewees and their possible contribution in each area. Interviewee selection can therefore be more objective.

40 Identify other sources of information such as existing systems (in addition to interviews/working sessions with users). Decide how much emphasis to place on them.

50 Decide the control structure of the project: leadership, control of progress and problems, reporting needs, quality assurance, stage sign-off procedures.

60 Review the plan for the analysis stage and revise it as required. This will involve adding more detail, but, if the estimates then differ substantially from the original, it may be necessary to review the scope or approach.

70 Establish the user management role. This may involve a user committee, or key individuals, participating in progress meetings/ feedbacks, and so on.

80 Publish/republish the plan to maintain commitment and keep interested parties (including those in other project/user areas) informed.

90 Brief project staff and users on this stage.

QUALITY ASSURANCE

The revised Terms of Reference and plan will be checked for feasibility by Information Systems management and for acceptability by users.

Deliverables

INPUTS
- strategy report and system development plan
- other sources of information
- Terms of Reference from strategy stage

OUTCOMES
System Deliverables
- *none*

Control Information
- *confirmed Terms of Reference*
- *revised system development plan*
- *agreed user roles*
- *business issues from strategy stage with actions*
- *matrix of function/user contribution*

Other Outcomes
- *interviewee list produced*
- *interview schedule*

ESTIMATES
Allow sufficient time for preparing and agreeing the plan, and for consultations and briefings: typically 2-6 man days.

RESOURCES
- sponsoring user
- project leader
- analysts

TECHNIQUES
- planning
- matrix planning (see Chapter 10)

TOOLS
- CASE*Method task list

CASE tools
- project planning tools

NOTES and COMMENTS

This is an important task for team building, ensuring that the project is going in the right direction and anticipating any needs or problems. Hence it is necessary to see that issues from the strategy stage are in user hands: any unresolved issues now will seriously prejudice the project's chance of success.

Similarly, ensuring that users understand, and agree, their part in working on and reviewing the project is vital. The plan should include a stage schedule, with subsets by individual or resource type. Assumptions on which the plan is based should be stated, and checkpoints highlighted. (Network diagrams and task descriptions are optional.) **Ensure that there is user commitment.**

It is also important that the users understand the approach to controlling the project. The project leader controls day-to-day issues, referring to the users where a business decision is required. Initially, change control is handled in this way; but at a later point (probably towards the end of the analysis stage) formal change control will be initiated and all changes will require change forms, impact analysis, user acceptance and planning. The users also need to determine how they will review progress: this involves the role of the sponsoring user and/or committee, and the content and frequency of reports.

TASK 30

*Review standards,
constraints and
potential design
issues*

DESCRIPTION

This task reviews decisions that need to be made or considered early in the project.

Activity 10 Determine standards required for:
- documentation levels
- naming conventions.

20 Determine the likely acceptance criteria for the system: these will be reviewed throughout the project and finalized in the transition stage.

30 Perform a high-level review of factors that might affect the subsequent design stage:
- preferred technologies
- user performance expectations
- user requirements for security (normal audit requirements will be dealt with in Task 80, but anything unusual should be considered here)
- cross-system support (e.g. the existence of an archiving strategy)
- technical constraints (e.g. current or preferred hardware, transaction processing monitor, database management system)
- working style issues for man-machine interfaces
- organizational concerns
- potential trade-off options and criteria.

QUALITY ASSURANCE

The project leader should ensure that designers have reviewed the intended approach, and that expectations are known and standards determined. Not all solutions will involve computers (heresy!). These opportunities must be identified and considered early.

Deliverables

INPUTS
- strategy report and system development plan
- folder of notes from the strategy stage
- information on current environment, systems and standards

OUTCOMES
System Deliverables
- *working style definition*
- *user acceptance criteria*
- *constraints and assumptions*

Control Information
- *awareness of design issues*

Other Outcomes
- *standards*

ESTIMATES
Allow time for designers to review the situation and discuss potential issues with analysts and users.

RESOURCES
- sponsoring user
- users
- project leader
- analysts
- designers

TECHNIQUES
- formulation of standards
- design evaluation

TOOLS

NOTES and COMMENTS

Designers need to be involved all through the project (just as analysts do not 'disappear' after the analysis stage!). However, until the detail of the function requirement is known (later in this stage) and the database management system and hardware options are evaluated, quantitative estimates are unreliable. Hence, avoid doing database sizing and performance predictions at this point.

User performance expectations can be documented as:
- **processing cycles:**
  note anything that has to be performed between two specific timed events.
- **functional area:**
  note preferred mode (interactive etc.) and throughput time for sets of work.
- **individual functions:**
  note preferred throughput time, immediacy (e.g. within a day) and the degree of integrity of information that is required.

TASK 40
*Investigate
detailed
requirement*

DESCRIPTION

This task encompasses detailed work with the user to extend and cross-check the Entity Relationship Diagram and Function Hierarchy, obtain volumes and frequencies, and identify transition issues.

Activity 10 Conduct detailed interviews (or hold working sessions) with users and/or Information Systems personnel. Use the function/user contribution matrix to help identify areas for questioning. Prototype possible requirements or ideas with a few to agree detail and as a means of discussing possible style of working.

20 Review the Entity Relationship Diagram and redraw/extend as required.

30 Review the Function Hierarchy and identify elementary business functions. Ensure that function descriptions are as complete as possible (including 'special cases' relating to input, processing, output, authorization, deadlines, etc.).

40 Cross-check entities and functions via a function/entity matrix and high-level function dependency diagram. Resolve any scoping issues in relation to the Terms of Reference and ensure that the high-level dependencies are understood. Produce entity life-cycle diagrams as a further cross-check for a few key entities.

50 Obtain details of any distributed requirements in the form of function usage by business unit (including entity volumes and function frequency) and performance expectations. Define or confirm the matrix of business units to geographic locations.

60 Identify those functions where complexity, function dependency (at elementary function level) or usage requires special attention. Draw function dependency, dataflow and state transition diagrams, and define function logic and potential design issues as appropriate. Discuss them with a designer.

70 Identify and record transition issues such as user competence levels, organization structure, existing systems, and so on. In particular, identify the manner of working that applies to different roles of user and what working style requirement would be appropriate for any new or revised system.

continues

Deliverables

INPUTS
- Entity Relationship Diagram
- Function Hierarchy
- awareness of design issues (from Task 30)
- systems boundary definition (from strategy stage)
- matrix of function/user contribution (from Task 20)
- agreed user roles
- working style

OUTCOMES
System Deliverables
- *agreed Entity Relationship Diagram*
- *agreed Function Hierarchy*
- *function/entity matrix*
- *function/business unit matrix*
- *entity/business unit matrix*
- *volumes, frequencies, performance expectations and other detail*
- *high-level function dependency*
- *function/responsibility matrix*
- *dataflow diagrams*
- *function logic*
- *working style requirement, by user role*

Control Information
- *final number of entities/ functions, for estimating purposes*

Other Outcomes
- *distributed/central requirements*
- *initial or further views on technical alternatives*
- *design issues*
- *transition issues*
- *entity life-cycle/history diagrams*
- *state transition diagrams*
- *revised system objectives*

ESTIMATES
Allow at least one day for each interview or working session, including model revisions and follow-up activities (multiply by numbers involved for man days).

Allow one hour per entity or function (whichever is the greater number) to cross-refer entities and functions.

RESOURCES
- analysts
- designers
- users

TECHNIQUES
- interviewing
- modelling
- checking correctness and feasibility (feedback, walk-through, desk check, etc.)
- function dependency diagramming

TOOLS
CASE tools
- screens for entity, attribute and function detail
- matrices for entity:function, entity:business unit, function:user, function:business unit, business unit: geographic location
- detail function logic screen

continues

continued

TASK 40

Investigate detailed requirement

DESCRIPTION

This task encompasses detailed work with the user to extend and cross-check the Entity Relationship Diagram and Function Hierarchy, obtain volumes and frequencies, and identify transition issues.

Activity 80 For existing systems to be re-engineered or with which new systems must coexist, analyze the processing logic and data usages and ensure that the new definitions encompass the same requirements, if they still exist.

90 Revise any system objectives for this phase if necessary.

Figure 4-5
Techniques to Use When a Function Requires Special Attention

	Function Description	Dataflow Diagram	Function Dependency	State Transition Diagram	Function Logic
Simple Functions	✓				
Functions interrelated by flow	✓	✓			✓(if complex)
Interdependent functions	✓		✓		✓(if complex)
Realtime functions	✓			✓	✓(if complex)

QUALITY ASSURANCE

Close liaison with the user should ensure that the information collected is accurate and comprehensive (users should see this as their responsibility). Feedbacks are less useful at this detailed level of working, but it may be helpful to hold reviews of each business area/potential sub-system.

The other area of quality assurance is checking technical correctness and ensuring that all documentation is completed and to the required standard, with particular emphasis on good function descriptions in easy-to-understand, unambiguous, user-oriented language.

Prototyping can be used during Activity 10 to help ensure that the user and analyst actually agree. It may also suggest styles of working that may be applicable later.

Remember, prototyping can be done on paper by sketching a potential form. This approach is often safer than using a computer screen. Users can get 'attached' to apparently finished software, which is only being used to help the analysis process. Ensure that computer prototypes used for this purpose are subsequently destroyed!

Deliverables

continued
RESOURCES

TECHNIQUES
– prototyping
  (see Appendix E)

TOOLS
– reverse engineering tools
– diagrammers for entity
  relationship, function hierarchy,
  dataflow, function dependency
  and state transition diagrams

NOTES and COMMENTS

It is important to capture as much useful information as possible, particularly in relation to function detail. This not only ensures that the business is understood, but forms the basis of design decisions on creating modules and required system controls. For simple standalone functions, a good function description may be sufficient to pass through to the design stage: for more complex functions, the description should highlight the need for further analysis and for special attention in design.

Complex functions that correspond to flow-oriented requirements will benefit from the production of dataflow diagrams. Interrelated functions may be modelled by function dependency diagrams, identifying triggering events. Whilst realtime requirements are often modelled using state transition diagrams. All complex functions may require the use of detailed function logic syntax (a pseudo-code/English-like language for defining functions).

Recording special cases against a function helps decisions on scope. It may be more cost-effective to explicitly exclude rare conditions and handle them by some special means (e.g. manually). On the other hand, an important exception correctly catered for at this stage may save an enormous expenditure later. It also provides information for defining the system test plan in the design stage and the user manual/training in the user documentation and transition stages. Often, some recurring function aspects are best recorded against the entity and/or attribute details to which they refer. Examples of these are:

– allowed values
– derivation of values
– integrity constraints
– consequential actions on change of information.

When analyzing existing systems one can occasionally use reverse engineering tools. However, this can be fraught with new difficulties when the existing systems are full of jargon, acronyms, badly-defined terms or are badly structured. In any event, the analyst and a knowledgeable designer from the old system need to work together closely on this activity.

Finally, volumes and frequencies are necessary for the database designer, and the performance expectations will form the basis of negotiations with the user, leading to agreed service levels by the end of the design stage. In rare cases it may be necessary to predict volumes and frequencies for several years to come, and even by different business units within the organization.

TASK 50

Review findings against Terms of Reference to confirm approach

DESCRIPTION

This task provides an opportunity to review the situation in the light of knowledge gained in Task 40.

Activity 10 Review findings, problems and ideas from Task 40 to ensure feasibility of the current direction and/or opportunities to vary the direction (e.g. change scope, review initial ideas on technical alternatives, vary development method).

20 Agree on the direction with the sponsoring user.

30 Revise the Terms of Reference and/or plan, as required.

QUALITY ASSURANCE

Any changes to the Terms of Reference and plan will be checked for feasibility by Information Systems management and for acceptability by users.

Deliverables

INPUTS
- Terms of Reference
- system development plan
- all deliverables to date

OUTCOMES
System Deliverables
- *none*

Control Information
- *confirmed Terms of Reference and plan for rest of analysis stage*
- *initial approach to design and build stages*

Other Outcomes
- *none*

ESTIMATES
Unless there are major difficulties/decisions, allow 50% of the time taken by Task 20.

RESOURCES
- sponsoring user
- project leader

TECHNIQUES
- review of existing material

TOOLS
CASE tools
- reports – see appropriate product reference manual for relevant reports

NOTES and COMMENTS

One of the most important project management responsibilities is to ensure that information is put to good use. This task is an important management checkpoint, where the knowledge gained in Task 40 is reviewed before committing to the time-intensive task of specification (Task 60).

It may be useful to write additional reports against your dictionary to speed up this process.

TASK 60
Provide detailed specification

DESCRIPTION
This task comprises documentation of attributes, function detail, function dependency and interfaces.

Activity 10   Record detailed entity/attribute descriptions.

20   Ensure that all attributes have been found by checking the current system and interfaces, and reviewing processing requirements for attributes used in selection, sequence, conditions, iteration or the definition of events.

30   Specify elementary business functions to the required level, as decided in Task 40. This may involve further analysis of dependencies, data usage, conditions or detailed function logic. Include preliminary notes in test folder.

40   Define dependencies (within and between functions) at all appropriate levels. This will entail elementary business functions and perhaps a higher level (to check interfaces). Dependencies may be due to time, data usage or system events (one function triggering another).

50   Review the options for functions affected by design constraints. Agree the degree of automation that is sensible for any function and outline the related manual procedures and interfaces. Review work distribution and distributed/central requirements to ensure feasibility and optimize efficiency.

60   Assist users to make decisions/check results.

Note: this could involve limited prototyping, such as demonstrations of the type of transaction associated with different levels of automation, sketches of screens and reports to decide content (not format: this is done in the design stage). Alternatively the specification may contain a storyboard to enable the analyst to walk the users through a possible solution.

70   Define draft 'look and feel' standards for forms, reports, menus, user documentation and any other form of user interface.

QUALITY ASSURANCE
Check the twenty or so most frequent functions and twenty or so most voluminous entities in great detail. Identify whether any significant relationships have unusual distributions and document accordingly. Seek out and record other peaks, troughs, limits and exceptions that may be vital during design.

Users must ensure that decisions on scope and approach are based on adequate information and reflect their needs. The other area of quality assurance is checking technical correctness; that is, that all documentation is completed and to the required standard (with particular emphasis on function detail).

Deliverables

INPUTS
- entity and function documentation
- outcomes from Task 40

OUTCOMES
System Deliverables
- *fully-documented entity model*
- *agreed function detail to appropriate level*
- *function dependency diagram*
- *outline of manual procedures*
- *test notes*
- *interface definitions*

Control Information
- *agreed levels of automation per function*

Other Outcomes
- *prototype*
- *storyboard*
- *draft 'look and feel' standards*

ESTIMATES
Allow 0.5 hours per attribute for documentation (assuming 5-7 attributes per entity, of which 2-3 may be documented already from the strategy stage). Allow 0.5 days per function for documentation, and 2 man days per interface.

RESOURCES
- project leader
- analysts
- users

TECHNIQUES
- there are various diagramming techniques to explore function dependency and detail within a function
- prototyping (see Appendix E)
- storyboarding

TOOLS
- computer graphics tool
CASE tools
- screens for entity, attribute and function detail
- screens and reports for completeness checks and impact analysis
- reports for user checking
- diagrammers for dataflow, state transition and function dependency diagrams
- detail function logic screen

NOTES and COMMENTS

Each function must be recorded within the Function Hierarchy and have an associated outline definition. Functions that are highly interdependent should be documented using a dataflow or function dependency diagram, as appropriate. Realtime requirements, that is, those which are heavily event driven, may be recorded via a state transition diagram. This is the main opportunity to ensure that sufficient function detail has been recorded. The project leader must ensure that the users understand the approach on each function (level of automation, likely performance on target hardware, implications of distributed/central requirements).

This task has little glamour attached to it. Try to find a way of keeping the analysts and users interested and committed, perhaps by introducing a degree of competition, humour, frequent goals to achieve, ... The use of both prototyping and storyboarding (on paper or using computer graphics) can help maintain commitment and improve quality.

TASK 70
Provide initial transition strategy

DESCRIPTION
This task ensures that while data and function detail are collected, the associated aspects of delivery and acceptance, data take-on, training, installation and cut-over are considered.

Activity 10   Define transition elements:

Delivery and Acceptance Plan: containing notes on what could be delivered, when, and the implementation mode. It will contain preferred phases of delivery (including function content, location considerations, temporary interfaces, etc.) and method of acceptance (e.g. extended system test, separate acceptance test, pilot, parallel run).

Acceptance testing, by a small, centralized team of expert users, should not be confused with pilot/parallel running, performed by a large, decentralized team of novice users who have just completed their training.

Training Plan: containing notes on any required organization changes (departments, roles, responsibilities, etc.), new/changed manual procedures, available training budget, preferred training methods, aptitude/availability of each category of user for training.

Data Take-on Plan: containing notes on source of data, ownership of data, the state it is in and any required actions (to collect or tidy it up), available data take-on budget and estimates of work required.

Cut-Over Plan: containing notes on how to change to the new system (e.g. timings, effects on current systems, who will be involved, assessment of risk, fall-back options).

Installation Plan: containing notes on required hardware, system software, timings/responsibilities for installing them. Remember to check both development and production requirements.

Critical Factors: containing details of key people, resources, dependencies without which transition will be at risk.

20   Review each section of the initial transition strategy and ensure that actions are in hand to make the required decisions in time to complete the strategy by the end of the design stage.

Deliverables

INPUTS
- initial ideas from strategy stage
- likely hardware, system software
- notes on transition issues from Task 40
- user acceptance criteria
- constraints and assumptions

OUTCOMES
System Deliverables
- *initial transition strategy*

Control Information
- *list of actions required to complete the transition strategy*

Other Outcomes
- *groups of functions to be developed together (based on delivery plan)*

ESTIMATES
Allow sufficient time for each section of the transition strategy to review plans and identify required actions.

RESOURCES
- project leader
- analysts
- designers
- users

TECHNIQUES
- planning

TOOLS

NOTES and COMMENTS
This formal task should take information collected during Task 40. It is essential to start preparing for implementation as early as possible, as some aspects require extensive planning and may include tasks of long duration (e.g. data clean-up).

QUALITY ASSURANCE
Users must ensure that the proposed implementation is achievable with available resources, and will produce a minimum disruption to the business. Information Systems personnel (including operations staff, technical staff, the data administrator and/or database administrator) must ensure that it is technically feasible.

Tasks

TASK 80
Define audit/
control needs

DESCRIPTION
This task ensures that functions are considered in the context of appropriate business control when they are designed in the next stage.

Activity 10 Define legal requirements and tests to ensure that business and legal specifications have been adhered to in the design.

20 Define access security requirements by user, function, time and location, and specify tests to ensure that they are met.

30 Define any other security needs (e.g. protection from fraud, protection of data in transit, provision of off-site storage or processing facilities).

40 Derive integrity controls.

50 Define application controls to be performed by users or by the system (e.g. daily reconciliation totals).

60 Define audit requirements, including audit trails, reports and security procedures.

70 Define any significant error handling (e.g. criteria for acceptance/ rejection of financial transactions and subsequent handling of them).

QUALITY ASSURANCE

Auditors are responsible for seeing that their requirements are incorporated. Information Systems personnel (including operations staff, technical staff, the data administrator and/or database administrator) must ensure that it is technically feasible and encourage the development of installation standards to fulfil these needs more efficiently.

Beware of specifying unnecessary or unwieldy auditing requirements that might act against the needs of the business. For each requirement ask the question, "Do we **really** need this and why?"

Deliverables

INPUTS
– initial ideas from strategy stage
– function details

OUTCOMES
System Deliverables
– *audit/control requirements*

Control Information
– *additional functions or sub-routines to provide controls (to be included in estimating remaining effort)*

Other Outcomes
– *requirement for additional forms, off-site facilities, etc.*

ESTIMATES
Allow sufficient time to discuss audit/control needs.

Note: it is expected that functions could undergo a 50% (effort) revision in the course of this stage. This is incorporated in Task 110.

RESOURCES
– analysts
– auditors

TECHNIQUES
– diagramming techniques used in Task 60 provide a helpful level of detail for discussing with auditors

TOOLS
CASE tools
– reports provide information to auditors

NOTES and COMMENTS
The project leader should be ensuring that liaison with interested parties takes place throughout the project; but at this particular point auditors become 'the user' in specifying their requirement. Their interest is wider than is sometimes assumed. They need to be satisfied that the system will meet business and legal requirements, as well as run and be used in a controlled way.

TASK 90
Define back-up/
recovery
requirements

DESCRIPTION

This task ensures that functions are considered in the context of operational issues when they are designed in the next stage.

Activity 10 Define data retention requirements. These should not only cover the intended production system, but also any produced software, CASE definitions or other development documentation which is really part of the full system.

20 Define the likely consequences should the new system become unavailable. Identify fall-back options and any special arrangements that are necessary (e.g. spare input forms for when an online system goes down).

30 Define requirements for back-up, recovery and archive storage of information.

40 Check with users and management that the envisaged back-up and recovery system will meet the business needs in cases of failure.

QUALITY ASSURANCE

Information Systems personnel must ensure that every effort is made in planning system availability and minimizing likely disruption from system failure.

Check that data retention periods specified are sensible. Users often specify long periods, 'just in case' anything should go wrong. When reviewed against the amount of physical or computer storage that might be needed, they often reduce the periods to more sensible values. The objective is adequate security, not massive storage problems.

Deliverables

INPUTS
- initial ideas from strategy stage
- function details
- installation standards for back-up and recovery

OUTCOMES

System Deliverables
- *back-up and recovery requirements*
- *data retention requirements*

Control Information
- *additional functions to provide back-up and recovery (to be included in estimating remaining effort)*

Other Outcomes
- *requirement for additional forms, off-site facilities, etc.*
- *fall-back options*

ESTIMATES
Allow sufficient time to discuss back-up/recovery needs.

In certain industries this task could result in extensive revisions of function specifications.

RESOURCES
- analysts
- users
- operations staff
- technical staff

TECHNIQUES
- specification of back-up/ recovery procedures

TOOLS

NOTES and COMMENTS

The project leader must ensure that the users understand the implications of a system failure and have considered loss of work in progress, loss of access to data, and the time needed to catch up after recovery. He must also ensure that data retention is handled sensibly: any information that is only required occasionally, or non-urgently, should be considered for archiving to another medium. (This could include fiche, a separate database, etc.) Archiving can also take the form of producing a consolidated record instead of individual details, but this is a non-trivial assignment, best handled by a separate project.

TASK 100

*Perform outline
sizing and predict
performance*

DESCRIPTION

This task provides early warnings of performance problems and is the first stage in responding to the required performance expectations discussed in Tasks 40 and 60.

Activity 10 Verify the consistency of information gathered on volumes/frequencies for entities/functions and obtain independent validation of the figures (e.g. statistics from another source).

20 Predict the likely size of the database and document assumptions, particularly those relating to data structure and module structure.

30 Predict the likely performance of the system and cross-check the sizing result against performance expectations. For frequently-used complex functions the performance prediction may require a detailed check against the actions carried out in the function, as defined by the detailed function logic. Record and adjust design assumptions and constraints, as required.

40 Investigate technical alternatives where there is a problem in achieving performance expectations.

50 Provide input to management on hardware and software requirements for development and operational environments.

QUALITY ASSURANCE

Remember the database may be a combination of clerical and computer files. Figures must be checked by a competent database designer. It may also be possible to compare with figures for the current system, applying known differences, to check that the order of magnitude is correct. Careful investigation of high-volume entities, textual attributes and data retention periods often helps you identify causes of problems.

Sizing experts often only use the most frequent and voluminous factors for their calculation, and then apply factors that they have used in the past to predict aggregate sizing figures.

Deliverables

INPUTS
- entity volumes
- function frequencies
- any relevant sizing statistics, for comparison
- function logic

OUTCOMES
System Deliverables
- *preliminary sizing*
- *proposed development and operational environment*
- *preliminary performance prediction*

Control Information
- *conflicts between predicted performance levels and user expectations (problems to pursue)*

Other Outcomes
- *sizing assumptions*

ESTIMATES
Allow sufficient time for the number of entities/functions (multiplied by the number of locations, for distributed data).

RESOURCES
- application designer
- database designer (assisted by analyst to explain volumes/ frequencies/ performance expectations)

TECHNIQUES
- sizing
- rules of thumb

TOOLS
CASE tools
- default database design and sizing utilities

NOTES and COMMENTS

This is an outline sizing only: it may assist choices on processor size and disk space requirements, but does not provide accurate performance estimates. Comparison with similar-sized existing systems will often provide a good cross-check.

During strategy, initial ideas of hardware and software requirements for development and the production system were produced. During this task, and subsequently during design, these requirements become refined and at some time the development staff and management must place the orders. This will often be a judgement based on current prices, group preference, service levels, learning curves and so on, but always constrained by these sizing and performance predictions.

Often gross assumptions must be made by the designers and analysts about the likely implementation method. It is essential to record these assumptions for the subsequent design stage. Purists could argue that this is a task best left to design, but experience has shown that risks are under better control when this task is carried out during analysis.

TASK 110
Review results of detailed analysis

DESCRIPTION

This task ensures that all parties have confidence in the direction of the project.

Activity 10 Review the further detail of the proposed solution (data require-ments, function detail, audit/control requirements, transition strategy, outline sizing) in terms of its impact on:

- other systems
- the organization (required premises, required staff, training needs, roles and responsibilities, disruption at cut-over)
- user expectations
- opinions of other groups associated with the project (auditors, technical staff, operations, data administrator and/or database administrator, other user areas, suppliers, etc.).

Ensure that the Terms of Reference are still appropriate in the light of further knowledge.

20 Agree Terms of Reference for the remainder of the project. Agree the approach to the design and build stages (including use of proto-typing). Ensure that all business issues from the strategy stage have been resolved and that issues from the analysis stage are in hand.

30 Ensure that the models are complete, have satisfied consistency checks and cover the agreed scope.

40 Ensure that there has been adequate user checking on each task and that follow-up actions have been carried out. Review any quality assurance reports.

50 Revise system deliverables, as required.

60 Revise 'look and feel' standards as required, remembering the user documentation as well as forms, reports and menu systems.

QUALITY ASSURANCE

This task is a checkpoint in itself, but it also underlines an important role for the project leader in taking responsibility for the state of the documentation (Activities 40 and 50).

Deliverables

INPUTS
- all deliverables to date
- Terms of Reference
- initial approach to design and build stages
- draft 'look and feel' standards

OUTCOMES

System Deliverables
- *agreed approach to design and build stages*
- *any revised deliverables*

Control Information
- *revised Terms of Reference*
- *approved quality assurance results*

Other Outcomes
- *revised 'look and feel' standards*

ESTIMATES
Each system deliverable (entity, attribute and function documentation) may attract an overhead of 50% of the original estimate in revising it as a result of quality assurance or in response to other changes.

The other activities (10-40) should take only minimal time if there has been continuing liaison between all groups associated with the project.

RESOURCES
- sponsoring user
- project leader
- analysts
- designers

TECHNIQUES
- any means of measuring understanding/confidence of all parties (meetings, walkthrough of selected deliverables, etc.)

TOOLS
- stage-end checklist

CASE tools
- plotting/printing for diagrammers
- reports as appropriate

NOTES and COMMENTS

The stages in systems development do not have 'automatic cut-off points', and this task is a test that sufficient work has been done to terminate the analysis stage. As well as checking for completion of the required tasks, it is important that there has been sufficient liaison and impact analysis (Activity 10) to ensure confidence in the way ahead.

TASK 120
Obtain stage-end commitment

DESCRIPTION

This task ensures confidence in the outcome of the analysis stage and the plans for the design stage.

Activity 10 Agree what needs to be documented at this stage for the transition strategy. This may include the draft Delivery and Acceptance Plan, Training Plan, Data Take-on Plan, Cut-over Plan and Installation Plan; and action points where discussion, authorization of expenditure or advance warning is needed. Publish the documentation.

20 Review costs, as required.

30 Produce a detailed plan for the design stage. This will involve adding more detail, but, if the estimates differ substantially from the original, it may be necessary to review the scope or approach. Revise the outline plan for the rest of the project. Publish plans, to obtain commitment and keep interested parties informed.

40 Produce a stage-end report or presentation, if required.

50 Obtain commitment to proceed.

60 Brief project staff and users on the next stage.

QUALITY ASSURANCE

Plans should be checked for feasibility by Information Systems management and for acceptability by users. In particular, ensure that the groups of functions make sense, since they will form the basis of work allocation and control in subsequent stages.

Deliverables

INPUTS
- initial transition strategy
- existing system development plan
- deliverables to include in report (if required)

OUTCOMES

System Deliverables
- *revised system development plan*
- *published initial transition strategy and actions*

Control Information
- *groups of functions to be developed together*
- *stage-end report, if required*

Other Outcomes
- *none*

ESTIMATES

Allow the same effort as for a feedback (up to 12 man days) for a stage-end report, if required. (The material should all be drawn from existing deliverables.)

Allow sufficient time for planning, obtaining commitment and briefing staff.

RESOURCES
- sponsoring user
- project leader
- analysts

TECHNIQUES
- planning
- report writing

TOOLS
- CASE*Method task list

CASE tools
- project control tools

NOTES and COMMENTS

Producing stage-end reports is costly in effort and should not be necessary if there has been close liaison with users throughout. An important part of the plan may be to identify groups of functions – these may be packets of work to be delivered at the same time (relating to a phased implementation) or handled in the same way (e.g. simple functions for 'incremental development').

Analysis Stage Summary

It has been ...

a tightly-controlled stage where analysts and users worked side by side collecting detail, confirming the approach, deciding the transition strategy.

We have produced ...

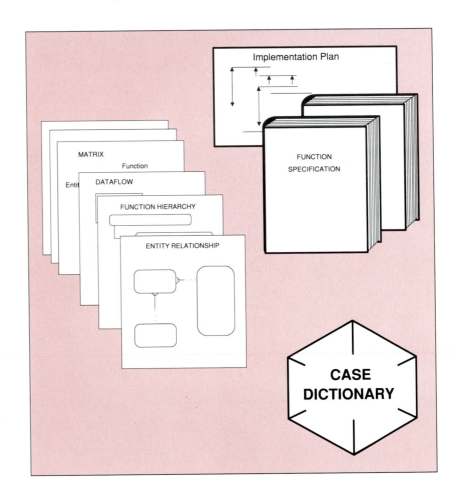

And now for ...

the design stage, which concentrates on 'how' instead of 'what' and produces a database, a system architecture, program specifications and other documentation to feed into subsequent stages.

Chapter

5

DESIGN STAGE

Aims and Objectives

The design stage will take the detailed requirements from the analysis stage and find the best way of fulfilling them and achieving agreed service levels, given the technical environment and previous decisions on required levels of automation.

Figure 5-1
The Design Stage in the
Life Cycle

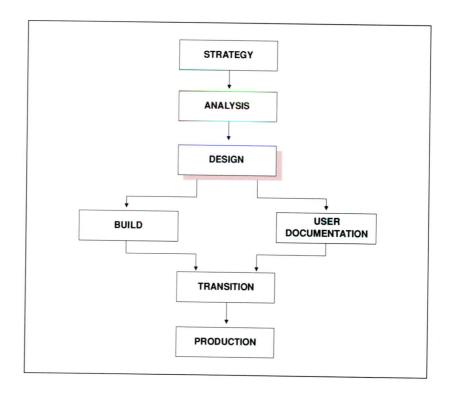

Description

The Entity Relationship Model will be turned into a database design and specification of non-database storage. Functions will be translated into modules and manual procedures, with required audit/control features and back-up/recovery points. Screens, reports and module linkages will be derived. Function usage will be employed to drive communications architecture design. Prototyping may be used to help make decisions on areas of doubt, but must be seen as a technique and not an end in itself. Finally, program specifications and a system test plan are produced, and the information gained in this stage is used to confirm the transition strategy.

Key Deliverables

- *System architecture*
- *Module design*
- *Logical and physical schemas*
- *Database and file design*
- *Detailed sizing*
- *Program specifications*
- *Specifications of manual procedures*
- *Draft user manual*
- *Agreed transition strategy comprising:*
  plans for delivery and acceptance, training, data take-on, cut-over and installation
- *System test plan*
- *Draft operations documentation*
- *Revised system development plan*

Critical Success Factors

The key factor is to produce a design appropriate to business needs, within the technical constraints. This involves:

- Knowing the capabilities of the hardware and possible delivery vehicles.
- Understanding the business needs.
- Making informed trade-off decisions.
- Identifying and resolving potential problems.

Approach

The process of design is predominantly an iterative one, where the requirements and ideas are taken and design alternatives tried until an acceptable compromise solution is found (see Figure 5-2). What **is** acceptable needs to be defined ahead of time, to act as objective criteria. Users, managers, operations, support and other staff may need to be presented with options for decision, to validate the designers' work and approve the final result.

Figure 5-2
Design – an Iterative Process

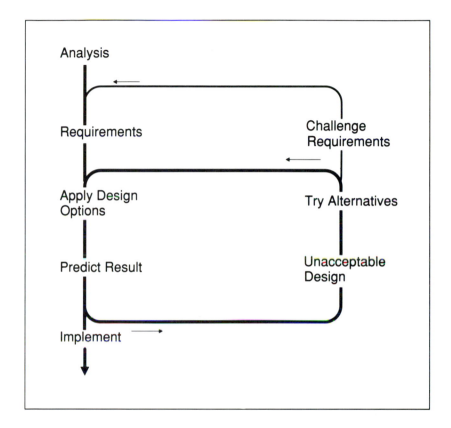

Analysis

Requirements   Challenge
                                Requirements

Apply Design   Try Alternatives
Options

Predict Result   Unacceptable
                                Design

Implement

In some cases there may be no practical or cost-effective way of meeting the requirements. This may be because of time, money, skill or other resource constraints, or may even be because the tools or techniques needed do not yet exist. In this case, it is important to go back to the user and analyst as soon as possible to see if the requirements can be modified to fit within the limitations of the technology and resource availability.

In practice, this iterative process is conducted in parallel for several aspects of the design. This is a sensible use of resources, but it must be remembered that assumptions made during database or application design may well affect the network design and so on.

Another reason for not achieving an acceptable system design is that although each separate aspect may be viable, there may be no practical combination. The following diagram (Figure 5-3) shows how the work can be organized to bring together these different aspects from time to time to examine their assumptions and interdependencies, so that an optimum system design can be created to encompass them all. Thus a vital part of the project leader's role is ensuring that the designers can work as a focused team and not in blinkered isolation on their pet topics.

Figure 5-3
Interdependent Design Aspects

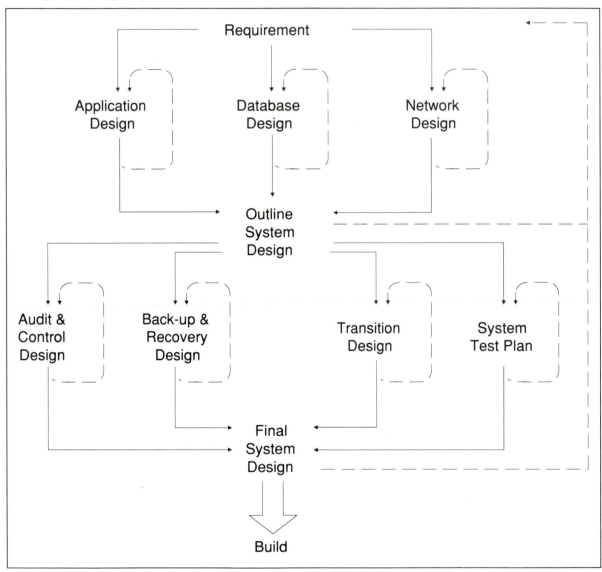

Finally, remember that this design process really started during strategy and continues on as a background task during all the other stages – at the end of the day the system must be well designed to meet the need.

List of Tasks

Figure 5-4
Network Diagram of the
Tasks in the Design Stage

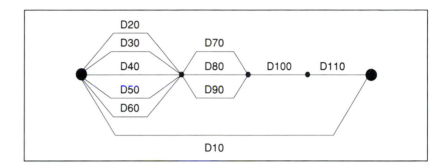

Key

D10	Project administration and management
D20	Design application
D30	Design and build database
D40	Produce network/communication design
D50	Design audit/control needs
D60	Design back-up/recovery needs
D70	Review outline design and produce program specifications
D80	Complete system test plan
D90	Complete transition strategy
D100	Review results of design stage
D110	Obtain stage-end commitment

TASK 10
*Project
administration
and management*

DESCRIPTION
This task comprises control, reporting, quality assurance and administrative activities performed by the team.

Activity 10 Review plan, monitor progress against plan and revise the plan if required.

20 Monitor the quality assurance results.

30 Liaise with other groups (auditors, technical staff, operations staff, data administrator and/or database administrator, other user groups, suppliers, etc.).

40 Monitor staff performance, give guidance, and so on.

50 Perform change control on analysis deliverables.

60 Report progress.

70 Hold periodic progress meetings with user management and/or the steering group (e.g. monthly).

80 Attend regular team meetings to provide status reports and to gather/disseminate information.

90 Maintain files, answer queries, and so on.
Note: this includes filing any material for use in subsequent stages.

100 Participate in quality assurance reviews.

110 Ensure that designers and the project leader have appropriate CASE and other tools.

120 Provide general administrative support (booking rooms, scheduling meetings, etc.).

QUALITY ASSURANCE

This is not a glamorous task, but contributes greatly to the success of the stage.

It is the project leader's responsibility to ensure that this task is performed well, which requires the ability to motivate all participants.

Deliverables

INPUTS
– system development plan
– timesheets
– unresolved issues
– deliverables from previous stages
– deliverables to be quality assured
– minutes of meetings
– Terms of Reference
– proposed development environment

OUTCOMES
System Deliverables
– *revised deliverables*

Control Information
– *progress reports*
– *quality assurance results*
– *change control log*
– *revised plans*
– *minutes of meetings*
– *revised system development plan*

Other Outcomes
– *orderly documentation*
– *awareness of staff strengths/ weaknesses*
– *good liaison with other parties to the project*
– *filed notes for subsequent stages*

ESTIMATES
Activities 10-60 will occupy most of the project leader's time for a team size of 5 or more (for team sizes in excess of 7 assistance will be needed).

Activities 70-100 will take up to one day per week for each team member.

Activity 110 is ideally delegated (e.g. to the sponsoring user's secretary).

RESOURCES
– project leader
– analysts
– designers
– programmers
– users
– secretary

TECHNIQUES
– quality assurance
– progress reporting
– project control
– man management

TOOLS
– quality assurance checklist
– timesheet forms
– progress reporting forms
– change control forms
– CASE*Method task list

CASE tools
– estimating and progress monitoring tools

NOTES and COMMENTS

A regular meeting is vital for keeping staff up to date and addressing required changes. (See Notes to Task 10, Analysis Stage.) It is also the best vehicle for keeping staff focused at a time when the team may be growing in size and working on separate groups of functions.

To ensure that dependencies between groups of functions are known (and met), invite anyone else who affects schedules (e.g. database administrator, users in charge of the training plan) to the regular meeting.

TASK 20
Design application

DESCRIPTION

This task translates functions into modules and provides specifications of them.

Activity 10 Assess the elementary business functions, and prepare a function/module matrix to ensure that all the functions necessary are implemented. Business functions should exist for the process of converting data and functions from existing systems.

20 Select the appropriate delivery vehicle for each module and decide the module structure (including manual procedures), using any available prototypes or storyboards from the analysis stage.

30 Design and document the application system architecture:

- menu structures
- screen dialogues
- batch procedures
- manual procedures
- user classes
- user interface and style for screens, reports and forms.

Document the design decisions and assumptions.
Note: include the interfaces identified in the analysis stage.

40 Review the architecture and module outline with users, database administrator, auditors, technical staff, and so on. Perform a structured walkthrough of the architecture with the users, to ensure that both computerized and manual procedures will do the job in a sensible manner.

continues

Deliverables

INPUTS
- outline system architecture from strategy stage
- function detail
- function dependencies (events and triggers)
- installation user interface standards
- function/entity matrix
- groups of functions to be developed together
- state transition diagram
- dataflow diagram
- function logic
- entity life-cycle/history diagrams
- working style requirement by user role
- prototype from analysis
- storyboard
- outline of manual procedures
- interface definitions

OUTCOMES
System Deliverables
- *system architecture*
- *module design and specifications*
- *documented design decisions*
- *initial module/table matrix*
- *menu structures, dialogue between screens*
- *screens, reports, forms*
- *additional documentation for screens (help text etc.)*
- *specifications of manual procedures*
- *draft user manual*

Control Information
- *early warning of module complexity (for estimating)*
- *reaction to prototype (if done)*

Other Outcomes
- *better awareness of technical environment and areas where trade-off decisions may need to be made*

ESTIMATES
Allow 3 man days per module if you have a reasonable range of simple, average and complex modules, and are familiar with the hardware and possible delivery vehicles. If not, load the estimates accordingly (unless you are using prototyping to resolve design issues and this task is only a 'first cut').

RESOURCES
- designers (including someone with expertise on delivery vehicles, hardware and design options)
- users

TECHNIQUES
- iteration of choices on splitting/combining elementary business functions and varying delivery vehicles
- logical to physical translation of accesses
- screen design
- report/form design
- design of screen links
- prototyping (see Appendix E)

TOOLS
- screen painters

CASE tools
- module definition and impact analysis screens and reports
- generator products for appropriate target computer language

continues

continued
TASK 20
Design application

DESCRIPTION

This task translates functions into modules and provides specifications of them.

Activity 50   For each module, define and document (as appropriate):

- draft layouts
- detail of processing, identifying how the delivery vehicle and in particular any complex functions defined by their detailed function logic will be used to perform each aspect of the function defined
- entity and attribute usage
- update procedures
- validation, control and reconciliation procedures
- back-up/recovery procedures
- error correction cycles, batch control procedures and dependent flows
- terminal sign-on/sign-off procedures
- special/exceptional procedures.

Prototype modules to check feasibility and best options. Document the design decisions, assumptions and likely complexity.

60   Cross-check module specifications against the Entity Relationship Diagram for completeness. Translate logical to physical accesses and ensure that the data design is feasible. Produce initial module(program)/table matrix to ensure that all aspects are covered.

QUALITY ASSURANCE

Module design should be fed back to the analyst who specified the function, to ensure that it meets the specification. The designer is responsible for ensuring good design.

Screen/report design should conform to installation standards (e.g. placing of common fields, standard function key usage for data manipulation within and between screens). The design must also be demonstrated to the user in such a way that he can assess its usability and determine the required procedures to support it.

Deliverables

Often, elementary business functions become modules, but it may be desirable to split or combine them, for performance or usability. The possible choices depend on the language and development/runtime tools available, and it requires skill and experience to make the best design decision for the business, in the given environment. Prototyping may be used to test the various options (see Appendix E). Modules may be a combination of computer programs and manual procedures.

Prototyping may also be used to evaluate the layout options. This can be a 'paper prototype' (i.e. a series of screen/report layouts, with real data) or can involve limited building of certain functions.

If prototyping is done, ensure that the requirement is understood, the work controlled and the prototype stopped (and discarded) when you plan to do so. Prototyping is a means of clarifying unknown factors that are deemed critical to the successful design. It is not an idle pursuit, but a disciplined trial of alternatives, to select the best option. Users must not 'adopt' the prototype. See Appendix E for further advice on prototyping.

It is usually beneficial to classify users (e.g. data entry clerks). Dialogues, menus, security and audit controls can then be built around these classes. User classes should be defined by user management.

The layout design is the users' interface with the system and will largely determine their perception of its usefulness. It is vital to understand the users' patterns of working, so that functions are grouped appropriately for access. For instance, dependent functions and those used by the same set of people should appear on the same menu. Highly dependent functions could be duplicated, so that one is included in the other, as well as occurring alone. Conversely, where the success unit is quite large (and the user would lose data if the system failed, and/or performance is a problem) consider splitting the transaction. In this case, ensure that the second transaction achieves data integrity.

Manual procedures need the same level of layout design and prototyping. Additional considerations must be borne in mind to cater for the restrictions of paper. Where will instructions and guidance material be placed? What about large fields that could be scrolled on the computer? Does a 'multi-line' section on the paper cater for ninety-five percent of all cases and have we allowed for continuation on other sheets? Have we considered two-part sets, weight of paper, colour, size, binding, logos, fonts, pictures, and so on? Do we need reference books? System and user documentation is an ongoing process: documentation on functions and manual/automated procedures from earlier stages is added to the documented design decisions from this task to form the basis of the draft user manual.

Finally, application design may, in part, involve the integration of an application package to carry out some of the functionality. The requirement definitions must be used to validate applicability and identify areas for modification or integration with other parts of the system.

TASK 30
Design and build database

DESCRIPTION
This task translates entities into tables and files, and then provides the required views, indices and clusters.

Given an Entity Relationship Diagram that represents the information needs of the business, database design is all about producing the most sensible compromise for holding the implied data on some medium or other. Possible implementation mechanisms include paper, manual files, conventional computer files and different types of database management systems (as illustrated opposite). Where data is only required for retrieval purposes, the use of microfiche, microfilm, optical layer devices, and so on may be appropriate.

The compromise on database design is normally derived by ensuring that it caters for the following 'representative' set of business functions:

the 10 most performance-critical functions

the 10 most complex functions

the 10 most urgent functions

and 20 other randomly selected functions.

continues

Figure 5-5
Database Design

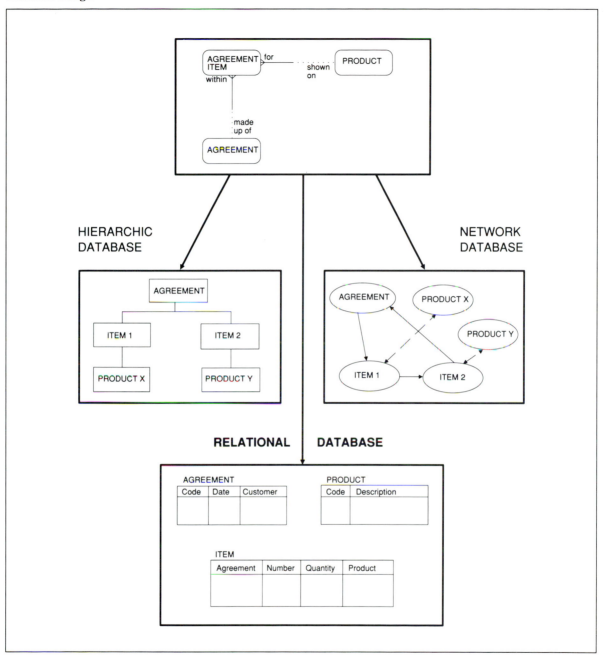

continues

continued
TASK 30
Design and build database

DESCRIPTION

This task translates entities into tables and files, and then provides the required views, indices and clusters.

Activity 10   Determine the implementation technique for entities: database tables, files or special media. Then assess whether each entity can be implemented as a single table or file for first-cut (initial) design.

20   Perform the first-cut database or file design.

30   Tune the database and file design for performance and storage needs. Add indexes and other access mechanisms. Vary space allocations, and predict the performance and size. Add distributed requirements. Iterate this task until acceptable.

40   Create temporary modifications to the design for data conversion, if necessary, and check module specifications for conversion and resetting to optimum database and file design. Similar work may be necessary on a more permanent basis to cater for coexistence with application packages or other systems.

50   Check and revise the module/table matrix as required. Derive user views.

60   Produce detailed sizing and capacity plan.

70   Perform a database and file design audit to predict whether performance is satisfactory. Agree service levels and storage requirements.

80   Build the database from the database design; for example, CREATE TABLE commands.

QUALITY ASSURANCE

The database designer must work closely with the module designer and the analyst who specified the function, to ensure that the right trade-off decisions are made in tuning.

On a complex design, prototype or benchmark the design against a representative or a simulated set of data to assure that performance will be adequate. Remember that performance can mean response time, throughput and the ability to do the entire job with the given resources.

Deliverables

continued

INPUTS

- Entity Relationship Diagram
- attribute details
- relationship details
- elementary function usage of entities and attributes
- data volumes and function frequencies
- function/business unit matrix
- entity/business unit matrix
- module/table matrix
- distributed/central requirements from analysis
- preliminary sizing and assumptions from analysis

RESOURCES

- database designer

OUTCOMES

System Deliverables

- *logical and physical schemas*
- *documented database and file design decisions*
- *detailed sizing*
- *the actual database*

Control Information

- *early warning of performance problems (for estimating a need for trials and tuning)*
- *result of prototype if done*

Other Outcomes

- *capacity plan*
- *agreed service levels*

TECHNIQUES

- database design
- tuning
- sizing
- prototyping (see Appendix E)
- data normalization and denormalization theory

ESTIMATES

Plan for a continuing involvement of one man day per week on database activities, from the design stage onwards.

TOOLS

CASE tools

- a default database design is useful for first-cut table production
- impact analysis reports assist design and tuning decisions
- sizing utility
- matrix diagrammer

NOTES and COMMENTS

It is helpful for the database designer to have attended the regular project meetings towards the end of the analysis stage, to become familiar with both the entity/function usage aspects and the business needs.

The trade-offs made in Activity 30 may involve denormalization via:

- aggregation
- duplication
- repetition

in order to meet performance objectives without constraining business needs. Prototyping may be used to test the various options.

Normally, you build the actual database at this time, as it only takes a short time once the design has been completed.

TASK 40
*Produce network/
communication
design*

DESCRIPTION

This task derives the network architecture and required network support procedures.

Activity 10 Establish the siting and type of terminals and processors, required protocols, network architecture (lines, devices, system software) for both subsequent development environment and the production system. Assess the need for and ease of reconfiguring and/or extending the network. Similarly identify the communication requirements to support manual procedures, for example, telephones, facsimile machines and other forms of office automation equipment. Build in redundancy, if required, for resilience or peak performance.

20 Predict line traffic (especially for peak utilization) and assess the impact on input/output devices and processors. Identify the likely performance profile (best, worst) and review the effect on other systems.

30 Review the provision for monitoring the system, fault diagnosis and correction on the network and provide appropriate procedures.

40 Obtain user agreement to the siting of equipment, performance levels, fault correction service and growth path of the network.

50 Provide input to the Installation Plan, as required (see Task 90).

60 Review and revise the database and file design, if required.

70 Draw up matrices of node/processor, program/processor, database/ node, user/node, geographic location/node, and so on, to check all aspects are covered. In particular, check for bottlenecks or components where a single failure would cause severe network disruption and re-design if possible.

80 Ensure relevant hardware and software exists or has been ordered for both development and production purposes.

QUALITY ASSURANCE

Technical checks must be done by outside experts (since this is a high-risk area, with expertise not commonly available). A 'what if' analysis should be carried out to predict what might be necessary if a node, communication line or other vital component is inoperable or becomes a bottleneck. The design may require inbuilt redundancy of equipment to cater for this. Questions need to be asked about other use of the network, including electronic mail, facsimile, telephones, video links and file transfers. See how other companies have done it and ask them about group patterns.

Deliverables

INPUTS
– data/function matrices and statistics by location
– network options, characteristics, constraints and costs
– back-up/recovery requirements
– facts about available protocols, line speeds, line capacity and terminal characteristics
– distributed/central requirements from analysis
– proposed development environment

OUTCOMES
System Deliverables
– *network architecture*
– *network control procedures*

Control Information
– *none*

Other Outcomes
– *agreed fault correction service levels*
– *capacity plan for the network*
– *cross-checking matrices as required*

ESTIMATES
These depend on the number of locations and complexity of the transaction mix. Derivation of the topology of a network based on full inputs will take a minimum of 5 days, to allow for exploring the design options.

RESOURCES
– network designer

TECHNIQUES
– network design

TOOLS
– spreadsheet

CASE tools
– designer matrices for entity:function
entity: business unit
function:business unit

NOTES and COMMENTS

Where a network is being introduced for the first time, there is a considerable effort in setting up a network control function, not least of which is acquiring the chosen processors and other hardware for the network architecture. Where the network already exists, it may be a stated (or perceived) constraint, and will directly affect the database design (Task 30).

Where no obvious network topology emerges from data and function patterns, it may be necessary to weight the testing estimates in the build stage to allow time to tune the network design (Build Stage, Task 50, Activity 50).

TASK 50
*Design audit/
control needs*

DESCRIPTION
This task designs the audit and access control requirements identified in the analysis stage.

Activity 10 Design tests to validate that business and legal requirements have been met (see Analysis Stage, Task 80). Discuss with the auditors. File in system test plan documentation.

20 Document access security provisions by user classification or user to be applied at program, record or field level, and ensure that there are procedures for controlling the security provisions (e.g. password allocation).

30 Document any other security provisions; for example, system software protection, tape encoders, off-site back-up, use of safes, secure zones in buildings, security guards.

40 Review the controls per module (see Task 20, Activity 50) and add in any system-wide controls; for example, date/version checks on programs and files, reconciliation totals checked between programs. Document any additional procedures required to ensure referential integrity.

50 Agree audit trails with auditors and ensure that any user needs are incorporated; for example, managers may want to track staff activities.

60 Ensure that any significant error handling is catered for; for example, criteria for acceptance/rejection of financial transactions, and subsequent handling of them.

QUALITY ASSURANCE
Solutions should conform to the installation standards, meet auditors' requirements and be agreed as feasible by operations staff.

Privacy requirements may be by named user, user role, location, device, data values, procedure and many other possibilities, dependent on the sensitivity of the system.

Deliverables

INPUTS
- audit/control requirements
- module design and specifications
- installation, business and legal standards for audit and security

OUTCOMES
System Deliverables
- *entries in system test plan*
- *revised module specifications*
- *additional control modules*
- *control/integrity procedures*
- *access security procedures*
- *draft operations documentation*

Control Information
- *audit criteria*

Other Outcomes
- *better awareness of vulnerable areas of the system (to highlight in user manual, operations procedures, help desk instructions, etc.)*

ESTIMATES
Allow at least one man day per sub-system to derive and agree controls. (In highly secure sites this task may well involve several months' effort.)

RESOURCES
- designers
- users
- operations staff

TECHNIQUES
- role playing an industrial spy or hacker

TOOLS
CASE tools
- design screens in query mode

NOTES and COMMENTS
Attention to controls will make the system more robust, and therefore reduce maintenance effort.

Subsequently, it may be found useful to ask a 'reliable' colleague to attempt to breach your security controls (perhaps given information to help him past your first line of defence).

TASK 60
Design back-up/ recovery needs

DESCRIPTION

This task meets the back-up and recovery needs identified in the analysis stage.

Activity 10 Document back-up/recovery procedures for the system. These should be compatible with the installation standards applied to other systems, but should reflect any special needs of this system.

20 Ensure that data retention requirements are handled. These should be compatible with the installation standards applied to other systems but should reflect any special retrieval needs of this system.

30 Ensure that fall-back options have been specified and that the responsibility to develop them has been allocated.

40 Review module specifications and revise/add new specifications, as required.

50 Provide an overview of programs and data, a schematic of the whole system, and initial thoughts on jobs, job links and processing cycles. Add additional material from Task 50 to form the draft operations documentation.

QUALITY ASSURANCE

Solutions should conform to the installation standards, meet auditors' requirements and be agreed as feasible by operations staff and anyone else concerned (e.g. database administrator).

Deliverables

INPUTS
- back-up/recovery requirements
- module design and specification
- installation standards for back-up and recovery
- data retention requirements from analysis
- installation standards for data retention

OUTCOMES
System Deliverables
- *revised module specification*
- *back-up/recovery procedures*
- *draft operations documentation*
- *fall-back options*
- *entries in system test plan*

Control Information
- *none*

Other Outcomes
- *better awareness of possible cause and effect of system failure (to educate help desk and operations staff)*
- *disaster planning*

ESTIMATES
Allow sufficient time to derive and agree back-up/recovery design.

This task may represent significant effort, depending on the complexity of the system, other systems in the same machine environment, the hardware capabilities and the nature of the organization.

RESOURCES
- designers
- operations staff
- database administrator
- users

TECHNIQUES
- create checklist of possible failure points in a distributed, multi-user computer system
- role playing an industrial spy or hacker

TOOLS

NOTES and COMMENTS
Attention to back-up/recovery will make the system 'safer' and reduce the disruption of a system failure.

TASK 70
Review outline design and produce program specifications

DESCRIPTION
This task ensures that module specifications reflect all previous tasks, and uses these specifications along with the database and file design and the interface design to form program specifications.

Activity 10 Walk through all aspects of the design:

- module design and specification
- database and file design
- user interface design
- network/communication design
- audit/control and back-up/recovery design.

Rework and review the efficiency of the modules, the predicted database and network performance, and the usability of the functions. Confirm service levels, archive policy, distributed/central requirements.

20 Revise the outline design to accommodate necessary changes.

30 Identify modules to be implemented by incremental development techniques (e.g. prototyping), and identify user authority and suitably skilled builders for each.

40 Prepare detailed specifications of implementation for each module that will not be incrementally built.

QUALITY ASSURANCE

Program specifications should conform to a standard layout and should provide the programmer with everything needed. Similarly, manual procedures and forms should conform to standard layout and style guidelines.

Each program specification should be reviewed by a structured walkthrough or formal inspection technique to ensure that it performs the required function and has criteria to cover the required degree of reliability and usability.

Deliverables

INPUTS

– module design and specification
– database and file design
– screens/reports/forms
– network design/architecture
– back-up/recovery and security procedures

OUTCOMES

System Deliverables
– *program specifications*

Control Information
– *initial reactions on complexity of programs (for estimating)*

Other Outcomes
– *confirmed service levels*
– *archive policy*
– *central/distributed requirements*

ESTIMATES

Activities 10-30 will depend on numbers and availability of users. These activities are unlikely to take less than 5 man days, and will probably use 25% of the time taken to prepare the outline design (Tasks 20-60).

Allow 2 days on average per module for Activity 40.

Note that complex modules (especially when using 3GL tools) can take over 10 days to specify fully.

RESOURCES

– programmers
– designers
– analysts (for information)

TECHNIQUES

TOOLS

– skeleton program specification
– specification standards

CASE tools
– design screens and reports

NOTES and COMMENTS

Specifications should derive from previous deliverables by the addition of detail by designers who are capable of performing the build work.

Note that job control modules for batch suites and menu modules are both types of program that need to be designed and specified here.

TASK 80
Complete system test plan

DESCRIPTION

This task collates test notes, and derives conditions, data and expected results sufficient to test the system thoroughly.

Activity 10 Derive test conditions appropriate to the design stage: data validation, missing/empty files, performance criteria.

20 Review notes on test conditions made in the analysis stage, and produce test conditions based on input, processing and output for each program.

30 Collate all test conditions and review against business and legal requirements, as specified in control/integrity procedures, and agree the condition list with users.

40 Define test plans for:

- standalone testing of interactive/non-interactive programs, manual procedures and other modules (limit and exception test plan is created during build stage)
- link testing of dependent modules and system exercise tests (for integration and system testing)
- performance, integrity, recovery and regression testing
- environment testing
- limit and exception testing
- integration with existing systems, packages and office automation facilities
- access control or other privacy aspects
- conversion from existing systems and take-on
- data distribution tests
- function distribution tests
- node failure tests
- disaster recovery procedures, if required.

Produce realistic and rigorous test data and expected results.

50 Agree the test plan with users. Allocate roles in testing: control schedule, conduct tests, document and co-ordinate change requests, correct code.

continues

Deliverables

INPUTS
- test notes and other conditions from analysis stage
- audit criteria
- entries in system test plan

OUTCOMES
System Deliverables
- *system test plan*

Control Information
- *number of tests (for estimating testing effort)*
- *test data*

Other Outcomes
- *requests for user involvement and machine resources*

ESTIMATES
Allow one man day per program for Activities 10-40, 60 and 70, and an additional 3 days for Activities 50, 80 and 90.

RESOURCES
- programmers
- analysts
- users
- designers

TECHNIQUES
- test planning

TOOLS
- test harness
- testing software

CASE tools
- test data generator
- configuration management tools

continues

continued

TASK 80

*Complete system
test plan*

DESCRIPTION

This task collates test notes, and derives conditions, data and expected results sufficient to test the system thoroughly.

Activity 60 Design the test pack: files, programs, data, job control language, scripts, human interactions.

70 Produce test documentation: task descriptions, online test scripts, batch test run schedules, results sheets, overall control matrix. If necessary, acquire or build test harness.

80 Plan the test environment: arrange for installation of hardware/software, book machine time, set up secure libraries for controlling data and program versions.

90 Walk through the test plan with the team, involving other Information Systems personnel experienced in system testing.

QUALITY ASSURANCE

Users should check that the test plan covers all conditions they perceive in the business; Information Systems personnel check for completeness in testing the program specifications.

Deliverables

continued
NOTES and COMMENTS

System testing should also 'try out' user and operations procedures, thus ensuring that the draft user manual and operations documentation will be available in time.

The team must understand how the system test will be conducted: the plan will be followed, although there will be dynamic replanning (if tests fail and have to be rescheduled) in order to satisfy testing dependencies.

TASK 90
Complete transition strategy

DESCRIPTION
This task revises the initial strategy produced (Analysis Stage, Task 120) in the light of further knowledge of the system, and as a result of actions carried out to verify the strategy.

Activity 10 Confirm Delivery and Acceptance Plan:
- phased delivery (function content, location considerations, temporary interfaces)
- method of acceptance, acceptance criteria and acceptance test plan
- resources, tasks and timescales.

20 Confirm Training Plan:
- sets of users to be trained, and scope of training for each
- training method (e.g. cascade, tutorial, on the job) and training responsibilities
- required sessions (schedules, locations, contents and materials)
- new staff to be recruited
- staff roles that will change (e.g. staff seconded to help desks, performing data administration roles, undertaking responsibility for ongoing training)
- required contribution from the project team (ideally this is to provide material for training and the user manual, which users will then take responsibility for)
- resources, tasks and timescales.

30 Confirm Data Take-on Plan:
- source of data (to be collected, existing manually, existing on other systems)
- state of data requiring clean-up, conversion, and so on
- data take-on method, complexity and effort required (user keying, use of bureau or conversion programs)
- required contribution from the project team
- resources, tasks and timescales.

continues

Deliverables

INPUTS
- transition strategy from analysis stage
- feedback from draft deliverables
  (e.g. via user discussions)

OUTCOMES
System Deliverables
- *Delivery and Acceptance Plan*
- *Training Plan*
- *Data Take-on Plan*
- *Cut-over Plan*
- *operational requirements*
- *Installation Plan*

Control Information
- *user responsibilities assigned for progressing plans (with critical milestones)*

Other Outcomes
- *required organization changes (new staff, changed roles)*

ESTIMATES
This task consists of two activities notoriously difficult to estimate – thinking and negotiating.

Expect to produce drafts and then review them. This cycle can easily be repeated for each plan.

Data clean-up may take elapsed months (see Notes and Comments).

RESOURCES
- sponsoring user
- project leader
- users
- analysts

TECHNIQUES
- planning

TOOLS
CASE Tools
- project control, estimating and planning tools

continues

continued
TASK 90
*Complete
transition strategy*

DESCRIPTION

This task revises the initial strategy produced (Analysis Stage, Task 120) in the light of further knowledge of the system, and as a result of actions carried out to verify the strategy.

Activity 40 Confirm Cut-over Plan (subject to revisions in the build stage):
- conversion 'window' in operational timetable
- parallel running
- dependencies
- fall-back options, what to do with 'old' data left in the system
- checkpoints, tests, responsibilities
- resources, tasks and timescales.

50 Confirm Installation Plan:
- building modifications
- installation of hardware, software, network/communications
- acquisition of consumables (e.g. stationery)
- resources, tasks and timescales
- control of third parties (suppliers, contractors, etc.).

60 Agree operational requirements:
- expected load on computers, including minimum, average and peak requirements
- storage requirements
- service, response and support required from operations staff.

70 Delegate control outside the project team, where appropriate (e.g. training, data take-on, user acceptance, installation), to ensure user commitment and simplify control of the system development.

QUALITY ASSURANCE

Ensure that the person responsible for each plan is confident about the tasks and timescales, that dependencies are highlighted and that there is adequate overall control (nominally by the sponsoring user, but essentially through liaison of all interested parties and clearly identified checkpoints).

Deliverables

continued

NOTES and COMMENTS

It is essential to co-ordinate these activities, so that implementation is as smooth as possible. A traumatic implementation affects user perception of the quality of the system. Although responsibility for developing and progressing the plans may be assigned to users, the team should hold a watching brief and assist, as required. In particular, ensure that the acceptance criteria are valid and achievable.

Where data conversion and loading (take-on) are non-trivial, a separate design and build of the take-on or conversion procedures should be conducted in parallel to the main project build, in order to be ready for transition (see Transition Stage, Task 50).

When data conversion requires a data clean-up exercise first (e.g. to bring name and address details up to date and to include unique or near unique identification codes), then existing systems may need to be changed. Many agencies exist to help such clean-up exercises. In any event, months of elapsed time may be necessary for this tedious but essential task.

TASK 100
Review results of design stage

DESCRIPTION
This task ensures that all parties have confidence in the direction of the project.

Activity 10 Review the translation process of the detailed requirement to the intended system:

- have the required decisions been taken?
- is everybody happy with them?
- is it a good design, is it elegant?
- is it flexible to changes in business requirements or technology?
- is it technically feasible?
- is there sufficient knowledge of the technical environment?
- does it fit into the working style of the users?

20 Review the intended system in terms of its impact on:

- other systems
- the organization (required premises and staff, training needs, roles and responsibilities, disruption at cut-over)
- user experience
- opinion of other groups associated with the project (auditors, technical staff, operations staff, data administrator and/or data-base administrator, other user areas, suppliers, etc.).

Ensure that the Terms of Reference are still appropriate in the light of further knowledge.

30 Perform a system walkthrough or dry run of the system to check for completeness and identify any bottlenecks. Try to resolve all design issues at this point.

40 Agree Terms of Reference for the remainder of the project. Ensure that all issues have been resolved prior to beginning the build stage (warn the user of the consequences of change from now on).

50 Ensure that there has been adequate user checking on each task and that follow-up actions have been carried out. Review any quality assurance reports.

60 Revise system deliverables, as required.

Deliverables

INPUTS
– all deliverables to date

OUTCOMES
System Deliverables
– *revised deliverables*

Control Information
– *revised Terms of Reference*
– *approved quality assurance results*
– *all issues now resolved*

Other Outcomes
– *change control is now instituted as a formal process (if not done earlier)*

ESTIMATES
All system deliverables (module specifications, screen/report/form design) attract an overhead of 50% of their original estimates in revising them as a result of quality assurance, or in response to other changes. The revision overhead is higher if iterative prototyping has been done. (See Appendix E.)

RESOURCES
– sponsoring user
– project leader
– analysts
– designers
– programmers
– users

TECHNIQUES
– any means of visualizing/ constructively criticizing the intended system (e.g. review of prototype, if done; or paper prototyping using mock-ups of inputs/outputs and any appropriate diagramming technique)
– lateral thinking

TOOLS
– stage-end checklist

NOTES and COMMENTS
Logically there is a clear cut-off between the design and build stages, but in practice the later stages of the development cycle may be dovetailed or even iterated for each group of functions identified in the analysis stage (see Analysis Stage, Task 120, Notes). This task of reviewing results may therefore be iterated for each group of functions, and it is vital to maintain an overall view of the system design.

QUALITY ASSURANCE
This task is a checkpoint in itself, but it also underlines an important role for the project leader in taking responsibility for the state of the documentation (Activities 50 and 60). It is an important time for identifying potential bottlenecks in the system as the cost of correction now can be very low in comparison with finding them later. Frequent system bottlenecks include data capture, sign-off clerks, disk input/output, and network traffic through a node.

TASK 110
Obtain stage-end commitment

DESCRIPTION

This task ensures confidence in the outcome of the design stage, and the plans for the build and user documentation stages.

Activity 10 Ensure that the areas of the transition strategy (split off in Task 90) are being adequately planned/controlled outside the main project.

20 Review costs, as required.

30 Ensure that change control procedures are adequate (include agreement with the database administrator about how and when versions of the database are released).

40 Produce detailed plans for the build and user documentation stages. This will involve adding more detail, but, if the estimates differ substantially from the original, it may be necessary to review the scope or approach. Revise the outline plan for the rest of the project. Publish plans, to obtain commitment and keep interested parties informed.

50 Produce a stage-end report or presentation, if required.

60 Obtain commitment to proceed.

70 Brief project staff and users on the next stages.

QUALITY ASSURANCE

Plans should be checked for feasibility by Information Systems management, and for acceptability by users. In particular, review the effectiveness of the groups of functions chosen in the analysis stage.

Do they still meet the need?

– packets of work to be delivered at the same time or handled in the same way.

Do they match the method of working?

– allocation of staff skills, responsibilities.

Are they on schedule?

– there will be dependencies between the groups of functions, and, if one is ahead/behind schedule, consider reallocating staff, unless this will be too disruptive.

Deliverables

INPUTS
- transition strategy
- system development plan
- deliverables, to be included in report (if required)

OUTCOMES
System Deliverables
- *revised system development plan*

Control Information
- *progress information from reviewing the areas of the transition strategy*
- *stage-end report, if required*

Other Outcomes
- *provisional agreement on development environment/ tools*

ESTIMATES
Allow the same effort as for a feedback (typically from 4-12 man days) for a stage-end report, if required. (The material should all be drawn from existing deliverables.)

Allow 1-2 man days for planning and 1-2 days for obtaining commitment and briefing staff.

RESOURCES
- sponsoring user
- project leader
- analysts
- programmers
- designers
- users

TECHNIQUES
- planning
- report writing
- evaluation of development environment/tools

TOOLS
- CASE*Method task list
- design stage skeleton report
- profiles showing use of different delivery vehicles

CASE tools
- project control packages

NOTES and COMMENTS
Producing stage-end reports is costly in effort and should not be necessary if there has been close liaison with users throughout. Plans are still fairly high level (for instance, by groups of functions): bottom-up estimating by program will be done in the build stage (Task 20).

Design Stage Summary

It has been ...

the stage where detailed requirements were translated into the intended system – the database, program specifications, network architecture and plans for delivery and acceptance, training, data take-on, cut-over and installation.

We have produced ...

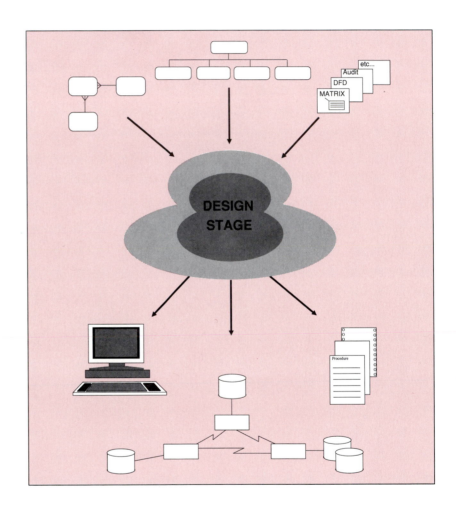

And now for ...

the build stage, which codes and tests the system, and the user documentation stage, which develops the required procedures and training in parallel. These stages will come together for system testing and transition.

Chapter

6

BUILD STAGE

Aims and Objectives

The build stage will code and test programs, using appropriate tools. These depend on the technical environment and the types of programs involved, but may range from conventional development to a 'quick build' approach using incremental development.

Figure 6-1
The Build Stage in the Life Cycle

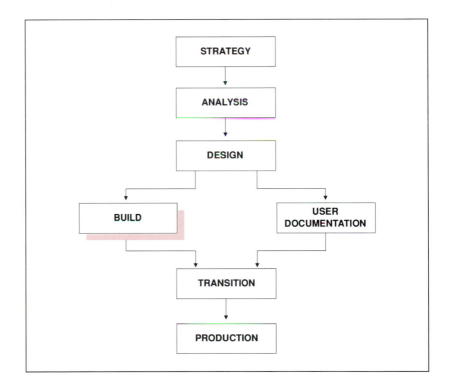

Description

Whatever the chosen approach, and it may vary by program, the build process involves planning, design of program structure, coding, bottom-up testing (unit and link tests), top-down testing (system test) and a disciplined approach to doing the work and controlling versions of programs, test packs, and so on.

Key Deliverables

- *Program design*
- *Tuned database*
- *Working, tested programs*
- *Revised transition strategy*
- *System test results*
- *Installed development hardware/software and early indications of performance*

Critical Success Factors

Important factors include:

- Ensuring quality work in tight timescales, where there are many dependencies.
- Picking up and reacting to early indications of performance; for example, network, input/output or processor bottlenecks.
- Tuning the database or programs.
- Testing limits and exceptions.

Figure 6-2
Critical Success Factors
and the Use of Prototypes

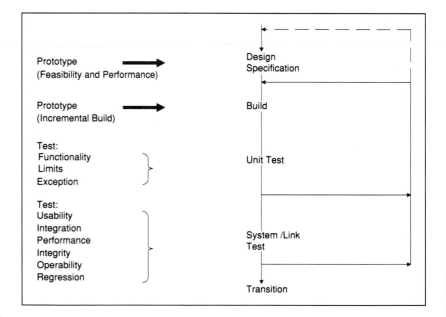

Approach

Staff develop the programs in relative isolation from the user, so it is important that any alterations of the specification are recognized and checked by the user/analyst (including recognizing the need to amend test plans and user manuals).

In addition the programmer will need to make many decisions. Most of these will be minor, but collectively the wrong choice can often accidentally waste a lot of effort reworking the system. The programmers should be encouraged to **really** understand what they are building. They

Figure 6-3
Build: the Process of Construction
Against a Design

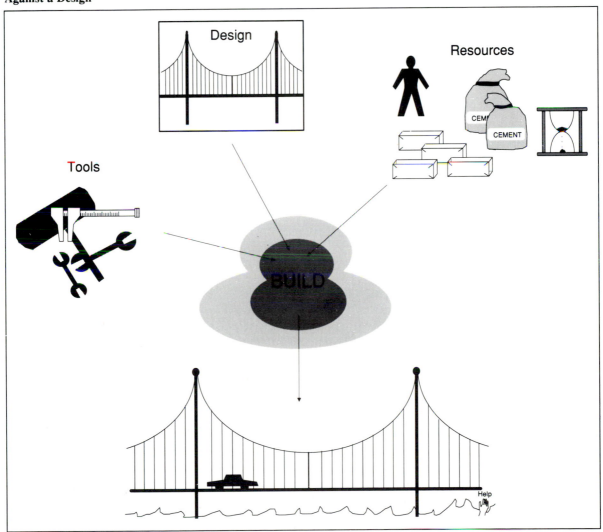

need to be given an overview of the whole system and an indication of how their bit fits into this total picture.

The users should have the opportunity to discuss some of the key things they want to get out of the system, and be kept informed about the performance, usability and other characteristics that are important and why. They will then be better placed to make more accurate decisions. They should be encouraged to document decisions and periodically review them with the analyst and/or user.

Whenever systems are built, apparently small constraints and limits get introduced during the build stage.

> "I can't imagine them ever needing more than 255!"
> "The biggest one I've ever seen only had seven line items."
> "I think I'll code those codes directly into the program to make it work faster!"

These items are ideally sought out and removed as early as possible. They can be difficult to find after the event and typically reduce the intended flexibility of the system. In fact, it is worth encouraging people to suggest ways of adding further flexibility.

The ideal place for such information is in a rule-base held in the database which can be changed directly by its own maintenance routines. It is meta data, which includes look-up codes, allowed values or ranges, discount or other business rules.

If and when limits have to be imposed directly by the program, the programmer must test them rigorously, rather than relying upon system testing to flush out any problems.

Programmers normally want to produce the perfect program: one that can be referenced when their career is next reviewed; one that has those few extra bells and whistles that enable them to say, "I wrote that, you can tell by the ..." These endeavours must somehow be channelled and balanced with the need for productivity, standard 'look and feel', and the different level to which programs need to be built dependent on their use. For example, a data take-on program to be used just once may have minimal (but adequate) documentation and exception handling; a program used only once a quarter may require more comprehensive hints, help messages and documentation so that its infrequent use does not detract from its usability. Programs of such different classes should be distributed between the programmers so that each has a mix of exciting challenges with the more tedious 'minimum adequate for the job' programs. The keener, brighter programmers can help to develop the look and feel standards, so the users will benefit from a really good common standard.

In parallel with this stage, analysts are helping to develop user manuals, training and operations hand-over documentation, and it is important that the system test pulls together the whole system, that is, procedures and documentation as well as programs. It should be as close to the live environment as a structured series of tests can be.

List of Tasks

**Figure 6-4
Network Diagram of the
Tasks in the Build Stage**

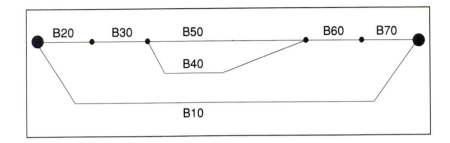

Key
B10   Project administration and management
B20   Prepare for build stage
B30   Review designs and estimates with programmer
B40   Produce programs
B50   Prepare, perform and review system test
B60   Review test results
B70   Obtain stage-end commitment

TASK 10
*Project
administration
and management*

DESCRIPTION

This task comprises control, reporting, quality assurance and administrative activities performed by the team.

Activity 10 Review plan and monitor the progress against plan and revise the plan if required.

20 Monitor the quality of coding/testing for structure, accuracy, annotation and standards.

30 Liaise with other groups (auditors, technical staff, operations staff, data administrator and/or database administrator, other user groups, suppliers, etc.).

40 Monitor staff performance, give guidance, and so on.

50 Perform change control on all design and analysis deliverables and reported errors with their associated corrections.

60 Report progress.

70 Hold periodic progress meetings with user management and/or the steering group.

80 Attend regular team meetings to provide status reports and to gather/disseminate information.

90 Participate in quality assurance reviews.

100 Ensure that system builders and the project leader have appropriate CASE tools, programming tools, database management system, other tools and the full development environment required for the job, in a timely manner.

110 Provide general administrative support (booking rooms, scheduling meetings, etc.).

QUALITY ASSURANCE

It is the project leader's responsibility to ensure that this task is performed well.

Deliverables

INPUTS
- system development plan
- Terms of Reference
- timesheets
- unresolved issues
- deliverables from previous stages
- deliverables to be quality assured
- minutes of meetings
- number of tests (for estimating effort)

OUTCOMES
System Deliverables
- *revised deliverables*

Control Information
- *progress reports*
- *quality assurance results*
- *change control log*
- *revised plans*
- *minutes of meetings*
- *revised system development plan*

Other Outcomes
- *good liaison with other parties to the project*
- *awareness of staff strengths/ weaknesses*

ESTIMATES
Activities 10-60 will occupy most of the project leader's time for a team size of 5 or more. It is important that the project leader simultaneously controls the technical cohesion of the project as well as its cost and timescales.

Activities 70-90 should take up no more than 0.5 days per week for each team member.

RESOURCES
- project leader
- analysts
- programmers
- users

TECHNIQUES
- progress reporting
- project control

TOOLS
- timesheet forms
- progress report forms
- change control forms
- quality assurance checklist
- CASE*Method task list

CASE tools
- module definition and weighting factor screens
- estimating and progress monitoring tools

NOTES and COMMENTS

The effort of co-ordinating activities increases throughout the development cycle. In this stage, the project leader may delegate certain areas of control:
- overall quality of program design (Task 30)
- technical sign-off to system test (Task 40)
- control of system test schedules (Task 50).

The stage plan cannot be completed until Task 20 has been completed, since the allocation of work packages to individual programmers can have a significant impact on scheduling.

TASK 20
Prepare for build stage

DESCRIPTION

This task verifies the plan produced at the end of the design stage by doing bottom-up estimating on each program (based on complexity and approach).

Activity 10 Review the program specifications and the estimates for build time, based on the latest metrics.

20 Review the groups of functions for the build stage (e.g. group online transactions, incremental development modules, modules using the same set of database views), as a basis for assigning work packages to builders.

30 Confirm the chosen development environment, tools, delivery vehicles for each function group. Document any technical decisions.

40 Publish detailed work schedules (by program and by programmer) for coding/unit test. Revise the stage plan if necessary.

50 Provide procedures for the chosen development environment, technical guidelines, programming standards and library system for controlling programs that are being built. Set up or revise 'look and feel' standards, balancing functional use with new ways of doing things. In particular, set up guidelines on the configuration of hardware, software, data files needed for different aspects of the testing and for subsequent transition, including unit testing, link and system testing, regression testing, demonstrations, training systems and specialized problems (such as privacy control or performance benchmarking). Brief staff.

60 Establish a suitable development environment for the team, and the tools and methods to be used. This activity may include the installation of hardware, and system and other bought-in software.

QUALITY ASSURANCE

The project leader is responsible for ensuring that the packages of work are given to appropriate people to do in agreed timescales with proven/understood technology. This may mean several iterations of Activities 20-40.

Time should be allowed in the schedules for the learning curves of programmers, where appropriate (i.e. learning curves related to the technology, the application and the environment).

Deliverables

INPUTS
- system development plan
- program specifications
- proposed development environment
- metrics

OUTCOMES
System Deliverables
- *hardware and system software*
- *revised program specifications*

Control Information
- *detailed estimates per program*
- *revised groups of functions*
- *detailed work schedules*

Other Outcomes
- *confirmation of development environment/tools*
- *technical guidelines/ programming standards for given environment*
- *revised 'look and feel' standards*
- *procedures for use of the development environment*
- *library control system*

ESTIMATES
The time taken to do a detailed examination of programs depends on complexity, staff skill, range of tools, etc. Allow 2 days minimum where the project is small enough to be fully known to the project leader. Probably at around 40 programs a second designer will need to be involved. Add 2 days for each additional 40 modules.

RESOURCES
- designers
- project leader
- technical staff (specialist in machine environment)
- programmers

TECHNIQUES
- estimating
- evaluation of development environment/tools

TOOLS
- profiles showing use of different delivery vehicles

CASE tools
- project control tools
- configuration management tools

NOTES and COMMENTS

Good program estimating is essential to controlling this stage. At least four weightings are needed: easy, moderate, complex, very complex. Complexity is based on the number of tables accessed, difficulty of access paths and the amount of processing (validation, calculation, reformatting, etc.). Estimates for each weighting depend on staff skill and environment. Metrics should be constantly reviewed/revised on the basis of actual performance figures for completed and accepted work. During this task adjustments may be made to estimates, and the schedules of individual programmers may be revised to allow for variance from 'standard' programmer productivity.

It should be noted that revisions and extensions to the test plans and data will occur during coding and testing (Task 40).

TASK 30

Review designs and estimates with programmer

DESCRIPTION

This task ensures that the programmer's approach is technically sound and can deliver the program in a predictable timescale, as specified.

Activity 10 Review the specification and estimates with the designer, and agree these with the programmer or senior programmer. (For incremental development this is informal; for the conventional approach it should be documented.) Ensure adherence to 'look and feel' or other standards and compatibility with other programs. Resolve any detailed design issues, and document decisions and changes.

20 For 'non-easy' programs and less experienced programmers plan the unit code and test (Task 40), providing at least one milestone per working week.

30 Draft the program test plan, and produce initial test data and expected results. Dry run the test data against your understanding of the logic to be performed, using structured walkthrough techniques. Agree this plan with the senior programmer.

40 Ensure that designs of common procedures are checked thoroughly and made known to programmers who are to use them.

QUALITY ASSURANCE

It is important to appoint one person (e.g. senior programmer) to review all designs for compatibility and adherence to standards. This is just as important if incremental development is being used, to save wasted iterations and/or substantial performance tuning later.

Deliverables

INPUTS
- module design and specification
- program specification
- any unresolved design issues (see Notes)

OUTCOMES
System Deliverables
- *revised program specification and detailed design*
- *program test plan*
- *expected results*

Control Information
- *early feedback on program estimates*

Other Outcomes
- *unit test plan*
- *design for common procedures*

ESTIMATES
Allow one man day per program for designing/checking.

RESOURCES
- analysts
- programmers
- senior programmer

TECHNIQUES
- program design
- structured walkthrough

TOOLS
- screen painters

CASE tools
- diagrammers for program structures

NOTES and COMMENTS

The menu system decided in the design stage (Task 20) and other mechanisms of invoking programs ('daemons', batch suites, test harness, etc.) should be fully designed, if not built, at this point, to provide a framework for testing, and to ensure early agreement with the user on methods of navigating the system, security issues, and so on. (For instance, menus may be customized to individual user classes.)

It would appear desirable to resolve design issues for all programs before commencing any coding (Task 40), to improve the overall schedule. However, this is rarely practical for two reasons. Firstly, rescheduling later may mean reallocation of work, which would then necessitate repetition of Task 30 with the newly assigned programmer. Secondly, it is more effective to conduct the review just before a programmer starts work on a new program (possibly overlapping with work on other programs).

TASK 40
Produce programs

DESCRIPTION

This task is done in different styles for the conventional approach and for incremental development, but always involves coding, unit/link testing and a program review.

Activity 10 Code and unit test each program. Do revisions.

In incremental development this is done by a series of iterations, but at some point the program should be formally tested.

20 Review each program.

For incremental development, this includes reviewing user response during the various iterations. For the conventional approach, the review will have two iterations where corrections are needed, and two repetitions (after code and test, and then after the link test). The review after the link test should only need a regression test against the unit test plan and against the link test criteria.

30 Refine and rework the code, as required, after unit testing and after link testing.

40 Link test a set of programs, ensuring that the linkages, controls and so on work together. For batch systems, test job streams; for online systems, test logical groups of functions. Testing should include system facilities such as load, back-up, recovery, archive and restore. Sign off programs for system test.

50 Revise matrices for program to tables, files, columns, business functions and check for completeness.

60 Document programs; in particular, any structured diagrams of program designs, imposed limits, use of special routines or procedures and any other aspect that will help with maintenance.

QUALITY ASSURANCE

It is essential that sub-standard programs are not released to system test, since it impacts complex schedules and impairs user confidence. It is the responsibility of the programmers to rigorously test any limits, exceptions or other aspects built into the programs because of their design or because of constraints of the tools. One person should be responsible for sign-off to system test, and approved programs should be documented and then made physically secure (e.g. by copying to a separate library).

Deliverables

INPUTS
- program design and specification
- function definitions
- function logic
- database design
- look and feel standards
- expected results

OUTCOMES
System Deliverables
- *first-cut code*
- *refined code and independently-tested programs*
- *unit/link test results*
- *revised program specifications*

Control Information
- *feedback on estimates*
- *user reaction to quick build iterations*
- *revised program matrices*

Other Outcomes
- *none*

ESTIMATES
Various estimating techniques are available in the market for the derivation of programming man effort and timescales. Some rely on guesses of lines of code. In practice, the only reliable technique is to categorize programs by type, language and complexity (simple, medium, complex and very complex should suffice). Then record the results of 'average' programmers and use these derived values for subsequent estimates.

For example, using SQL*Forms for a fully tested and documented code, the following values may apply:

simple	2 days
medium	5 days
complex	16 days.

RESOURCES
- programmers
- user and analyst, to help on incremental build
- person to control sign-off to system test

TECHNIQUES
- incremental development (see Appendix E)
- coding
- unit/link testing

TOOLS
- any useful programming language
- 4GLs

CASE tools
- matrices
- test harnesses

NOTES and COMMENTS

It is important to appoint one person to control the system test schedules: this person will need to be aware of 'late' programs and try to minimize the impact.

Eliminate the learning curve before using derived estimates; for example, the very first program written by a programmer in a new language.

TASK 50
Prepare, perform and review system test

DESCRIPTION
This task ensures that the system (programs, documentation and procedures) is proved adequately before hand-over to the user.

Activity 10 Prepare test environment: data, program libraries, network/communications and other equipment, operating system and other support software.

20 Perform a set of tests as per test script (online test) or test run (batch test).

30 Document the test results and record any bugs/errors or other deficiencies.

40 Control the system test schedules: ensure correct sequence of tests, controlled error fixing, rescheduling of tests, completion of results documentation.

50 Correct errors, tune database or programs, resolve hardware or network problems in response to system test, including network architecture.

60 Maintain library control: programs are booked into the system test library after technical sign-off, and booked out again on the authority of the system test scheduler – either to return for error correction, or to be copied to an 'acceptance' library when approved.

70 Monitor system test problems and ensure required quality of programs and testing. This includes amending test conditions/expected results where these are found to be inadequate.

80 Determine the end of the system test: required level of confidence achieved.

QUALITY ASSURANCE

There are two roles:
- the person controlling the test schedule must ensure that it is completely and correctly carried out.
- the team doing the test (including users) must ensure the quality of both tests and results.

The help of one of those people who can always find fault in others' work can be invaluable during this task.

Quality of testing may naturally decline if successive retesting is necessary. To protect against this, rigorous use of checklists, automation of as many of the tests as possible, use of a regular intake of new testers and a highly professional attitude are required.

Deliverables

INPUTS
- completed system
- system test plan
- expected results
- draft user and operations manual from design or user documentation stages
- network design/ architecture

OUTCOMES
System Deliverables
- *system test results*
- *tested systems*
- *tuned database*
- *error/bug list*

Control Information
- *feedback on feasibility of implementation timescales*
- *feedback on system quality (technical and functional)*
- *feedback on quality of documentation and training*
- *feedback on system performance*

Other Outcomes
- *revised network architecture*

ESTIMATES
Allow 80% of the actual (not estimated) program development time for system test.

RESOURCES
- analysts
- programmers
- person to control system test
- users

TECHNIQUES
- testing
- evaluation of documentation/ procedures

TOOLS
- test results log
- source code control system
- log/tracking system
- error log
- change control system

NOTES and COMMENTS

System testing is arduous, but a lot can be gained if it is well run and users participate fully. Ideally, test data is created by the new system (to prove validation), but loading data can be used to test data take-on procedures. Ensure authentic data is used. The aim is to detect as many errors as possible in the shortest time. It is tempting to be diverted by "wouldn't it be nice if the system ...?", but the team must focus on the task in hand. Genuinely required changes should be raised via change control, not done 'on the fly'. Part of management of the system test will involve classifying changes as 'bugs' or user-requested function changes, based on function definitions delivered in analysis. The changes need to be given an order of priority ('must have/wish list') and the schedule controlled carefully.

Individuals carrying out the system test must follow the test script (online) or test run (batch). When there are errors, they should carry on testing as far as possible (to reduce iterations), and document test results fully (including error diagnosis if possible). The person controlling the test must monitor initial program quality, thoroughness of testing and efficiency of error fixing. He must optimize the use of resources (deploying people to other tests if there are delays for error fixing), ensure sufficient machine time, and report on progress to timescales, since problems may mean implementation has to be rescheduled. Involving users (key representatives from user departments) provides the additional benefits of testing user documentation and an opportunity to train the trainers early.

TASK 60

Review test results

DESCRIPTION

This task ensures that all parties have confidence in the system.

Activity 10 Review the completeness and accuracy of the system. Check that the corrections to bugs have been appropriately made, and that any implications on future work are recorded as new requirements.

20 Review the suitability of the system: fulfilment of objectives, acceptability to all parties.

30 Review the procedures and documentation used in the system test, as these may be used again when implementing subsequent phases.

QUALITY ASSURANCE

This task is a checkpoint in itself, but it also underlines an important role for the project leader in taking responsibility for the completion of all agreed tasks; the user expresses confidence on the basis of what he has seen (system test) and what the project leader assures him has, or will have, been done before hand-over for acceptance test.

Deliverables

INPUTS
- test results
- error/bug list and their corrections
- outstanding errors

OUTCOMES

System Deliverables
- *none*

Control Information
- *level of confidence in system*

Other Outcomes
- *none*

ESTIMATES
Allow time to obtain the views of all interested parties. There can be considerable debate concerning the classification of errors found during testing as bugs or deficiencies. Impact analysis must be done to clarify the extent of any potential changes, and thus their relative priority.

RESOURCES
- sponsoring user
- project leader
- analyst
- all interested parties

TECHNIQUES
- impact analysis

TOOLS
CASE tools
- reports and query screens

NOTES and COMMENTS

This is in preparation for handing the system over for acceptance test; it is not the final 'OK to implement'.

In theory, if there are any outstanding changes then the build is not finished and a further iteration of Task 50 is needed. In practice, low priority changes may be deferred in order to keep on schedule.

TASK 70

Obtain stage-end commitment

DESCRIPTION

This task ensures confidence for proceeding to the transition stage.

Activity 10   Review plans for transition instigated in the design stage (see Design Stage, Task 90):

- Delivery and Acceptance Plan
- Data Take-on Plan
- Cut-over Plan
- Installation Plan
- Training Plan.

Confirm that actions performed externally to the project are completed. Revise the plans as a result of these actions and expand the outline plans to sufficient detail for the transition stage.

20   Review and complete system documentation.

30   Agree project team involvement during the transition stage.

40   Confirm the cut-over date.

50   Brief staff.

QUALITY ASSURANCE

All interested parties must approve the planning and timescales for acceptance testing, data take-on, installation and cut-over.

Deliverables

INPUTS
- the transition strategy comprising:
- Delivery and Acceptance Plan
- Data Take-on Plan
- Cut-over Plan
- Installation Plan
- Training Plan

OUTCOMES
System Deliverables
- *revised deliverables and plans*
- *revised transition strategy*

Control Information
- *confirmed transition approach/timescales*

Other Outcomes
- *if any official notification of transition is required, it can now be given, e.g. 'public relations' within company, confirmed dates to third parties, etc.*

ESTIMATES
Allow time to focus all interested parties on the need for liaison during transition; for example, if other projects are being implemented at the same time, or multiple locations are involved.

If a comprehensive data dictionary has been used throughout, the system documentation (Activity 20) should be nearly complete. If not, this can be a very arduous activity.

RESOURCES
- sponsoring user
- project leader
- all interested parties

TECHNIQUES

TOOLS

NOTES and COMMENTS

The project team involvement during transition may be quite small if users are controlling acceptance tests, data take-on and installation. The project team must, however, control cut-over. It is worth emphasizing the delicate timings involved in performing transition, to minimize disruption to the business.

If maintenance is the responsibility of a separate group of people, then they should be involved in the review of system documentation to ensure that the system is maintainable.

Build Stage Summary

It has been ...

the stage where the system was completed and reviewed, prior to handing over for user acceptance. It has been conducted in parallel with the documentation stage.

We have produced ...

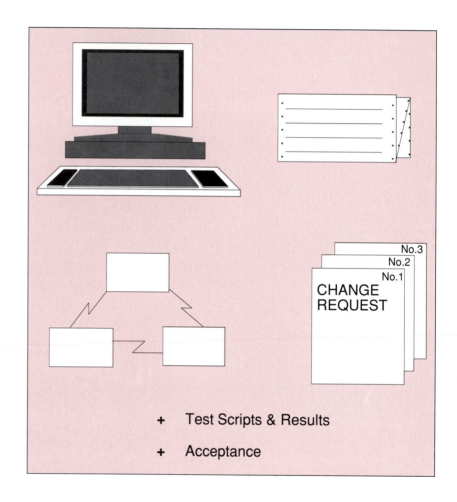

+ Test Scripts & Results

+ Acceptance

And now for ...

the transition stage, where the system finally goes live!

7

USER DOCUMENTATION STAGE

Aims and Objectives

The user documentation stage will deliver user manuals and operations hand-over documentation. These must be sufficient to support the system testing tasks in the concurrent build stage, and documentation must be completed before acceptance testing in the transition stage.

**Figure 7-1
The User Documentation
Stage in the Life Cycle**

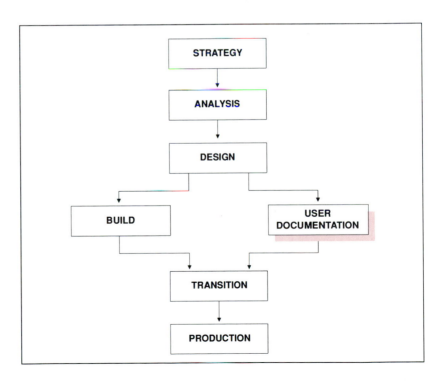

Description

During the strategy and analysis stages, all the functions were identified and documented, including those that are wholly manual, and those that involve an interaction of automation and user procedure. This interaction was investigated further in the design stage. Outline operations hand-over documentation was also produced during the design stage and service levels agreed. All this information is now brought together to ensure that the users and operations staff are fully prepared.

Key deliverables

- *User documentation*
- *Operations hand-over documentation*

Critical Success Factors

It is important to involve users and production systems operations staff as much as possible so that:

- The documentation is appropriate and effective.
- Users and operations staff are confident about taking on the system for acceptance testing.

Approach

Documentation of any system has to be an art more than a science if it is to be useful and appropriate. This book, for instance, is designed to encourage structured thinking and a methodical step-by-step approach to building systems. If a similar style was used to provide training and education to users for a new system they would find it inappropriate, and frankly would become bored with it very quickly. However, a tutorial in a storyboard manner with plenty of practical examples would be far more acceptable and effective.

It helps to start each aspect of the documentation by thinking, "Who is going to read it and what for?" If you were the reader, what would you need, how would you need to access the information, what would be superfluous? A well-structured contents list, an index and/or other form of navigation to the relevant information may be necessary. For example, should there be a fault in a production computer system does the online or paper documentation help the process of rapid diagnosis, fault correction, call-out of specialists or escalation?

Operations documentation is best done by providing background information and assisting operations staff in writing their own procedures. Similarly, user manuals are prepared by providing function descriptions, screen/report/form layouts, validation tables, error messages and any general information appropriate to understanding the system and assisting users to write their own manual.

The user documentation should include a full reference manual for users of the system. For each facility offered by the system, the manual should include what is expected of the user and what is the meaning of, and appropriate reaction to, each error message produced. It is often valuable to provide a tutorial, which can help new users gain an understanding of how the system works and, by use of suitable case studies, how the system serves the organization. In many modern systems, much of the documentation may be available online as help, hints, comprehensive error messages and in-context reference information.

Figure 7-2
Documentation for Training, Use, Support and Maintenance

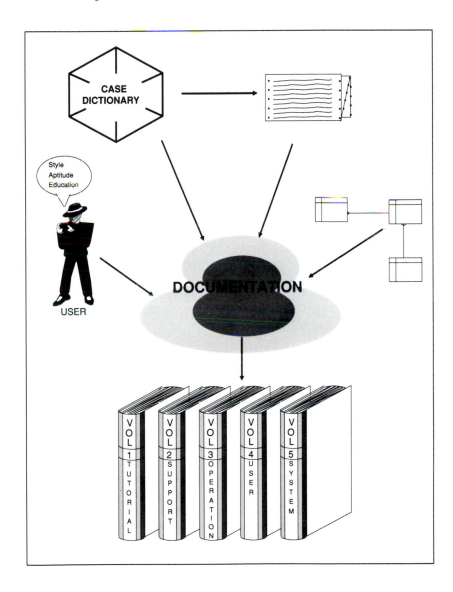

The operations documentation should provide a brief guide to day-to-day operations. In large production environments it is often vital to produce a support manual. This is essentially an extract from the system documentation, and should provide internal details of the system such that diagnosis of problems can be carried out by operations staff when the problem occurs. This is particularly important for 'twenty-four hour a day' operations, to enable the operations staff to correct the problem without the need to call out the development staff at three o'clock in the morning!

List of Tasks

Figure 7-3
Network Diagram of the Tasks in the User Documentation Stage

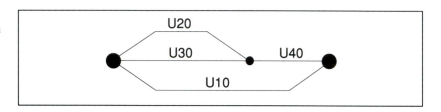

Key

U10	Project administration and management
U20	Complete user documentation
U30	Provide operations hand-over documentation
U40	Obtain stage-end commitment

The tasks and deliverables for the user documentation stage begin on pages 7-6 and 7-7.

TASK 10
*Project
administration
and management*

DESCRIPTION
This task comprises control, reporting, quality assurance and administrative activities performed by the team.

Activity 10   Monitor progress against plan and revise the plan if required.

20   Monitor the quality of the documentation for accuracy, legibility, completeness and usability.

30   Ensure that the documentation produced adheres to house standards where appropriate (audit, operations, data administration, database administration, user departments). Ensure that where new standards are to be established the appropriate groups are informed/consulted.

40   Monitor staff performance, give guidance, and so on.

50   Report progress.

60   Attend periodic progress meetings.

70   Provide general administrative support (scheduling rooms etc.).

80   Ensure that the team has appropriate CASE and other tools, in particular, configuration management and/or version control facilities.

QUALITY ASSURANCE

It is the project leader's responsibility to ensure that this task is performed well. Quality of documentation is always difficult, as the authors of this document have found – care must be taken to assure that the documentation is of a standard acceptable to the target readership and accurate in its use of terminology.

Deliverables

INPUTS
- system development plan
- timesheets
- unresolved issues
- steering group directives
- policy directives
- documentation standards
- minutes of meetings
- Terms of Reference

OUTPUTS

System Deliverables
- *none*

Control Information
- *information about progress*
- *minutes of meetings*
- *revised system development plan*
- *change control log*

Other Outcomes
- *good liaison with other parties to the project*
- *awareness of staff strengths/ weaknesses*

ESTIMATES
Activities 10-50 will probably occupy no more than half of the project leader's time for a team of up to 4.

RESOURCES
- project leader
- analysts
- programmers

TECHNIQUES
- progress reporting
- project control
- change control procedures

TOOLS
- timesheet forms
- progress reporting forms
- change control forms
- CASE*Method task list

CASE tools
- estimating and progress monitoring tools

NOTES and COMMENTS

It is important that staff involved in this stage realize the importance of documentation to the success of the system: it is not a 'soft option' and will often require the skills of the most articulate and knowledgeable analysts and users.

Tasks

<table>
<tr><td>

TASK 20
*Complete user
documentation*

</td><td>

DESCRIPTION
This task comprises revisions to the draft user manual and online documentation, and arrangements for the production and maintenance of manuals.

</td></tr>
</table>

Activity 10 Review the draft user manual from the design stage. Decide further material needed, required layout, responsibilities for producing the manual.

20 Complete and revise the draft manual. Input, check and revise any online hints, help messages, error messages and in-context reference information.

30 Obtain feedback by using the documentation during the system test.

40 Review the documentation against the definition of the business functions and objectives, and modify both, as appropriate.

50 Rigorously check and then agree the final version of the user manual and online information. Cross-index the manuals, if required.

60 Arrange for production and distribution of the user manual.

70 Agree responsibility and procedures for updating the user documentation (for future changes to the system and procedures).

80 Prepare tutorials and input, if required, for a training database.

90 Optionally, revise job definitions for users, cross-referencing the business functions and objectives that the job is intended to satisfy.

QUALITY ASSURANCE

Users should be responsible for the manual, but the project leader must ensure that it is of the requisite standard and reflects proper understanding of the use of the system. Cross-check the flow of words, ease of understanding, terminology, completeness, relevance, style and ease of finding information.

Cross-referencing job definitions to business functions and objectives is an excellent way to complete the loop between a system and its users; but care and sensitivity is needed as job definitions may not always exist, and in some cases you may identify jobs that have no perceived relationships to business functions or objectives!

Deliverables

INPUTS
– draft user manual
– function definitions
– look and feel standards
– feedback on quality of documentation
– feedback from system test

OUTCOMES
System Deliverables
– *finished user manual*
– *online documentation*
– *draft tutorial*

Control Information
– *feedback on whether the system and procedures interfaced well during system test*

Other Outcomes
– *draft training database details*

ESTIMATES
The team's contribution to the manual (layouts etc.) already exists, but allow time to liaise with interested parties (see Task 10, Activity 30), proof-read the manual and provide assistance, as required.

RESOURCES
– analysts
– users
– standards department

TECHNIQUES
– technical writing

TOOLS
– word processor or desktop publishing tool
– data entry screens for online documentation
– written reports against views

CASE tools
– reports against views
– diagrammers

NOTES and COMMENTS

The manual should be consistent with others, be written in the users' style, and contain everything they need (including their own working standards): hence it is best written by users themselves. If the manual is split into reference and tutorial, the tutorial should be based on realistic case studies, which should be provided by the users.

Many desktop publishing tools can accept output from CASE tools and screen dumps, terminals, personal computers and workstations. These can be used very effectively to illustrate points, act as storyboards or convey meaning via a picture.

TASK 30
Provide operations hand-over documentation

DESCRIPTION

This task ensures that the operations staff are confident about running the system and have the appropriate documentation to do the job.

Activity 10 Review the draft documentation from the design stage – decide on any further material and/or instruction needed.

20 Provide material and/or instruction.

30 Obtain feedback by using hand-over documentation during the system test.

40 Assist, as required, until operations staff are confident about running the system on their own.

Topics that may need to be covered include:

- installation of the hardware, software and other components of the system
- system initialization and checks
- regular start-up and close-down procedures
- system reconfiguration and online changes
- back-up, archive and recovery procedures
- error handling and support procedures
- operating network
- operating network security
- installation at other sites if appropriate
- regular review definition for aspects such as performance, integrity and audit trails
- procedures for communication and interfacing with other systems.

QUALITY ASSURANCE

Operations staff must agree that they are ready for acceptance testing.

Deliverables

INPUTS
- draft operations
  documentation

OUTCOMES
System Deliverables
- *operations (hand-over)
  documentation*

Control Information
- *assessment of how prepared
  operations staff are for
  acceptance testing*

Other Outcomes
- *none*

ESTIMATES
Allow time for instructing
operations staff and providing
additional material; for example,
user role in controlling system (run
requests, input of parameters, etc.),
known problem areas.

RESOURCES
- senior development team
  member/s
- operations staff
- standards department

TECHNIQUES
- technical writing

TOOLS
CASE tools
- reports as available

NOTES and COMMENTS
It helps if operations staff have been kept informed since the beginning of the
project (the project leader has a task to liaise with other groups), and can assign
someone to get involved at the design stage and take responsibility for the
hand-over documentation.

Tasks

TASK 40
Obtain stage-end commitment

DESCRIPTION

This task ensures confidence for proceeding to the transition stage.

Activity 10 Review documentation and obtain the commitment of the users and operations staff.

20 Provide any required input to the review of plans carried out during the build stage (Task 70).

QUALITY ASSURANCE

Both the users and the project team must be confident that this stage has been satisfactory.

The users should ensure that the documentation provides everything they need for induction of new staff to the system, for defining day-to-day procedures and for quick reference when users have become familiar with the system.

The team must ensure that the user manual is accurate, complete and well written, and that the arrangements for maintaining it are satisfactory. They must also ensure that operations documentation is accurate and sufficient.

Deliverables

INPUTS
– system development plan

OUTCOMES
System Deliverables
– *none*

Control Information
– *confidence that the users are adequately prepared for acceptance testing*

Other Outcomes
– *none*

ESTIMATES
Allow sufficient time to ensure that users and operations staff feel their documentation needs have been met. Typically, this can take 3-4 days on a medium-sized system.

RESOURCES
– project leader
– sponsoring user

TECHNIQUES
– completeness checking
– reviews and walkthroughs
– 'test marketing'
– standards checking

TOOLS

NOTES and COMMENTS
The user documentation stage effectively dovetails with the build stage at this point.

User Documentation Stage Summary

It has been ...

the stage where the user and operations documentation was completed, prior to handing over for the acceptance test. It has been carried out in parallel to the build stage.

We have produced ...

And now for ...

the transition stage, where the system finally goes live!

Chapter

8

TRANSITION STAGE

Aims and Objectives

The transition stage performs all tasks necessary for implementation and provides an initial period of support for the system. Transition must be accomplished with minimum disruption to the business, and must leave the users confident and ready to exploit the new system.

Figure 8-1
The Transition Stage in the Life Cycle

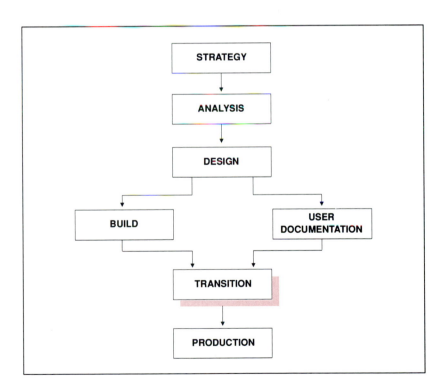

Description

Training is provided and the user is assisted in performing an acceptance test. Data take-on and hardware/software installation are then completed, and there is a final review of all details, since this is the most critical part of the whole project. Cut-over involves loading new data, file conversions and a series of tests to ensure that it is safe to run production work: final tidying-up (e.g. catch-up runs for old data in the system) may take several days. The initial period of support involves assistance to users, careful checking of the system and its performance, and fault correction.

Key Deliverables

- *Training and educational material*
- *Trained users and operations staff*
- *Installed and fully operational system*
- *Converted data*
- *Operations fault log*
- *Post-implementation review report*
- *Support facilities (e.g. help desk)*
- *Completed system documentation*

Critical Success Factors

It is important to:

- Ensure that the training is appropriate and effective.
- Ensure that the user does sufficient acceptance testing to prove the system operationally and become familiar with it.
- Co-ordinate the implementation, which is complex and time-critical.
- Ensure that operations, technical support and application support staff have sufficient training and documentation to be able to understand the system, how to diagnose problems and what actions to take in the event of a hardware or software failure.
- Schedule the implementation to fit the business requirements and ensure the availability of key users, developers and support staff.
- Ensure that integration or coexistence with existing systems, packages, office automation or other operational aspects is thoroughly planned and tested.

Approach

As far as the users and management are concerned, transition is often the most traumatic stage. During this period they may be asked to run two systems simultaneously and to still meet their business objectives. It is a little like having a new bathroom and kitchen installed in a house at the same time, only worse! Change in itself is often difficult to accept. There is nothing more difficult than learning a new way of doing things, especially in the more conservative-oriented institutions. There will be resistance. This must not be seen as a negative reaction to the new system, but as a real challenge to overcome so that the intended business benefits can be fulfilled.

The problems to overcome can be numerous. They have to do with attitudes, resources, timing, continuity, deadlines, business pressures and a wealth of small unforeseen issues. Planning of this stage is, therefore, crucial. Identifying every possible obstacle and deciding what to do with each can help. But the most dramatic aid is to enlist the full and informed help of the users and management themselves. If what needs to be done is carefully and professionally laid out, they will in nearly all cases be more than willing to help – it is in their interest to do so, after all.

Minimum disruption to the business is a goal that can only be achieved by co-operation of all parties, so the users should be involved months ahead of any planned implementation. They must get used to more rigorous data validation, cleaning up of current data, revision of some of the old procedures and working closely with the development staff. It may be useful to extract data from old systems into a query-only database so some of the benefits of the new system can be realized early, and a little of the potential of the new system will be demonstrated.

As implementation gets closer the approach is for even more user involvement. Development staff with a flair for training can help key users set up realistic training data, educate the training classes, and ensure that user documentation is pertinent and intelligible. The intention is to get the key users to train other users, so their understanding of the business and the old and new systems is crucial. Training by the project team is the fall-back option, but rarely as successful as training given by these key users.

The new system will be owned by the users, therefore it must be accepted by them. Proper acceptance is gained when the users thoroughly understand what they are being given, including the problems as well as the benefits. It is a fact of life that people get used to new benefits quickly: they soon accept them as normal and forget what it was like before. They may vent considerable pent-up feelings on apparently trivial problems. (If you have ever had a new car with lots of lovely new gadgets, but the indicator switch is just in the wrong place for your liking, and the radio doesn't pick up your favourite station, and ... then you'll know what we mean. You overlook that it starts first time every cold morning, and forget that you used to nearly flatten the battery trying to get the old model started.)

Getting acceptance is a process of give and take, based on mutual trust and understanding. Development staff must be prepared to resolve the irritants quickly. Users must put in the 'up-front' effort to flush out problems early. Careful planning and full commitment by all parties are needed. Acceptance testing should be controlled by the users, with full support and guidance from the development staff.

Figure 8-2
Transition Issues

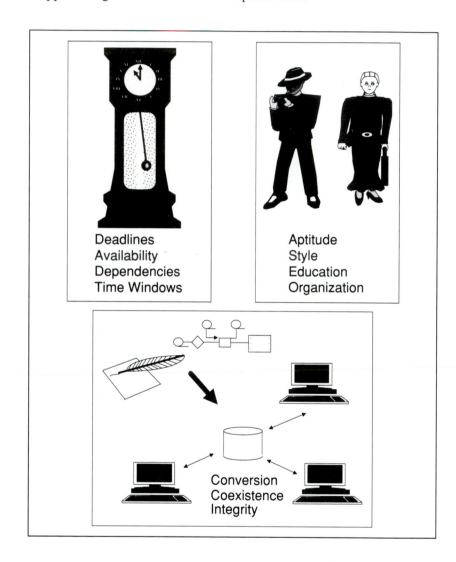

Deadlines
Availability
Dependencies
Time Windows

Aptitude
Style
Education
Organization

Conversion
Coexistence
Integrity

The acceptance test should be used to prove operational aspects of the system; for example, using equipment in situ (not in the Information Systems department), reacting to real data, performing processing cycles with deadlines, volume testing, solving faults via the help desk (not 'hands-on'). It should, therefore, be run by users and operations staff, as if 'for real', with support from the team. Responsibilities for data take-on and hardware/software installation may be shared between user and team. Cut-over is planned and managed by the team, with users to check the tests and give the final permission to go live.

The timing of cut-over is important. It is often discussed in terms of **time windows** when it is sensible in business terms to go live on the new system. These windows will need to be agreed with senior management, and the impact of any delays or serious problems must be fully understood. Where large-scale computer systems currently exist, it is important to seek the opinion, advice and help of operations staff. Where many users are involved it may prove beneficial to ask for the participation of unions or other bodies representing employees.

List of Tasks

Figure 8-3
Network Diagram of the
Tasks in the Transition Stage

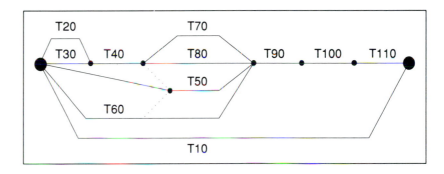

Key

T10	Project administration and management
T20	Train users
T30	Prepare for acceptance testing
T40	Support acceptance test
T50	Perform data take-on
T60	Carry out installation of hardware, system software, and other components of the production configuration
T70	Perform any other pre-implementation trials
T80	Prepare for cut-over
T90	Perform cut-over
T100	Support system during the critical period
T110	Perform post-implementation review

Figure 8-4
An Incremental Approach to Transition

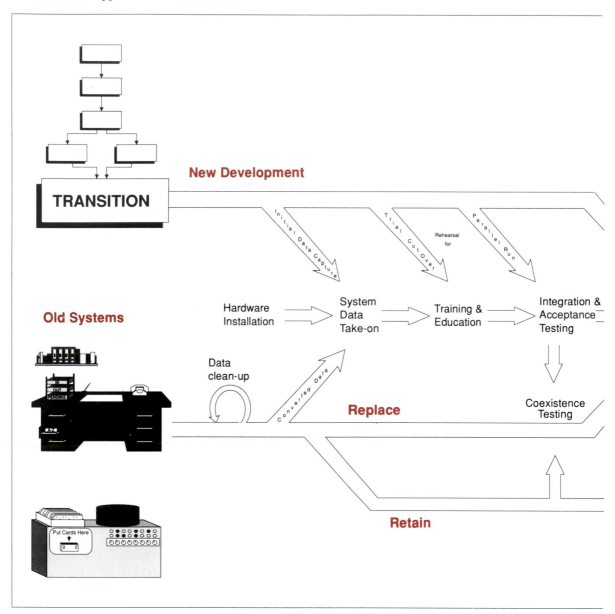

The New System

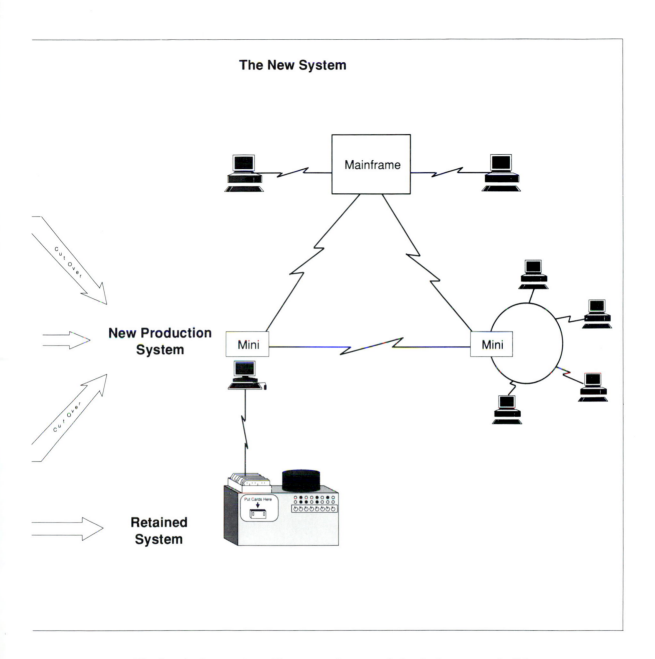

Phasing the integration of human, software and physical resources builds credibility, promotes co-operation and reduces risk. Each step is planned as a rehearsal for the next.

TASK 10
Project administration and management

DESCRIPTION

This task comprises control, reporting, quality assurance and administrative activities performed by the team.

Activity 10 Monitor progress against plan and revise the plan if required. If the 'go-live' date has to change, notify the users and managers as soon as possible – there may only be a few other viable alternative dates or time windows, which must be met.

20 Monitor problems and resolve them. At this stage tactical solutions may be required, with a more complete solution scheduled for a later date.

30 Liaise with other groups (auditors, technical staff, operations staff, data administrator and/or database administrator, other user groups, etc.).

40 Monitor staff performance, give guidance, encouragement and help.

50 Perform change control on all system deliverables.

60 Report progress; in particular, on user understanding, timescales, dependencies and issues to be resolved.

70 Conduct project and steering group meetings. Often, informal meetings will be required daily during this stage.

80 Provide general administrative support (scheduling rooms etc.). It may be useful to help the users find temporary staff to cover the existing system, as they may have old and new systems to support for a short period.

90 Ensure that the team has appropriate CASE and other tools, in a timely manner.

QUALITY ASSURANCE

It is the project leader's responsibility to ensure that this task is performed well. In particular, during this stage the close liaison with users, development, training and support staff is vital. Early planning for data clean-up and collection may be required, sometimes months before the 'go-live' date. The plan must include how to cater for coexistence with existing systems, integration with automated office systems and any other operational aspects. Ensure everyone's expectations are set correctly for this complex stage of 'bringing it all together': **if it can go wrong, it will!**

Deliverables

INPUTS
- system development plan
- all system deliverables
- timesheets
- minutes of meetings
- Terms of Reference
- transition strategy

OUTCOMES
System Deliverables
- *revised system deliverables*

Control Information
- *information about progress*
- *change control log*
- *minutes of meetings*
- *revised system development plan*

Other Outcomes
- *good liaison with other parties to the project*
- *awareness of staff strengths/ weaknesses*

ESTIMATES
This task will occupy most of the project leader's time.

Activities 60-70 should normally take up one day per week per team member.

RESOURCES
- project leader
- analysts
- programmers
- a sense of humour
- the ability to juggle with hundreds of issues at the same time

TECHNIQUES
- progress reporting
- project control

TOOLS
- timesheet forms
- progress reporting forms
- change control forms
- CASE*Method task list

CASE tools
- estimating and progress monitoring tools

NOTES and COMMENTS

The regular team meeting should be continued until the end of the stage, as a means of collecting/giving information.

Tracking system deliverables can often be controlled well by the use of a white board showing all the deliverables, with columns marked up for **produced, tested, checked, approved, integrated, complete,** and so on.

TASK 20

Train users

DESCRIPTION

This task comprises whatever contribution to education and training has been decided in the Training Plan.

Activity 10 Arrange the training sessions, including agreeing on trainers, attendees, dates; publish the training schedule, hire and equip rooms, agree session content. Ideally, the development staff train a group of knowledgeable and keen users, who then train the other users.

20 Prepare the sessions, including slides, handouts, exercises, hardware and software environment, demonstrations, follow-up question-naires. Ideally, a complete dummy training database should be used, with data as close to reality as possible. Ensure that material not only covers what to do but why.

30 Rehearse and give training, remembering to reset the training material at the beginning of every session.

40 Assess the effectiveness of the training: follow up each session informally, or via staff managers, or by using questionnaires or by running 'spot checks'. If there are areas of uncertainty, schedule additional training, possibly on a 'one to one' basis when required.

50 Set up the mechanism by which new users will be trained and educated in the future (e.g. formal sessions are not suitable for very small groups, ones and twos). The use of the training database and scripts can help. An amateur video of training classes, with copies of the handouts, is often very useful.

QUALITY ASSURANCE

Responsibility for training was assigned in the Training Plan (Design Stage, Task 90, Activity 20): users must agree that they are ready for acceptance testing, and the team should have confidence that training was successful (since ill-prepared users will not be satisfied with the system).

If there is a training department in your organization obtain their help, if only for the production of material, logistics and guidance on how to train.

Good quality training material should include humour, plenty of worked examples, regular scheduled breaks, and so on. Think of all the bad training you have received and learn from it!

Deliverables

INPUTS
- Training Plan
- system documentation
- demonstration material
  (e.g. from system test)
- user manual
- draft training database
  details
- draft tutorial

OUTCOMES
System Deliverables
- *tutorials and other training
  and educational material*

Control Information
- *training schedule*
- *questionnaires*
- *assessment of how prepared
  the user is for acceptance
  testing*

Other Outcomes
- *feedback on effectiveness of
  training*
- *training database and scripts*

ESTIMATES
Training material is drawn from existing documentation (overviews, user manuals, system test scripts, etc.), but may need supplementing with training scripts, a training database for practice, and notes for trainers and users. Allow 10-15 days' preparation time for each day of training. With a new system, the preparation of the script and training database may increase these numbers by a further 5 days per day of training needed. Allow time between each session to revise the material if necessary. This should be weighted towards the early sessions, where a rework for a day's session may require a further day or so of effort.

RESOURCES
- analysts
- external accommodation/
  equipment
- users
- professional trainers,
  if available

TECHNIQUES
- lecturing
- tutorial
- self-study
- demonstration

TOOLS
- overhead projector
- terminals
- video equipment
- desktop publishing
- equipment for making materials
  for audio/visual presentation

CASE tools
- dictionary outputs

NOTES and COMMENTS

Ensure that the training sequence is suitable (e.g. managers before staff) and timing is such that attendees can assimilate what they have learned, but are not trained so far in advance that they forget their training before they use it. Remember to train them in what to do and educate them in why! This is an opportunity to re-emphasize the business aims and objectives the system is attempting to address.

System documentation will have been created and revised during analysis, design and build. It should have been organized in a development dictionary, which will ease the task of collating and preparing the training material. The user manual will form part of the training material for users, who will also need to be trained in using this manual effectively. Desktop publishing (DTP) of the training and user manual can be very effective, especially if large numbers of users need high-quality training. Many such DTP tools can include diagrams, reports and sample screen-shots from CASE tools or other systems.

TASK 30
Prepare for acceptance testing

DESCRIPTION

This task ensures that users and operations staff have planned for an acceptance test that will sufficiently prove operational aspects of the system.

Activity 10 Review the Delivery and Acceptance Plan (see Design Stage, Task 90, Activity 10).

20 Assist planning and preparation of the acceptance test. This includes:

- the evaluation of users' acceptance criteria
- the provision of any data needed
- the provision of any equipment required
- advice on the approach (including volume and performance testing)
- criteria for evaluating the correct conversion from existing data and procedures
- ensuring that the users have arranged a means of logging incidents and reviewing results of the acceptance test
- arranging the means by which the project team will correct faults: they need timely access to the system and files but without endangering control (i.e. access will probably be via the database administrator).

30 Set up support facilities, in particular a help desk for acceptance testing, cut-over and the ultimate production stage.

QUALITY ASSURANCE

Users determine whether the scope of the planned acceptance test is satisfactory; the project team ensure that it is feasible, and help the users identify things they might otherwise miss.

Test the quality of the support facilities/help desk by enacting simulated problems.

Deliverables

INPUTS
- Delivery and Acceptance Plan

OUTCOMES
System Deliverables
- *revised Delivery and Acceptance Plan*
- *support facilities (e.g. help desk)*

Control Information
- *assessment of degree of support needed for acceptance test*

Other Outcomes
- *none*

ESTIMATES
Allow sufficient time to verify details of the acceptance plan. This will often take around 3-4 days for a simple extension to the system plan, or up to 5-10 days when a full parallel run is needed.

RESOURCES
- analysts
- users
- project leader
- sponsoring user

TECHNIQUES
- testing

TOOLS
- test results log
- source code control system
- error log/tracking system
- change control system

NOTES and COMMENTS

The project team must 'stand back' to allow the users to determine the scope of acceptance testing, but they should advise if they foresee difficulties.

Acceptance testing may range from being an extension to the system test to a full-blown pilot site or parallel run. Users will probably need help in planning, setting up and running tests. In particular, the criteria for acceptance, agreed during the design stage (Task 90, Activity 10), must be clearly defined in terms of the planned tests. This is not a prototype, where the user comes back with suggested revisions. Change control will operate, as normal, but changes at this stage must be assessed jointly with the users, to reflect a balance of need, timescales and severity of impact.

TASK 40
*Support
acceptance test*

DESCRIPTION

This task ensures that the users test operational aspects of the system.

Activity 10   Assist the users in running the acceptance test.

20   Run the acceptance test.

30   Log problems, faults, queries.

40   Correct faults.

50   Resolve problems and answer queries.

60   Review the user log of the acceptance test.

70   Review the results of the acceptance test.

80   Recommend additional training, where identified.

90   Obtain acceptance sign-off.

QUALITY ASSURANCE

The team must be confident that operational aspects have been adequately tested: it may not be possible to do all things (e.g. volume tests, whole processing cycles) but there should be sufficient to infer results.

Remember that users will not be experienced in filling in test result logs – sit with them and help them through the first few. The users have the final responsibility for approving the outcome of the acceptance test: this should be against acceptance criteria laid down in the plan – it will rarely encompass changes they have thought of while using the system (which must normally be scheduled as 'new' requirements).

High-quality acceptance testing can be arduous for the users. Ensure that they get breaks and there is a high degree of good-natured humour and patience. They may get upset by things not working perfectly – **you** must not!

Deliverables

INPUTS
- Delivery and Acceptance Plan
- operational system
- user manual
- operations hand-over documentation
- support facilities (e.g. help desk)

OUTCOMES
System Deliverables
- *accepted system*

Control Information
- *feedback from all parties involved*
- *faults, required changes*

Other Outcomes
- *users/operations staff familiarization with system*

ESTIMATES
Allow at least one full-time resource for the duration of the acceptance test to ensure satisfactory user support.

Data take-on can take between 2-3 days; but if a parallel run is required it may be necessary to encompass a complete business period such as a financial month.

RESOURCES
- analysts
- users

TECHNIQUES

TOOLS

NOTES and COMMENTS

The project team must be supportive without 'taking over' (unless the users experience extreme difficulties). Users should log everything they do so that the team can assess whether they have used the system thoroughly/properly, whether the operations interface is satisfactory, and if there are problems.

It is important that the acceptance test includes interfacing live data to and from other systems and ensuring the integrity of the stored database.

Faults must be corrected as quickly as possible, ensuring that the corrections are properly planned and tested and that any changes to the documentation are also done.

TASK 50
Perform data take-on

DESCRIPTION

This task provides start-up data for the new system, by data entry, conversion or using input screens.

Activity 10 Prepare for data take-on. This may be:

- collecting/cleaning up data required for keying into the system
- writing/testing conversion programs
- providing bulk data-entry facilities.

20 Perform data take-on.

30 Check data take-on; for example, by running reports on the old and new systems.

40 Check the actual volume of each type of data and assess against the original design assumptions. If the volume for a given type has changed dramatically, it may affect sizing, file placement, performance, and so on. Adjust design and implementation of files as necessary.

50 Obtain user sign-off of data take-on.

QUALITY ASSURANCE

The team should carry out system checks; for example, perform record counts, carry out dry runs with the new data, produce user reports and demonstrate data integrity. The final responsibility rests with the user, and may also involve auditors.

An internal audit should also review the take-on data (take-on to a new system often exposes inadequacies of an existing system). When using a computer system with powerful query/reporting facilities, it is often useful to prepare several different special reports that cross-check the data from different user perceptions.

Deliverables

INPUTS
- raw data, or existing data/files to be converted
- Data Take-on Plan
- support facilities (e.g. help desk)

OUTCOMES
System Deliverables
- *start-up and converted data*

Control Information
- *any user problems in 'translating' unstructured data*
- *effectiveness of system validation (see Notes)*
- *user approval*

Other Outcomes
- *user familiarization with input facilities of system*

ESTIMATES
These depend on the state of the data and the take-on method. Where fields have to be derived from unstructured data, or codes converted, it can be a lengthy process. Estimate by taking a small sample, converting it and then grossing up for the volume required.

RESOURCES
- analysts
- programmers
- external agencies for bulk entry
- users

TECHNIQUES
- conversion

TOOLS
- load/merge software tools
- specially written programs

CASE tools
- configuration management facilities

NOTES and COMMENTS

To save time (and to test the system validation) any special programs for data take-on should make use of validation code from the system input transactions. Where there were problems translating unstructured data, ensure that user procedures are made more explicit.

If the programs necessary for data conversion and loading are non-trivial (as identified in Design Stage, Task 90, Activity 30 and Notes), then this task should have been conducted in parallel to the new system development to shorten the overall timescales. In which case, Activity 30 of this task can take on all the complexity of a full Design and Build.

Schedule the conversion of reference data several weeks ahead of the main bulk data. During the intervening period, update reference data on both old and new systems.

TASK 60

Carry out installation of hardware, system software, and other components of the production configuration

DESCRIPTION

This task provides the facilities and products needed for the new system. (See Design Stage, Task 90, Activity 50.)

Activity 10 Perform the installation work; for example, new hardware, system software, cabling, moving or refurbishing of premises, building alterations.

20 Check the installation work, including testing hardware, software and network/communications in situ.

30 Ensure that any consumables are provided (e.g. printer tapes, paper, diskettes) and arrange responsibilities for ongoing supplies.

40 Obtain user approval of the installation.

QUALITY ASSURANCE

Technical staff are responsible for approving hardware/software installation; and users should approve aspects that affect them. The supplier will often conduct his own installation quality assurance programme, but this is only a start.

Installation of hardware can be a complex task and may well require a sub-project of its own. The major problems are nearly always those of missing components and bad control of dependencies. Remember that installation often includes reconfiguring wiring, air conditioning, telephones, communications networks, and so on, whilst the users are trying to get on with their jobs. They may finish up with two sets of equipment side by side for a period. Patience and consideration are essential.

Software installation needs careful control of management issues such as access control, directory structures, interrelated versions, configuration to selected hardware, and so on. Once more careful planning and the use of third-party experts will help.

Deliverables

INPUTS
- Installation Plan
- network design/architecture
- network control procedure
- operational requirements
- existing or new hardware, software or network components

OUTCOMES
System Deliverables
- *working operational hardware*
- *operational system and network*

Control Information
- *any problems with hardware/software*
- *user approval*

Other Outcomes
- *none*

ESTIMATES
This depends on the extent of installation work. Allow at least one man day per location for testing hardware/software in situ.

RESOURCES
- programmers
- technical staff to test hardware/software installation
- users
- third-party hardware, software and other suppliers

TECHNIQUES
- testing

TOOLS

NOTES and COMMENTS
Where there has to be work on user premises, ensure that they agree the arrangements well in advance and try to minimize disruption.

TASK 70
*Perform any other
pre-implementation
trials*

DESCRIPTION
This task encompasses any other tests it is necessary or desirable to do.

Activity 10 Plan the trials.

20 Perform the trials.

30 Review the results of the trials.

40 Perform any remaining adjustments to the system
(functionality, usability, performance).

QUALITY ASSURANCE

Staff carrying out tests must ensure their validity.

Brainstorm ahead of time to identify any site, user, system or other special trial that
may be required.

Deliverables

INPUTS
- operational system
- feedback on system performance

OUTCOMES

System Deliverables
- *performance benchmark*

Control Information
- *results of trials*

Other Outcomes
- *none*

ESTIMATES
These depend on the type of trial, but be conservative in estimating: set-up, re-runs, and so on always take a lot of time.

RESOURCES
- analysts
- programmers
- technical staff

TECHNIQUES
- benchmarking
- regression testing
- simulation of crash or trial disaster

TOOLS

NOTES and COMMENTS

Some or all of the following activities will be necessary, depending on the circumstances:

- parallel running
- performance benchmarking
- regression testing (ensuring that the new system has no adverse effect on other systems or previous versions)
- sending tapes, reports, etc. to external agencies that may need to approve them (e.g. legal returns, magnetic media for banking systems)
- back-up and recovery testing
- disaster testing.

Tasks

TASK 80
Prepare for cut-over

DESCRIPTION
This task comprises everything for implementation, except the activities that have to be done in the 'conversion window'.

Activity 10 Confirm cut-over timings; for example, timings of production cycles before/after cut-over, business deadlines, availability of users and staff, machine availability.

20 Hold meeting(s) of staff involved, to confirm the checklist of activities in the Cut-over Plan, assign responsibilities (and stand-ins for 'key players'), identify checkpoints and fall-back options.

30 Review previous sign-offs: check that approval of all prerequisites is complete; for example, installation, data take-on, user acceptance test, other trials.

40 Review requirements for live running: security arrangements, such as passwords, operations schedules, support for help desk, and so on.

50 Produce back-up and/or archive copies of any old systems, often in the form of paper, microfiche or magnetic tape copies. Ensure that all procedures and programs are copied, along with the data.

60 Perform loads (programs, files, etc.), check successful loads, and ensure that a consistent and secure environment exists.

70 Agree to proceed with the cut-over from old systems to the new.

QUALITY ASSURANCE
All staff involved in cut-over are responsible for performing their activities, and reviewing the impact on other activities. It is vital for everyone to be vigilant and rigorous about the outcome of these tasks.

Deliverables

INPUTS
- Cut-over Plan
- operational system
  (to load)

OUTCOMES
System Deliverables
- *none*

Control Information
- *agreement to implement
  the system*
- *progress details recorded
  against Cut-over Plan*

Other Outcomes
- *back-up copies of old system*

ESTIMATES
One person needs to be assigned full-time to manage the Cut-over Plan.

RESOURCES
- project leader
- analysts
- programmers
- person to control cut-over
- technical staff
- users
- sponsoring user

TECHNIQUES
- control of a detailed schedule

TOOLS

NOTES and COMMENTS
Control of the Cut-over Plan is so critical that it is useful to institute a 'countdown'; meetings each morning for, say, five days before, to ensure that tasks are done, dependencies maintained and staff are fully briefed.

TASK 90
Perform cut-over

DESCRIPTION
This task comprises the final activities to make the system live.

Activity 10   Perform the activities in the Cut-over Plan (see Design Stage, Task 90, Activity 40).

20   Monitor and control the activities in the Cut-over Plan.

30   Review cut-over and obtain commitment to go live.

40   Ensure that the system and project documentation is complete.

50   Declare the new system 'live' and celebrate.

QUALITY ASSURANCE

Timing is often critical in cut-over; for instance, conversion windows. Particular attention should be paid to progress timescales and dependencies during cut-over. The person controlling cut-over must also be able to respond to problems by calling in additional resources, re-scheduling, finding alternatives, and so on, and must monitor checkpoints and decide whether to go on.

Users have the final decision on whether to go live, based on the recommendation of the person controlling cut-over.

Deliverables

INPUTS
- Cut-over Plan
- operational system

OUTCOMES
System Deliverables
- *fully operational system*
- *completed system documentation*

Control Information
- *completed cut-over schedule (including incident log)*
- *completed project control documentation*

Other Outcomes
- *user response to implementation (very significant to the perceived success of the system)*

ESTIMATES
During cut-over (minimum of one day) all resources should be assigned full-time, since staff may have to stand by if there are re-runs, and so on.

RESOURCES
- analysts
- programmers
- technical staff
- person to control cut-over
- project leader
- sponsoring user
- users

TECHNIQUES
- control of a detailed schedule
- rigorous use of checklists *

TOOLS

NOTES and COMMENTS

Activity 40 ensures that documentation is finished off and filed. There are two sets of documentation – the system documentation (models, specifications, design decisions, technical material, etc.) and the project control documentation (plans, Terms of Reference, progress information, quality assurance results, etc.).

System documentation is for operating and maintaining the system. Control documentation is needed for the post-implementation review, to follow up queries on what was included/excluded from the system, to assist future projects, and to assist historical analysis of estimates (e.g. via a metrics database).

TASK 100
Support system during the critical period

DESCRIPTION

This task includes assistance, bug fixing, removal of irritants and review of the live system.

Activity 10 Visit the users and help them pro-actively at their place of work; operate the help desk. Remind them of the reasons for the new system and the benefits that will ensue.

20 Seek out irritants to the users and, whenever possible, put in place changes to remove or minimize them.

30 Identify, log and correct bugs. Supply circumventions (or 'work-arounds') to unresolved problems.

40 Control changes to the live environment.

50 Review the service to the users: monitor the incident log, turn-round on problems.

60 Assess the success of live running: down-time, service levels, number of faults.

70 Assess the success of the system: fulfilment of business objectives, success criteria, number of required changes/enhancements.

QUALITY ASSURANCE

The project leader must ensure that incident and change control logs are monitored, down-time is recorded, service levels are measured, and that every effort is made to support the user and bring the system quickly to a state where it can be handed over to full production.

Deliverables

INPUTS
– live system
– support facilities
  (e.g. help desk)

OUTCOMES
System Deliverables
– *required changes/*
  enhancements
– *operations fault log*
– *definition of circumvention*

Control Information
– *incident log*
– *change control log*

Other Outcomes
– *user response to system*

ESTIMATES
Allow one full-time resource to support each group of users in the early weeks.

RESOURCES
– analysts
– programmers
– technical staff
– users

TECHNIQUES
– system support

TOOLS
CASE tools
– query screens and reports

NOTES and COMMENTS

Staff should either man or support the help desk and ensure that advice is available, incidents are logged, and problems are routed to the appropriate resource and solved quickly. Operations staff should keep a log of system faults.

Sometimes temporary staff are required to take some of the burden of work during this difficult period, when the users are undergoing a learning curve on the new system yet still responsible for satisfying their corporate objectives.

TASK 110
*Perform
post-implementation
review*

DESCRIPTION

This task collects responses on the conduct of the application development life-cycle and on the resultant application system from all interested parties, performs a feedback and follows up recommendations.

Activity 10 Interview all interested parties (users, auditors, technical staff, operations staff, data administrator and/or database administrator, project team, third parties, e.g. customers).

20 Collate interview material into categories; for example, methods and standards, conduct of the project, success of the system.

30 Produce feedback material.

40 Perform a post-implementation feedback.

50 Provide a post-implementation report, including recommendations.

60 Follow up on recommendations.

70 Obtain agreement to end the initial support period and move the system to full production.

80 Move the system to production: copy to production library, remove access rights of project staff, redeploy project staff, perform hand-over to maintenance function and get ready for support (and the next one).

90 Send a 'thank-you' note to developers, management and users involved in the project.

QUALITY ASSURANCE

Users and staff should be satisfied that the post-implementation report is a fair assessment of the project/system, and that the recommendations are useful.

Deliverables

INPUTS
- help desk incident log
- operations fault log
- change control log
- Terms of Reference

OUTCOMES
System Deliverables
- *post-implementation review report*

Control Information
- *none*

Other Outcomes
- *recommendations to apply on methods, standards, training, user roles, quality assurance, etc.*
- *debriefing of all interested parties to the project*
- *thank-you note*

ESTIMATES
Allow 0.5 man days per interview, 12 man days to prepare and do feedback and 1-5 man days to prepare and follow up the report. This is not a trivial task.

Allow at least one day to move the system to production.

RESOURCES
- project leader
- all interested parties

TECHNIQUES
- interviewing
- conducting feedback
- report writing

TOOLS
- post-implementation interview checklist
- post-implementation report

NOTES and COMMENTS

A great deal of benefit can be obtained from this review: it motivates staff, uncovers problems, reinforces lessons learned and effectively reviews and improves the effectiveness of the Information Systems department. It also reassures users and encourages ongoing commitment.

Transition Stage Summary

It has been ...

the stage where the completed system was implemented, supported and finally handed over to production.

We have produced ...

And now for ...

the production stage, where the system continues to run (with minimum maintenance!) until business changes or the need to update hardware/ software occasion another project ...

Chapter

9

PRODUCTION STAGE

Aims and Objectives

The production stage will ensure smooth running of the system, with minimum intervention from operations or support staff, and monitor its use and performance at each live running site. Necessary changes should be introduced in a non-disruptive manner and everything possible done to ensure maximum user enthusiasm and commitment.

**Figure 9-1
The Production Stage in the
Life Cycle**

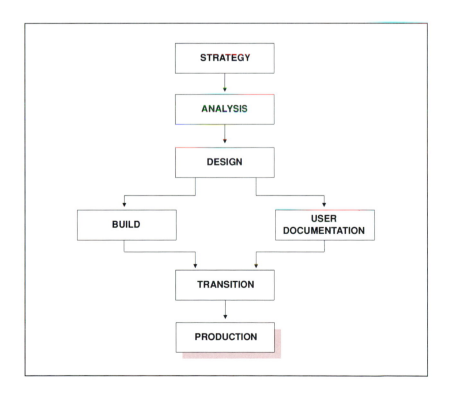

Description

Operations staff provide the agreed service levels for the system, and support staff respond to problems and user queries/requests to assist this process. Service levels are monitored, and any additional required technical checks are performed. Faults are corrected and changes performed in a controlled way. Management decides system audits, based on monitored results and plans to enhance/replace systems.

Key Deliverables

- *Back-up, recovery and archive files*
- *Change control log*
- *Fault reports*
- *Amendments to the system*
- *Performance statistics*
- *New requirements*
- *System audit results*

Critical Success Factors

The critical success factors that are essential to a successful production stage include:

- Commitment to achieving high levels of service.
- Timely response to user queries and requests.
- Good change control.

Approach

During this stage, operations and support staff are responsible for providing service levels, but development project staff should be available to perform a back-up role.

CASE tools can be useful for two main purposes during the production stage. Firstly, when changes are requested the CASE dictionary or repository can be examined bottom up to determine the likely impact of the change, to check to see if it is within the system objectives and to plan for the change. Secondly, when subsequent phases of development are undertaken or major enhancements are planned the dictionary can be used top down to assess impact and fit into the existing system. CASE tools may also be used for configuration control during change, project control and to help review and monitor procedures. Analyzing the online system and recording details in the dictionary can help gauge the effectiveness of the system against its expectations.

Figure 9-2
Using CASE Tools to
Produce the Best System

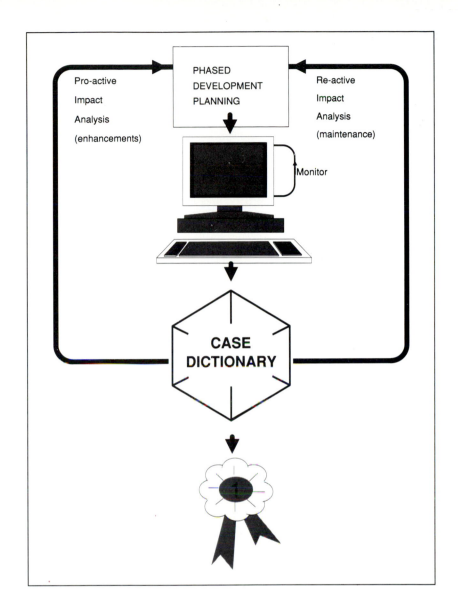

Occasional reviews show interest and commitment and will tease out irritants, minor problems and may help pre-empt larger issues. The aim is to provide minimum intervention, so that the system truly 'belongs' to the users; that is, they control system parameters, batch run requests, additional printing, and so on, and monitor usage and performance.

It is all too easy to consider the development task complete when a system goes into production. A successfully operating system is our ultimate goal, but for really contented users regular attendance to their irritants and problems is essential, especially during the first few weeks of any implementation.

This stage may be the end result of many months of work. Don't let it become soured by lack of interest.

List of Tasks

Figure 9-3
Network Diagram of the Tasks in the Production Stage

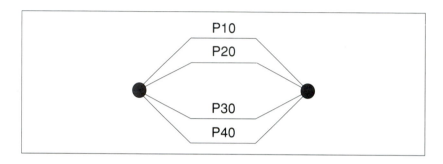

Key
P10	Provide operational service
P20	Respond to user requests
P30	Monitor/review performance
P40	Assess the future of the system

The tasks and deliverables for the production stage begin on pages 9-6 and 9-7.

TASK 10
Provide
operational service

DESCRIPTION

This task ensures that service levels are met and that the business is adequately supported.

Activity 10   Log faults – this can be initiated by operations staff, users or support staff (whoever encounters or suspects the faults), but is controlled by operations staff.

20   Diagnose faults and decide action – diagnosis can be by operations staff or users, but should be confirmed by support staff, who review all fault reports. The fault reports should contain the solution(s) and impact analysis, so that users can approve required actions.

30   Correct faults or recommend a circumvention, either of which must then be recorded in the user and system documentation.

40   Regression test and release amended component. This will normally be a program change, but could equally well be a change to the computer network or even to manual procedures.

50   Run the system: that is, carry out defined operations procedures plus any reasonable variations due to day-to-day conditions.

60   Support the user: this includes the help desk function, and a reasonable level of casual interaction with support staff for help and advice.

70   Take back-up, recovery and archive copies of all or part of the system and recover the system after any failure.

80   Ensure the team has appropriate CASE and other tools, in a timely manner.

QUALITY ASSURANCE

The responsibility for achieving service levels rests with operations staff, who can call on support staff (or, as a second line, development staff) to assist. Support staff must ensure the quality of all changes.

On correction of an error a test should be run to establish that the fault has been corrected. A special test, called a regression test, should then be run to ensure that other components of the system have not been affected by accident. Several corrections may be collected together, tested and implemented as a group to minimize effort and disruption.

Deliverables

INPUTS
- fault reports
- operations log
- users' comments (formal and informal)
- minutes of meetings
- operations (hand-over) documentation

OUTCOMES
System Deliverables
- *amendments to system and/or documentation*
- *definition of circumvention*
- *fault reports*

Control Information
- *awareness of quality of system*
- *change control log*
- *back-up, recovery and archive files*
- *minutes of meetings*
- *operations log*

Other Outcomes
- *none*

ESTIMATES
Allow sufficient allocation of analysis/programming staff to provide fast turn-round on faults.

The rate of faults occurring should decrease exponentially with time. A budget of 5-10% of the development effort should be allocated for a well-engineered system during the first few weeks.

RESOURCES
- operations staff
- support staff
- help desk

TECHNIQUES
- change control
- fault diagnosis
- impact analysis
- regression testing

TOOLS
CASE tools
- reports and query screens
- matrix diagrammer
- configuration management tools

NOTES and COMMENTS
Reacting to faults and releasing changes must be done in a manner that minimizes the impact on the business. This may mean out-of-hours working and being seen to be responsive to users. Change control is especially critical where multiple systems are involved.

TASK 20
Respond to user requests

DESCRIPTION
This task analyzes requests and decides whether a change or a new project (such as a major enhancement) is needed.

Activity 10 Investigate requests and decide action: enhancements should be treated as requests for further development projects (albeit potentially very small). Changes/bugs should be dealt with directly by support staff.

20 Agree urgent changes or add them to the change control log or record them as new requirements.

30 Perform the urgent changes.

40 Test these changes, regression test the system and release the amended component (e.g. a program).

50 Revise documentation and training.

QUALITY ASSURANCE

Support staff must ensure the feasibility of the change and provide a quality update; users must ensure that the change is really needed, including anticipating any related changes that may be better handled in one go.

Deliverables

INPUTS
- users' requests
- system documentation
- user documentation
- system audit results
- change control log

OUTCOMES
System Deliverables
- *amendments to system and/or documentation*
- *new requirements*
- *change control log*

Control Information
- *awareness of how appropriate the system is*

Other Outcomes
- *none*

ESTIMATES
Allow sufficient time to analyze each request, and sufficient analysis/programming staff to provide a reasonable response to agreed changes.

RESOURCES
- support staff

TECHNIQUES
- change control
- impact analysis
- estimating and planning

TOOLS
CASE tools
- impact analysis screens and reports

NOTES and COMMENTS
Changes identified in this way are usually more far-reaching than faults (see Task 10), and need analysis of options and careful checking that all affected areas (including training) are updated.

TASK 30
Monitor/review performance

DESCRIPTION
This task ensures that all relevant measures are taken and reviewed.

Activity 10 Refine or define performance measures. These may include:
- utilization of the system (volumes processed)
- machine utilization
- capacity requirements
- technical performance (e.g. timings of batch runs, start-up, response time)
- reliability (machine down-time, system down-time, level of faults)
- service levels.

20 Provide performance statistics (actual versus the level set as acceptable).

30 Review the ease of use. This may include checking procedures, identifying duplication, keystroke patterns, sequences of events, and the availability of relevant information at the time it is needed.

40 Review the service levels and decide action, including change requests.

50 Perform required actions to improve performance or usability, address the problem (e.g. increase capacity) or change the system to reflect the actual (rather than predicted) work load.

QUALITY ASSURANCE
Operations and technical staff are responsible for ensuring that monitoring is done. Users may assist in providing data (e.g. log of down-time, terminal utilization).

Deliverables

INPUTS
- system monitor results
- embedded performance monitor outputs
- timings from users or monitoring staff
- audit criteria

OUTCOMES
System Deliverables
- *performance statistics*
- *tuned system*
- *change requests*

Control Information
- *awareness of accuracy of capacity and performance predictions*

Other Outcomes
- *tests and results*

ESTIMATES
Allow time for regular collection of statistics, so that trends can be spotted.

Schedule a review of a new system a few weeks after implementation, with about 20% of the development team available for approximately a week to solve major problems.

Smaller reviews should be planned subsequently on a regular basis of, say, 3-monthly intervals.

RESOURCES
- operations staff
- technical staff

TECHNIQUES
- performance measuring
- tuning
- watching users at their work

TOOLS
- monitoring software

NOTES and COMMENTS
It is important to test all predictions about the system. Thus not only can performance issues be addressed, but future predictions can be improved. Where service levels are not being met, the results, reasons and courses of action must be discussed with the user.

The numbers gathered here are inputs to capacity planning. The changes in the usage figures will indicate a future need to act before that need becomes critical. However, other more qualitative variables concerning usability and user satisfaction should also be identified and tracked.

TASK 40
Assess the future
of the system

DESCRIPTION
This task monitors how well the system is still supporting the business.

Activity 10 Ensure that business models are up to date, in particular the business objectives, aims and performance indicators. This activity is conducted by carrying out a mini strategy study.

20 Decide the assessment criteria for a system audit, taking account of any benefits that were originally used to justify the system.

30 Measure the system against the assessment criteria and against the general business objectives, both original and updated.

40 Make recommendations on the future of the system and prepare a system audit report if required.

QUALITY ASSURANCE

The project leader must ensure that assessment criteria for the system audit are appropriate and measurable, and that the audit is a 'fair trial' of the system. Criteria include a match to requirements (by comparison of old/new models), service levels, technical and performance criteria, the contribution to strategic hardware/software directions, acceptability to the users, resource levels used, and so on.

Deliverables

INPUTS
- existing business model
- change requests
- system statistics

OUTCOMES
System Deliverables
- *updated business models*
- *system audit criteria*
- *system audit results*
- *system audit report*

Control Information
- *awareness of suitability of system*

Other Outcomes
- *none*

ESTIMATES
A system audit is conducted as a 'cut-down' strategy and analysis. See the Strategy and Analysis Stages, Chapters 3-4. A budget of between 10-15 man days is normally acceptable.

RESOURCES
- project leader
- business analyst
- user managers
- users

TECHNIQUES
- modelling
- assessment against criteria
- interviewing
- monitoring feedback

TOOLS
CASE tools
- impact analysis reports to help update and comparison of models

NOTES and COMMENTS

Auditing a system periodically is the best way of ensuring that models are kept up to date and that the system continues to address the business needs.

A system audit can use information gathering, modelling and feedback techniques to review and, if necessary, revise the business model. The degree to which the new business model diverges from the implemented model represents the mismatch of the needs and the system. It is inevitable that such a gap exists; it represents the lag between evolving business needs and system maintenance/enhancement. The usefulness of a system can be measured by the magnitude of that gap and the rate at which it changes over a period of time. As long as the gap remains small the system can be regarded as responsive to the business.

Production Stage Summary

It has been ...

a stage where the system was maintained and monitored, to ensure a continued useful life in support of the business.

We have produced ...

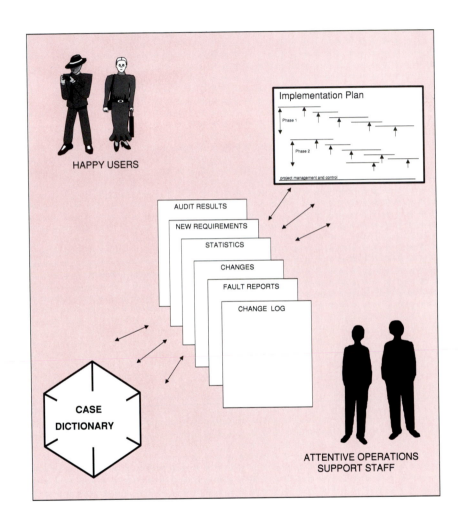

The system will eventually go full circle, and at one of its system audits (or as a result of user project requests) the need to replace it will be recognized.

The development cycle will start again ...
or, more accurately, continue its never-ending cycle.

10 PROJECT MANAGEMENT AND CONTROL

Introduction

Every project or system development is unique. Planning for each should be treated as a mini-project in its own right, with clearly understood objectives. This chapter is designed to generate awareness of some of the key issues in running any project. It covers the setting up of the project, several techniques to help thinking in this and many other situations, different-sized projects and different starting points in CASE*Method.

Setting Up Any Project

The success or otherwise of most systems engineering projects is determined by how well they are set up, managed and controlled. Clearly, the accurate deployment of the appropriate human, physical and financial resources is very important. The development environment must be correct; appropriate tools must be brought to bear; and relevant education, training and external expertise must be put in place. But all of this is to no avail unless the project sets out to achieve the right results with the right plan.

The starting point of any project is, therefore, to thoroughly analyze the requirement and explicitly state the project overview, objectives, aims, constraints, priorities and those factors critical to its success.

Project objectives are the things that the project must achieve and for which the achievement can be measured. These may include the delivery and acceptance of a certain component by a specific date. Less tangible aims may also be essential to the success of the project. Often these are to do with commitment and acceptance by the users, and may include such things as gaining the commitment and help of the key opinion leaders, or setting the right level of user expectations. If these 'intangibles' are important, they should be sought out, discussed, agreed and explicitly made known to the project managers and team members. **If the team does not know the project objectives and aims they are unlikely to achieve them!**

There are often many ways of planning a project. Details of priorities, constraints and available resources must all be made available to the project planner so that the best compromise plan can be formulated. Certain things will stop the achievement of even the most vehemently-defined goal. Facts will be necessary to substantiate the best dates that can be attained, and to help identify trade-offs and alternative approaches that can be taken. When all the planning data is known, a very useful starting point is to produce a **resource-unlimited** network, based purely upon the inter-dependency of any of the tasks and activities. This can then gradually be modified into a plan by the addition of known constraints (such as the availability date of a new computer), the number and capability of available development staff, the management requirement for a demonstration to a steering group on a specific date, the earliest start date, ...

Work Breakdown

With this overall understanding of what the project must achieve and an early indication of dependencies and possible timescales, the next activity is to identify in detail all the deliverables that must be produced, along with their acceptance criteria. The project must then be rigorously broken down into components that are small enough to be easily understood, estimated and controlled. Typically, tasks of between three and ten man days' effort are ideal, as these enable progress to be assessed easily and problems remedied in a timely manner, without being too small to cause excessive overheads in project control.

It is a good idea to check this work breakdown from several perspectives:

- from a top-down viewpoint, to ascertain the key deliverables and milestones
- from a bottom-up approach to ensure that the people doing the job have identified all the things that need to be done
- by comparison with similar tasks. Cross-check against this and any other book, and by any or all of the risk-containment procedures mentioned further on in this chapter.

To estimate the work, each task and set of deliverables must be assessed for complexity, and the skill type and level that must be deployed. **Fit for the purpose** is a useful consideration, as it may not be sensible to produce a 'Rolls-Royce' solution for something that is only going to be used once.

Over a period of time it is possible to build up a matrix of task type and deliverables by complexity against skill type. This book has some guidelines on these, but it is important to set up ones that apply to **your** organization, against **your** standards and that work with **your** people. A design job given to a really top-class designer with relevant experience and skills may only take a few hours; the same task given to a good designer may take days; and to someone straight off a training course it could take weeks (perhaps without even achieving the required result). So the next job is the accurate deployment of available resources and the revision of estimates, based on either the type of person (role) to be used (including skill level and experience) or the specific person to be assigned. This process can make a fifty percent difference to project costing and timescales, so it is worth a lot of attention.

When time is of the essence and true costing is being done, the accurate and focused deployment of third-party experts can be of real benefit.

But beware

- Are they **personally** real experts, or simply consultants from a company with a good reputation?

- Does the cost and quality of the two days the expert will need balance the ten-day effort for one of your own people to do it?

- And will you understand what has been achieved and how?

Estimation also includes a high degree of subjectivity and trade-offs. Similar projects should be used as rule-of-thumb comparisons. Budgets and timescale constraints may force the rephasing of work, a change of content or an alteration to the way in which the work is to be done. This may affect the quality, performance or some other usability aspect of the resulting system, and thus may require the correct setting of expectations and the scheduling of further work to raise the system back to the correct quality. If short cuts need to be taken, scheduling short balancing tasks by experts can minimize the potential damage that may be caused. The simple expediency of getting an expert to spend a few minutes checking something at the right point in the project can prevent real problems later.

Whenever possible you should err on the side of putting extra effort into requirement definition and design. **The build and testing tasks to produce a good system can take a tenth of the time when using well-proven designs.**

Contingency time must be included in the plan. Management do not like to see this, but it is good practice to allocate time and resources explicitly for the unexpected, for re-working, for correcting problems identified during a review or quality check, and so on. But don't waste this time! If it is not needed, deliver the project early. It can be done!

Before this work breakdown is completed, various risk-containment actions can be carried out as described below. But the most important one is to go back to the real objectives of the project and see if they are still being met. In addition, are the hidden objectives being met? These may include an early illustration of tangible progress, something for a key user to show his colleagues at an important meeting, and so on.

The process then continues with the production of dependency networks of tasks, critical-path analysis, milestone or Gantt charts, accurate resource allocation, full task definition, management-level charts, assumption definition, and so on, to the standards used in the organization. Project management and control software can obviously help, but it is still always better to put a rough plan together manually and compare it with one produced by some automatic scheduler than to rely purely upon a computerized system: the problem being that one inaccurate dependency, for example, could cause an order-of-magnitude error in an automated schedule, but it can be very difficult to determine the cause of the error.

Risk Containment

Before any plan is put under formal change control a period of time considering risks is fruitful. The more obvious technical risks and dependencies will often have been catered for. A simple, but effective technique is to identify some key deliverables and see what happens to the plan if they are not available on the necessary dates. What would happen if your top designer was ill for three months or resigned?

There are various techniques that you might wish to deploy to aid risk containment and the accurate definition of a project. Each of those mentioned below is there purely to aid the thinking of the project leader, either as a means of divergent thinking to ensure that all aspects have been considered or convergent thinking to help focus on relevant aspects that project members must bear in mind.

Categorization

Think about the project very carefully and set up a loose-leaf folder and/or computer system with sections labelled for various obvious components.

These would typically include:

- Project Terms of Reference, including:
  - description
  - objectives
  - aims
  - key deliverables
  - critical success factors
  - major milestones
  - key personnel
  - priorities
  - specific exclusions
  - major issues

- Plans, including:
  - estimates
  - assumptions
  - dependency networks/Gantt charts
  - milestones

- Task definitions and deliverables
- Budget and costs incurred
- Quality assurance
- Project members and timesheets
- Physical resources and availability
- Project and management reports
- Minutes of meetings
- Risks
- Change control documents
- Ideas
- Unresolved issues
- Problems
- Key actions
- Dependencies
- Contents list.

Use some of the other techniques mentioned below (such as interviewing) to identify any other general, organizational or project-specific factors that must be considered. Set up categories for each major new area and then record all relevant checklists under these headings.

For example, if you are building a small computer system, the category **Availability** might well apply to:

- Hardware:
  - development machine
  - operational machine
  - terminals
  - air conditioning
  - network
  - printers, plotters

- System software:
  - operating system
  - editors
  - network software
  - system monitors
  - back-up/recovery

- Development software:
  - database management system
  - CASE
  - project control system
  - compilers
  - de-bugging aids
  - monitors
  - electronic mail
  - storyboard facilities
  - word processors/desktop publishing packages

- Development environment:
  - chairs, desks, filing cabinets, ...
  - lighting
  - power and computer points
  - air conditioning
  - photocopiers
  - telephones, facsimile machines

- People:
  - users
  - team members
  - quality assurance experts
  - industry experts
  - consultants

- contractors
- trainers
- operators
- management
- key players for any specific task

• Financial resources:
  - budget
  - cash
  - executives for 'sign-off'.

As categories are added, with lists of things to remember or consider under each, a more complete picture emerges. After a while the same topics come up under different headings from a different perspective. The successful project leader will take each of these categories and use them to cross-check the others. Omissions and gaps will be filled in so that within a few hours the project leader has a comprehensive set of aspects to consider, enabling him to set up the project much more accurately. During the project these categorized lists can be used as a constant aide-mémoire to ensure that even the least important aspects get reconsidered from time to time – occasionally they can suddenly become important. Add to the lists at any time. Periodically discard the irrelevant ideas and consolidate sections. File control documents and changes, and essentially get the project to treat this book or system as the definitive repository and guide for the project.

This method is designed to give the project leader maximum opportunity to identify and solve problems early.

Interviewing

Conduct a brief interview of each of the people who have a say in the set-up and success of the project. Find out their expectations, motivation and measures of success. Ask them for advice, guidance, tips and hints, things to remember. Get them to identify who else can help the success of the project, and run through any of the categories that have already been established.

Role Playing

Consider the project from different perspectives. Think yourself into the role of management, user, team member, contractor, acceptance person, data administrator, operator, supplier, administrator, or any other role that might affect the success of the project or be affected by it.

What is important to these people?
What will they be looking for?
What could cause them to become enemies?
What will help them to stay allies?
Have they any preconceived notions or expectations?

Brainstorm Session

A very fast way of getting ideas is to hold a ten to twenty minute brainstorm session with people who can think freely and have a general knowledge of the area of interest, the specific project or any of the techniques that might be employed. Brainstorming works by word association, both verbally and by seeing the written word.

In its simplest form the technique is as follows:

- Set up a room with whiteboards and/or flipcharts.
- Gather together five or six relevant people.
- Lay down the rules:
    - when told to start the following apply
    - say whatever comes into your head
    - keep it short
    - no interruptions
    - no questions
    - keep it going
    - a fixed timescale.
- State the problem in simple terms that keep the subject wide open.
- Start.
- One person writes down any word or phrase said **without question**.
- Keep writing everything down very quickly. After a while someone else may need to help by sticking the flipchart sheets that are already filled onto the walls – it is useful to be able to see everything all the time. (Alternatively use memo-stickers as mentioned under cluster analysis below.)
- When no new ideas are forthcoming use a predefined checklist to stimulate further ideas.

At the end of this proces there will be an unstructured list of words and phrases – typically in the region of three to four hundred such entries. These can now be classified using the categorization method mentioned before, or cluster analysis techniques.

Cluster Analysis

This is a process of taking a random selection of ideas or an unstructured list and grouping them subjectively. The outcome should be a number of useful categories, and lists of things to be considered within each category.

There are many ways to carry out this process, one of the most effective being by means of small memo-stickers and a large wall (ideally made of glass, as the stickers often fall off other surfaces!). Most offices have pads of these memo-stickers on which people write reminders and notes, and typically stick them on other people's telephones or terminals. (Some people have been known to write them whilst driving a car, but this is not to be recommended.)

The technique is as follows:

- Write each word or phrase on a separate memo-sticker.

- When complete, cluster the stickers (most effectively done by a single person).

- Place the first sticker in the centre of the wall.

- Place the second sticker by the side of the first, if it is **directly related**. If not, place it above or below.

- Place subsequent stickers by the side of existing ones if they are directly related, or start a new group above or below, as required.

- At any time during this process, create new stickers with a useful name for a group that is emerging and put these to the left of the group.

- At any time add new stickers on any subject or aspect that comes to mind.

- Periodically reposition stickers or groups of stickers into more sensible positions. In effect, allow similar ideas to migrate to the same part of the wall.

- Before the process is finished, group the groups into a hierarchy, so that at the end there is a single, project hierarchy of all the ideas decomposed into sensible groupings.

When complete, the density of stickers under any group indicates the subjective priority placed on it by the source or combined sources of the ideas – remember this may be biased.

As can be seen from the illustration (Figure 10-1), it is often sensible to put the highest density grouping uppermost to aid this subjective grouping process.

This technique can be used to help categorize information in many circumstances. In particular, it is useful during the strategy and analysis stages to perform cluster analysis on business functions, to produce function hierarchies.

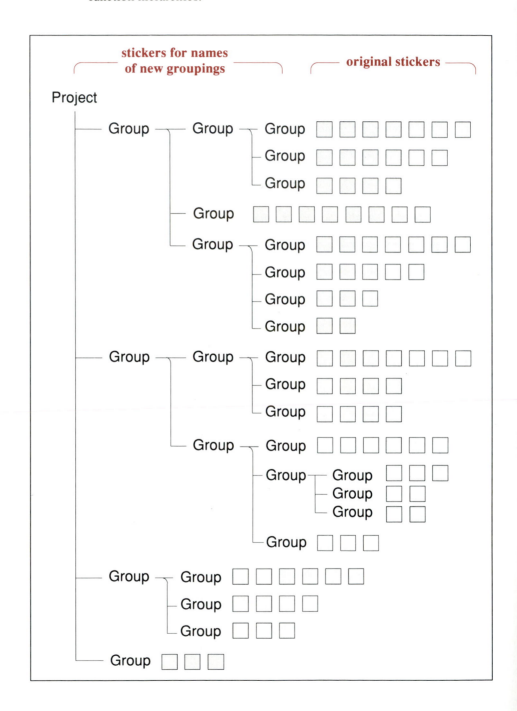

Figure 10-1
Cluster Analysis

Matrix Planning

Categorization is very useful, but does not help with related concepts. Two-dimensional matrices can be used to help to identify the sometimes complex interrelationships between different aspects of a project.

The technique is simple: squared paper, a large whiteboard or a matrix diagrammer is required. Identify two related lists of objects, and fill in the description for one as headings to the columns and for the other as side headings to the rows. Define the interrelationship on each intersection. Sometimes this is as simple as a 'tick' to remind you that it needs to be considered. At other times the interrelationship needs to be qualified.

The example below shows a people-to-task matrix on a strategy study, with the intersection identifying their likely roles. This is a useful precursor to project planning.

		Matrix: **Strategy Stage Tasks by Roles**				
Role	Name	Administration	Scoping	Plan	Briefing & Interviews	Modelling
Team leader	B.Jones	✓	✓	✓	3	
Analyst	A.Smith		✓		Lead	3
Analyst	R.J.Townsend				Notetaker	
Consultant	C.Longman				✓	Quality
Industry specialist	P.Towers					Terminology and completeness
IS Manager	G.Garside			Budget	Control	
Data Administrator	B.Chen					Cross-project issues
Secretary	L.Ellis	Smooth running			Information source	
Users	–		Interviewee selection			
Sponsoring user	R.Acheson		Scope	Timescale		

Another matrix useful during detailed analysis planning is one of all the business functions in the selected phase of the project against all the potential users for interview. Typically, this can be fifty or sixty functions against twenty or thirty users. In the intersections, identify whether or not the user is a key source of information on a given business function. The objective is to identify the smallest number of users who collectively cover all the functions, with a degree of overlap.

Presentation

Finally, in this short section on techniques to help the planning process, the use of various presentation techniques is strongly recommended. Any presentation of ideas to other people forces the presenter to prepare, think about the issues, structure the presentation and in the process of delivery to explain or rationalize any material presented. Good project leaders will err on the side of identifying their doubts or concerns, so that these can be addressed and hopefully resolved at the earliest opportunity.

Examples of useful presentations during project planning or review are:

- a peer-group check with another project leader
- a start-up meeting for members of the team
- a feedback of the scope and approach to the sponsors
- management review meetings
- sub-contractor meetings.

The presentations can be in various forms such as verbal, written or using overhead projector slides. Being able to read about the issues as well as hear about them doubles the likely feedback that will be attained, and thus improves the quality.

Technique Summary

Each of these ways of thinking should only take a few minutes or hours at the most. More complete details of these and other techniques are covered in another book in this series, and by training courses and books from various suppliers.

The important thing is to get everything out into the open so that all issues and points can be considered. It is then up to the project leader to use his judgement to plan and run the project when armed with this, perhaps, wider view.

| **Different-sized Projects** | In essence there is no difference between a large project and a small one, other than the **degree** to which things are done and the emphasis on project control, quality, integration and other such issues. |

Large Projects

For very large projects, say fifteen to five hundred people in a team (possibly with multiple sub-contracts), the key to success is to break the project down into smaller more manageable sub-projects. Ideally, this subdivision should be based on overall data, function and resource dependencies to ensure continuity and maximum progress at all times.

Reviewing project objectives will bias the parallelism of sub-projects to achieve the required periodic expenditure, end dates, milestones or to meet the resource availability constraints that may apply.

Control will be of the essence.

Project management and control can take as much as thirty percent of the entire effort on a large project. Much of this effort will be spent in liaison between sub-projects, with users and keeping management aware of the issues. Things change continuously, and the management team will need the ability to juggle with hundreds of conflicting issues and priorities on a week-by-week or even day-by-day basis. A very small group of people who can be given the authority to make rapid decisions is essential. They need fast access to all the key players to help them assess risks and alternatives, and they must then take the responsibility to ensure that all interested parties are informed of any outcomes in a timely manner. Tools and techniques that can help are suggested below:

- a project control system with multi-project and what-if capability
- integrated spreadsheets
- matrices and prioritized lists
- CASE dictionaries to act as the central repository of information
- electronic mail, facsimile, voicemail, and so on
- rapid dissemination of planned changes with urgent response from affected people
- rigorous sign-off, change control, dependency control and configuration management.

It is very difficult to maintain good communication, understanding and culture.

Typically there is a continual turnover of people. As a project builds up or it moves into a new phase, everything is new to most members of the team. Often, one is building a new system with new technology, new methods, new ways of running the business and thus an ever-changing team membership.

The only solution is management commitment to communication, education and training. Before a new phase starts hold a briefing meeting to cover the scope, objectives, approach and give an understanding of how this phase fits into the global picture. Make sure people know what is expected of them. Hold regular mini training classes on new techniques, lessons learnt so far, how to use deliverables prepared in early stages. These short sessions can often be held at lunchtime or in the early evening and should be given informally by team members to their colleagues.

Ensure that each role in the project has clear responsibilities laid down. Team members must know how they should work with others and how they will be judged. Each person in every role should receive similar training, be conversant with the same techniques for modelling, building, group activities and presentation. It would seem ludicrous to expect five electricians to work together if they each used different colours of wire for the same purpose and could not understand each other's layout diagrams. Yet it is amazing how rarely the Information Systems industry takes standards and training seriously when building strategic information systems for large corporations.

On a team of fifty or so, there are often about five or ten key people who make the difference between success and failure. Their time must be used strategically. This may involve them in cross-project peer-group checking, key design tasks and balancing complex alternative ways forward. These people can be most beneficial in aiding communication, by explaining their thinking processes and vision to their colleagues, who are then less likely to make poor decisions when left to their own devices. They should be encouraged to take personal responsibility for the technical aspects of projects, and along with the team or project leaders carry out regular 'walk-around' sessions to see what is going on, to help, advise, and encourage team members. This also acts as an early warning for impending problems.

Politics and personal aspirations can get in the way of success. There are no easy answers to this, other than ensuring that management is aware of these issues and can plan accordingly to pre-empt and minimize them. There are many projects where the lack of control of such issues has doubled timescales and costs.

Projects of this scale often require multi-site working. This may require a lot of preplanning to set up wide-area network communication capability to, say, a multi-user CASE dictionary and to make cross-project electronic mail practicable. In addition, regular face-to-face meetings cannot be over-emphasized as a vital communication tool. For very large international projects, video-conferencing facilities may be cost justified to complement expensive long-distance travel arrangements.

Small Projects

With small projects of say less than five people and a timescale of around three to six months then the emphasis changes. **Multiple roles suddenly become very important.**

As the project is small, each team member may need to play more than one role. But these should be clearly visible and played carefully to ensure that things do not get missed. The roles may include:

- project leader
- technical leader
- devil's advocate
- performance guru
- cross-project integrator
- analyst
- designer
- usability guru.

The danger is that a person may simultaneously have two roles that are normally in gentle conflict. For example, an analyst/designer may compromise the requirements for ease of design. Someone responsible for performance and ease of use may sacrifice one for the other without the necessary debate. In such cases the responsibility rests with the project and technical leader, along with the user, to check that such balances are adequately made.

Much of the administration, project control, change control and communication can be simplified. These activities can be reduced to five or ten percent of the resources effort deployed. This is not short cutting these important issues: it is relying upon the fact that a small team working together in close proximity is a more efficient way of working than a large organization; that is, as long as each team member remembers to take responsibility to keep the communication channels open at all times.

Small projects can often amalgamate tasks into a much simpler structure. Dependencies and milestones may be met by a simple note in the diary or a verbal report to management. **It does not mean that they do not get done** – it simply means that the mechanism is easier. For example, a project report could be a one-sided piece of paper recording key actions, relying upon the open communication channels mentioned above, whereas on a large project a similar report might run to twenty or thirty pages.

In some cases complete stages of CASE*Method can be merged. This should not be entered into lightly, but there are circumstances when it is valid. By way of illustration let us examine three different scenarios, each of which is a small project.

Merged Strategy and Analysis

The two stages of strategy and analysis may sometimes be merged. The most obvious example is when a previous strategy is already in place, and an analysis stage is being planned for phase four of a long development. In this case a very short confirmatory strategy can usefully precede and coincide with the detailed analysis. This may appear as the following activities at the beginning of analysis:

- Identify two or three strategic information and directional interviewees.

- Interview them using strategic analysis questioning techniques, such as **open** questioning.

- Consolidate the information gathered with previous strategic architectures and revise plans.

- Optionally, conduct a short feedback session with the interviewees and selected users from the original strategy, concentrating on differences and new aspects.

- Revise the terms of reference for this analysis activity.

In the process, if the interviewees happen to be relevant for the detailed analysis stage, extend the interviews to encompass the required detail; for example, questions about volumetrics and detailed functionality.

The second frequent case of merged strategy and analysis is when the project is to replace an existing small system, perhaps using new technology. The time may not be appropriate for a wide strategy, so the objective is to replace the system with appropriate technology in as flexible a manner as possible, such that any future strategy or interrelationship with other systems is minimally compromised.

The approach is very similar to the first example. The top-down direction and architecture are again obtained from two or three key people. This is balanced with a detailed bottom-up analysis of the existing system and any requirements or wish-list items placed upon it. Good generic modelling techniques and expert analyst/designers are needed to create flexible data structures, data-driven functionality and identify potential re-usable components. This can be considered as the first stage of detailed analysis, but without the investment in a strategic plan or long-term information architecture.

Pilot Project

When switching to structured methods or adopting some major new software or hardware technology, there is often a need to try out the new ideas quickly, prior to committing major resources. In these cases the method is to set up joint development techniques with real experts in the new approach. Scope out a small, but significant project and rely upon regular, personal, project updates and on a few key people to ensure that the project is meeting its objectives. This group would typically comprise a user, a technical expert, a strong project leader and a responsible manager.

Sometimes the intention of a pilot project is not to prove an entire process, but to test out feasibility, approach and interdependent technologies. In which case, it may not be necessary to deliver a complete system, and a representative core that exercises all major components and technologies will suffice.

For such a pilot study, an expert project leader should draw up a one-off project plan and use this book to ensure that nothing important has been omitted; and that all aspects have at least been considered.

Rapid prototyping techniques can also be used in such pilot schemes. In Appendix E alternative prototyping approaches are discussed. These can be used to good effect to speed up understanding and illustrate possible techniques. They can also be used in an incremental build to construct small systems rapidly against rigid standards for look and feel. The use of a CASE dictionary and generator products to enforce integrity checks, domain validation, style and environmental processing will provide very acceptable solutions in many cases. Once more, caution is recommended as these potential short-cut techniques can 'come home to roost' later in the shape of performance problems, unhappy users because they were not consulted, missing functionality, and so on; that is, any of the things a rigorous, structured analysis tries to avoid.

Different Starting Points

Consultants are often faced with a situation where a client has already completed an early stage of development such as a strategy study, a feasibility study, a statement of operational requirement or similar. In fact, in large organizations with regular movement of staff, a new team may be faced with exactly the same situation within its own organization.

What should they do?

Would you trust a third party you do not know when you have no evidence that they have done their job correctly? Your future career might depend on the success of this project.

On the other hand, do you think anyone will allow you to do it again? Increasing the cost for no perceived value to management will not endear you to your boss!

The issue **must** be discussed openly. **You** must have confidence in your starting point, and there are two well-tried methods for handling it.

The first is to audit the results of the previous work and check for quality, completeness, professionalism, coherence and rigour. This task has to be scheduled into the project, along with a review with management and an amount of resource set aside to remedy any problems.

The alternative, and perhaps better approach is to do a confirmatory strategy or feasibility study with a few, really carefully chosen users.

This relies on the fact that if twenty or thirty people were involved with the earlier work, you would only need to see two or three of them to synthesize your own top-down model of the need. Then you will be equipped to carry out the above audit, armed not only with logic but also with your own clear understanding.

In either case, the project must have a short, sharp, early set of activities before the next stage can sensibly be addressed.

Software Package Integration

In some cases it is very sensible to implement one, or perhaps several parts of a system using proprietary software packages. Typically these would cover general topics such as financials, human or physical resource management; or in vertical industries specialized packages such as manufacturing. How are these integrated and where do they fit within the life-cycle?

The optimum solution for an organization will be found by conducting a strategy study in the normal manner to ensure the enterprise requirement and business direction are fully understood. With this framework in place, alternative implementation vehicles may then be accurately assessed for their specific applicability and their ability to fit in with the wider picture.

In particular, the entity relationship model and its back-up attribute definitions can be used to check whether a package addresses the appropriate data. In this process it is important to check for those exceptions which were carefully identified during feedback sessions. One way or another each exception must be capable of being handled, at worst by some manual procedure with a computerized cross-reference.

The function hierarchy can be used to ensure that the package facilities cater sufficiently for the business needs. It is also valuable to check the critical success factors, business objectives and so on; which of them can be ascertained or controlled via the packages?

Finally, look at the **way** the package works. Is the look and feel acceptable? How will its user interface fit into other parts of the system which may be built internally? If several packages are envisaged, how will they fit together; does this imply a different style of working per package? Who will own the problem when a cross-package problem occurs?

If a package is subsequently chosen, the analysis stage changes to include the following (as necessary):

- detailed package facility assessment

- matching of facility to requirement

- requirement definition for aspects not covered by the package or to ensure that the package can coexist with other parts of the business

- specification of changes required to the package, exception-handling techniques and package acceptance criteria

- transition analysis must also cover these integration and conversion issues, along with defining the special learning curves associated with adapting external software.

Key Resource Management

This chapter would be incomplete without considering the important issue of key resource management. This can be as simple as ensuring that computers, rooms, telephones are all being exploited in an optimum manner or that key people are being utilized to best advantage. In some organizations, if the key people are being used for the correct balance of strategic and tactical work then the projects may be considered to be running in an optimum fashion.

How is this achieved? The first step is to deploy the people accurately. Know their strengths, weaknesses, aspirations and motivations and aim to maximize their contribution. Whenever a top technical person is carrying out petty administration; whenever a strategist is fighting fires; whenever a top project manager is on a technical critical-path activity there is every probability that the balance is wrong. Regular, short planning sessions are a useful way of determining where people can be deployed to most effect. The results of such a session might identify a mix of roles on a collection of sub-projects. It may include key tasks and activities that they must assure. It may provide them with project-wide key objectives or critical success factors for which they take personal responsibility.

When your key resources are well utilized you may be working in a most effective manner.

Likely Problems

Before leaving this subject it is a good idea to look at some typical problems that may need to be considered when setting up and running complex projects.

Have the expectations of the users been set too high?

Have dates already been promised?

How visible must the project progress be?

Are the team members properly motivated?

Is the mix of skills available adequate for the job?

Has responsibility been allocated for each aspect of the work, including bringing it all together as a coherent whole?

Is this project the one that is seen as the opportunity to regain credibility after some disaster? If so, can that be assured?

Have staff turnover figures, holidays, sickness and other reasons for unavailability been considered?

Requirements **will** change. Are there activities to seek out the changes and control them, without disrupting the project?

Summary

This chapter was not intended to give a detailed tutorial on project estimating, control and management but to raise awareness of the risks and approach that need to be considered to be successful.

Projects often fail badly because of unknown facts that could easily have been catered for at the outset. It is **not** an acceptable excuse to say, "Well no one told me!" if the questions were not asked. Thus the really important thing to remember is that good projects are delivered by people who seek out by many means all the relevant facts, and then use other techniques, such as peer-group check, to ensure that what they are about to do is correct.

Chapter

11

QUALITY ASSURANCE

The majority of this book concentrates on the tasks that have to be performed and estimating factors, which gives project leaders the information they need to determine plans and timescales. This chapter complements the quality assurance notes found elsewhere to address the key issue of **quality** and how it can be **assured**.

Quality

What is quality?

In this context, a dictionary definition in terms of **degree of excellence or worthiness** would be appropriate. Many people tend to use the word quality as a synonym for high quality; thus they refer to a quality product or a person of quality. Of course, without further qualification the word itself gives no indication of the degree – good, bad or indifferent!

Quality Assurance

Quality Assurance, in system development terms, is about making sure that any system being built will competently fit the purpose for which it was intended, is value for money and is within the constraints of any installation, legal or other standards.

Put another way, quality assurance is about sleeping comfortably at night.

It must start off with a clear understanding of the need and constraints without which it would be impossible to assess **'real' quality**.

Assurance of quality also includes checking whether or not the correct procedures have been followed, that the components have been constructed to standard, that documentation is complete, consistent and adequate to understand what has been built, why and how it could be changed. Good practice comes into this equation, which could cover aspects such as naming standards, re-usable components, common usage of techniques, approved style, testing procedures, standard ways of using specific tools (e.g. a programming language).

In some organizations quality is **only** perceived as being this rigid adherence to standards, possibly made worse by allowing 'none-doing' people to continually devise new and revised standards. This is the problem of 'standards for standards sake'. Experience has shown that useful quality standards are best drawn up by very busy, quality-oriented doers with help from their peers. The standards must add value to the result: otherwise why bother? But remember, the result will often include the ability to intervene and change things in the future.

For the above, and other reasons, quality assurance as a separate subject is often held in disrepute. Yet to show how vital it is we only have to look at the cost of correction after a poor-quality system has been installed. The symptoms are common – system development departments that spend seventy, eighty or even ninety percent of their effort on maintenance and creeping enhancements, causing an unacceptable backlog in new work. The target should be no more than twenty percent of development effort dedicated to maintenance.

The costs of failure can encompass many aspects:

- the cost of repair
- loss of credibility
- the cost of re-implementation and training
- the cost of delays to the organization in the expected system benefits.

For a small fault the cost of repair has frequently been measured between five hundred and a thousand times the cost of doing it correctly at the outset. But the really high costs are rarely measured, being the cost to the organization of delay, unavailability or, in the worst case, total abandonment of a new system. These costs often start in the ten million dollar range!

So how should quality be assured in a practical way?

It requires a combination of approaches, where the emphasis varies depending on the scale.

Quality Approaches

In rough priority, the following approaches can most affect the quality of any system.

1. The capability, motivation and dedication of a skilled system development team.

   Requirement: a high emphasis on recruitment, retention, project communication, training and accurate management of key resources.

2. User involvement to ensure that the system meets their needs and is **owned** by them.

   Requirement: credibility of system development staff, top-level management and user commitment, active user participation in interviews, feedbacks, reviews, acceptance, training and trade-off decisions.

3. Powerful modelling, presentation and other techniques to identify the requirements, check detail, synthesize new and better ways of doing things, identify things that are common and opportunities for simplification, to tease out that full understanding which helps assure success and simplifies automation of many of those error-prone tasks.

   Requirement: state of the art presentation, divergent and convergent modelling techniques, and the skills for their effective use. These should be supported by a powerful computer-aided systems engineering (CASE) facility to enforce modelling standards, carry out tedious, error-prone tasks, and add further embedded expertise and quality checks.

4. Constant early warning and error correction techniques within the framework of a structured method.

   Requirement: the adoption of a proven, structured method. Regular reviews or structured walkthroughs should be planned at the earliest opportunity, to be carried out by the most appropriate people in the organization. This group always includes peers and users, and will frequently include management, industry and technical experts.

5. Standards against which quality can be measured.

   Requirement: as in the engineering industry, for each technique used, for each build process, type of documentation, and so on, there should be a set of guidelines of good practice. These might take the form of rule-of-thumb examples, material on training classes, checklists and computer.enforced/suggested rules.

6. A separate quality assurance group to objectively assist other groups acquire the appropriate level of quality.

   Requirement: for large projects or departments with many projects, a separate, highly-skilled and respected group, which conducts peer-group checks, sets up quality plans, polices standards and separately adds value to system development projects. This group can also act as a catalyst for removing problems, in particular identifying their root causes and corrective actions. **The focus of such a group is on prevention rather than cure.**

7. The audit.

   Requirement: the ability to mount special audit projects to rescue projects or learn from the experience of recently-completed projects.

Quality Plan

A Quality Plan is a document, produced at the beginning of a project, with twin aims: to explain to people outside the actual project that the project team knows how to do the job, and to describe how those outsiders will be assured (at regular intervals) that the intended route will deliver the expected results. It also serves to direct the project team along the intended route, avoiding the obvious risks inherent in the project.

To achieve these aims a set of tasks is selected to fit the combination of the project expectations, skills to be deployed, management requirements, critical safety aspects, legislative requirements and chosen methodology. This is recorded as the Quality Plan for the project. The tasks include assessment of work done, measuring the process as well as the end-product, pre-emptive actions and defect prevention, escalation to senior management, change control, damage containment and defect repair.

These assurance tasks are distributed throughout the stage-by-stage tasks of CASE*Method, and can lead to specific quality assurance deliverables. The full system development plan encompasses not just the actual system development tasks but the quality assurance tasks, essential for the production of a satisfactory system.

The Quality Plan is a policy to provide practical guidance in the process of development, and a schedule of significant defect prevention and assessment tasks. It should highlight the times when the developers need to step back and specifically review some aspect of their work to date or intended way forward. As well as providing practical guidance, it is often important to be seen to be working in a quality-oriented way. Users find this reassuring and it may be a required manner of work in your organization.

The plan defines the policy for assuring the system-production tasks. It contains such criteria as:

- the type of conformance assessment to apply to different types of production activity

- how to measure whether assessment criteria have been met

- the circumstances under which problems should be escalated to senior management

- the types of change that can be decided by the project team, by the project management, by the contract negotiators.

In planning terms it may help to identify the sequence in which the development tasks are carried out. It specifically identifies prevention and safeguarding activities to be carried out by the project or a third-party team. It identifies how any reports of the quality assurance activities will be made available for review.

Prevention Tasks

Prevention tasks are analogous to paying for an insurance policy or servicing a car. They involve investing resources before a problem arises to prevent the occurrence of defects at a later stage. The intention is to promote attitudes that minimize risk and heighten consciousness in aspects such as security, integrity and quality.

Costs of prevention are caused by tasks that would not be necessary if we had a purely enlightened world of highly-skilled all-rounders who were able, risk free, to tackle any task at any time to an expert level. These experts would also need to have assimilated all the information about the requirements (political, technical and commercial), about the interface and protocol standards, and about the status of all the other workers' tasks. Such a world exists only in small craft shops or Utopia; but being mere mortals, **we** need a sound engineering discipline.

Prevention tasks include:

- training in subjects relevant to forthcoming tasks
  (both technical and managerial)

- staff selection and recruitment to obtain the required skill mix

- risk assessment and openly-documented decision making
  (ad hoc, unsubstantiated decision making is often a symptom of a failure to plan adequately)

- rigorous planning, re-planning and contingency planning

- estimating

- refining the estimating process by collecting statistics on the duration of tasks

- selection or generation of standards

- adoption (and adaptation) of good working practices as standards for the project

- generation and update of checklists to be used in review procedures (see Chapter 10 for ideas on generating checklists)

- procurement of tools (or their production if not yet in existence) which would reduce the margin of error

- investigative prototyping

- investigating the development process and refining it for the installation or particular types of project.

Cost-effective changes are more welcome to management than cost-increasing changes. However, a quality improvement that satisfies the heightened expectations of the user or reduces business costs will tend to improve business performance and may even contribute to competitive edge.

Safeguarding Tasks

The work in progress must be kept safe from accidental or unauthorized modification.

The tasks to supply these safeguards are also partly covered under the heading of configuration management, and are often considered separately from quality-related tasks. They are listed here since their absence can nullify the effect of the prevention and review tasks, and they must be planned together with those tasks to achieve the quality of the deliverables.

Safeguarding tasks include:

- identifying stage-by-stage deliverables

- establishing naming conventions for uniquely identifying all items

- safeguarding the development environment (e.g. from hackers)

- publicizing the library convention for the development environment to ensure correct storage, archiving and use of documents and computer data

- safeguarding the items under work

- safeguarding the items that have completed the review procedure

- making available the completed items that are ready to be used in a later stage: and preventing the use of incomplete items
- disseminating information about agreed changes of requirements; prevention of propagation of speculative changes.

Typical Contents of a Quality Plan

When writing the quality plan at the start of a project, it is useful to take a checklist of headings from a typical, large-scale plan, such as the list given below:

Introduction

Scope of the Quality Plan

Reference Documents

Prevention of Loss of Quality

Project Objectives and End Deliverables

Constraints, Standards, and Risks

Methodologies and Techniques

Planning

Tasks and Responsibilities

Organization and Management

Resources

Working Practices and Conventions

Appraisal of Quality

Documentation of the Development and Transition Stages

Reviews and Audits

Verification and Validation

Records Collection, Maintenance and Retention

Safeguarding Achieved Quality and Regression Testing

Software Configuration Management

Code Control and Release Packaging

Development Environment Protection

Repair of Defects

Problem Reporting and Corrective Action

Problem Escalation

For simple, low-risk projects the quality plan may be simplified to tasks included in the main project which address:

- the quality objectives of the product from this project, such as:
  - high reliability for a life-critical or business-critical system
  - a fast path for a demonstration throwaway system
  - high flexibility for pilot investigation into usability
  - high-performance or some other quality attribute

- the means to evaluate the degree of achievement of these quality objectives

- special items anticipated to affect quality (i.e. foreseeable risks)

- definition of each phase of incremental delivery

- definition of each stage of the development life-cycle, including:
  - entry criteria to the stage
    (e.g. completeness of key deliverables from a previous stage, partial completeness of some deliverables)
  - exit criteria from the stage (e.g. client sign-off)
  - major quality activity during each stage
    (e.g. strategy feedback, design reviews, code walkthroughs, system test of integrated programs and user documentation)
  - the organization unit responsible for the stage
    (e.g. for the combined design, build and transition activities; for providing the requirements and interfaces; for the review, test and quality assurance activities; and for the resource provision and co-ordination management)

- development plan creation and update procedures

- the testing and validation plans

- systems integration procedures

- the maintenance and support plan (for use during the production stage).

On large projects, however, it may be essential to have a second parallel monitoring project with the primary objective of assuring that quality system development processes are used to produce high-quality and relevant deliverables. Such a quality plan needs to be compiled and implemented with sensitivity: few people like being checked on by third parties. Checklists that identify mandatory and optional items can easily lead to a transcription without thought, a 'no-brain' exercise, to comply with producing a so-called Quality Plan. The objective is to encourage people to build quality in during all tasks, as opposed to thinking they have achieved quality by ticking all the items on a checklist.

It will be recognized that all of the above tasks appear either in the actual tasks defined for each stage of CASE*Method or in the project control aspects mentioned in the previous chapter. It is only because of the fallibility of particularly large teams that this separate, focused exercise is important. In the end, the finest quality systems are built by high-calibre people.

The Audit

An audit to check out another project, or the system that is being or has been delivered, is a formal project in its own right. Typically, it addresses all the issues covered in this chapter, but does so during a short, sharp activity. The word 'audit' nearly always makes people defensive, so great sensitivity is needed if it is used.

Experience has shown that the mechanism of using an audit project is rarely as effective as building in quality in the first place or monitoring it as we go along.

Post-implementation Review

A useful form of audit is the post-implementation review, which can take the original objectives, requirement and standards and check that each has been met to the satisfaction of interested parties. Deliverables from such an audit should include a list of corrections to the system, to the standards and to the methods employed.

Emergency Audit

If all else fails, an emergency audit can help get a project back on the right track. These are very difficult to do successfully, and require highly-competent and experienced staff. Their efforts will be seen as interference; and because it is an emergency the deliverables they can audit will rarely be consistent or complete. However, as a last resort an emergency audit can be very effective.

Summary

Quality is as important as timeliness and cost on any system development project. In the end, poor quality of the delivered system and the subsequent repair entailed can delay the intended benefits of the system. This delay can cost the business orders of magnitude more in lost opportunity than the original development cost.

The age-old maxim that prevention is better than a cure applies to quality assurance, even with the most sophisticated of modern tools.

Quality starts with, *"Are we doing the right thing in the right way?"* and finishes with, *"And is it acceptable?"*

Appendix

A

Summary of Tasks

STAGE	TASK	
Strategy	10	Project administration and management
	20	Scope the study and agree Terms of Reference
	30	Plan a strategy study
	40	Briefings, interviews and other information gathering
	50	Model the business
	60	Prepare for feedback session
	70	Conduct feedback session
	80	Consolidate results of feedback session
	90	Complete documentation of the business model
	100	Evolve information system architecture and make other recommendations
	110	Determine forward system development plan
	120	Prepare verbal report
	130	Report to senior management
	140	Prepare and deliver written report
Analysis	10	Project administration and management
	20	Plan detailed analysis
	30	Review standards, constraints and potential design issues
	40	Investigate detailed requirement
	50	Review findings against Terms of Reference to confirm approach
	60	Provide detailed specification
	70	Provide initial transition strategy
	80	Define audit/control needs
	90	Define back-up/recovery requirements
	100	Perform outline sizing and predict performance
	110	Review results of detailed analysis
	120	Obtain stage-end commitment

STAGE		TASK
Design	10	Project administration and management
	20	Design application
	30	Design and build database
	40	Produce network/communication design
	50	Design audit/control needs
	60	Design back-up/recovery needs
	70	Review outline design and produce program specifications
	80	Complete system test plan
	90	Complete transition strategy
	100	Review results of design stage
	110	Obtain stage-end commitment
Build	10	Project administration and management
	20	Prepare for build stage
	30	Review designs and estimates with programmer
	40	Produce programs
	50	Prepare, perform and review system test
	60	Review test results
	70	Obtain stage-end commitment
User Documentation	10	Project administration and management
	20	Complete user documentation
	30	Provide operations hand-over documentation
	40	Obtain stage-end commitment
Transition	10	Project administration and management
	20	Train users
	30	Prepare for acceptance testing
	40	Support acceptance test
	50	Perform data take-on
	60	Carry out installation of hardware, system software and other components of the production configuration
	70	Perform any other pre-implementation trials
	80	Prepare for cut-over
	90	Perform cut-over
	100	Support system during the critical period
	110	Perform post-implementation review
Production	10	Provide operational service
	20	Respond to user requests
	30	Monitor/review performance
	40	Assess the future of the system

Appendix

B

STANDARD STRATEGY
REPORT CONTENTS LIST

Purpose

Every strategy study is unique, because every business is unique. The final model of the business and the recommended information systems strategy will reflect this. It is, however, helpful to have some guidelines for writing the report of the strategy study to be presented to the client.

Remember, during the beginning of the strategy you may have agreed a set of Terms of Reference that includes things for you to comment upon.

Examples are
- assessment of existing systems
- organizational implications of any changes
- how any recommendations might apply if the organization were decentralized (or centralized!).

During the study it may have evolved that the full report should only go to a few people, whilst a management summary with minimal back-up information is distributed more widely.

Thus the first step is to define the contents of your report without reference to this appendix. **Then** take this appendix as a checklist of possibilities that may or may not apply.

Target the document to have a thin management report (a maximum of 30 or so pages), with back-up appendices. Many of the appendices may be reports produced directly out of CASE*Dictionary or diagrams from CASE*Designer. Additional 'fuzzy model' diagrams should be added to convey concepts to decision makers.

Standard Strategy Report Contents List

Contents

1. Management Summary

2. Introduction/Aims and Objectives

3. The Business Model

4. Information Systems Strategy

5. Costs and Benefits

Appendices

1. Management Summary

1.0 Introduction

1.1 Problem Identification/Findings

1.2 Recommendations Summary

1.3 Cost/Benefit Summary

1.4 Decisions Required

1.5 Unresolved Issues

1.6 Conclusion

Note: formal subheadings may not be necessary in the Management Summary.

2. Introduction/Aims and Objectives of The Study

2.1 Background to/Reasons for Study

2.2 Acknowledgements/Interview List

2.3 How to Use the Report

2.4 Terms of Reference

2.4.1 Scope
2.4.2 Deliverables
2.4.3 Exclusions
2.4.4 Targets
2.4.5 Staffing/Reporting/Control

2.5 Variations to Terms of Reference

2.6 Project Constraints/Assumptions

2.7 Method of Working

2.8 Other Findings

3. The Business Model

3.1 Business Background

3.1.1 Business Direction
3.1.2 Operational Concerns, Problems, Needs
3.1.3 SWOT Analysis (Strengths, Weaknesses, Opportunities, Threats)
3.1.4 Business Constraints
3.1.4.1 External Constraints/Deadlines
3.1.4.2 Internal Constraints/Deadlines
3.1.4.3 Technical Constraints

3.2 Aims and Objectives of the Business

3.2.1 Business Aims
3.2.2 Business Objectives
3.2.3 Critical Success Factors
3.2.4 Key Performance Indicators

3.3 Information Model (high-level only)

3.4 Function Model (high-level only)

3.5 Business Model Maintenance

4. Information Systems Strategy

4.1   Outline Solution

4.1.1   Implications/Effect on End Users

4.1.2   Business Priorities

4.1.3   Logical Dependencies

4.1.4   Recommended Implementation Method
(e.g. Package Evaluation, Prototypes, Pilot System, Parallel Run)

4.1.5   Possible Hardware Types and Sites

4.1.5.1   Factors not Sized

4.1.5.2   Hardware

4.1.5.3   Development Machine

4.1.6   Communications Requirement

4.1.7   Possible Software Types

4.1.8   Support/Production Considerations

4.1.8.1   Change Control

4.1.8.2   Security

4.1.8.3   System Control

4.2   Alternatives Considered (Note: include 'Do Nothing' Option)

4.3   Proposed Development Plan

4.3.1   Phasing

4.3.2   Planning Assumptions
(Task Breakdown with Time/Resource Estimates and Costs)

4.3.3   Development Schedule/Milestones

4.3.4   Transition Overview and Issues

4.3.5   Staff Requirements and Training Needs

4.3.6   Installation Schedule

4.4   Management Issues/Prerequisites

4.4.1   Phasing

4.4.2   User Involvement

4.4.3   Policy Issues

4.4.4   Dependencies

4.4.5   Resources

4.5   Next Steps/Actions

4.6   Future Possibilities

4.7   Tactical/Interim Solutions

5.   COSTS AND BENEFITS

5.1   Benefits

5.1.1   Benefit Identification (Linked to Functions/Key Performance Factors)
5.1.2   Benefit Quantification (Note: should be done by or at least explicitly endorsed by users)

5.2   Cost Breakdown

5.2.1   Development Cost Estimates
5.2.2   Implementation Cost Estimates
5.2.2.1   Capital
5.2.2.2   Revenue
5.2.2.3   Software Licence Costs
5.2.3   Running Cost Estimates
- Computer
- Clerical/Other

5.3   Cost/Benefit Analysis

5.3.1   Full Implementation of Recommended Solution
5.3.2   Alternative Implementation Scenarios:
- 'Do Nothing' Option
- Reduced Functionality
- Reduced Number of Sites Implemented
- Spread over Longer Time

APPENDICES

A.1   Key Performance Factors (detail)

A.2   Current Business Systems and Shortcomings

A.3   Function Hierarchy (detailed)

A.4   Key Performance Factors: Function Matrix

A.5   Full Entity Model

A.6   Entity Definitions (Detailed with Significance, Synonyms, Relationships and Important Attributes)

A.7   Function: Entity Matrix

A.8   Details of Costs and Benefits

A.9   Detailed Development Plans

A.10   Glossary

Appendix

C

SET OF STANDARD FORMS

This section covers a paper-based 'dictionary' concept, which was the predecessor of CASE tools. The forms provide a simple introduction to documenting most aspects of the life-cycle, but nowadays the use of a full-coverage CASE tool must be recommended for ease of use, quality controls and the wealth of utilities and active support one gets.

The use of the CASE tools from Oracle is covered in Appendix D, along with a few pictures of the contents of screens to illustrate how paper systems have been superseded.

Standard Forms

C1	Blank form for business level
C2	Application (system)
C3	Domain Definition
C4	Geographic Location
C5	Business Unit
C6	Entity Definition
C7	Entity Volumes (general volumes)
C8	Entity Volumes (distributed requirement)
C9	Full Attribute Definition
C10	Business Function Hierarchy
C11	Elementary Business Function Definition
C12	Business Function Frequency (general frequencies)
C13	Business Function Frequency (distributed requirement)
C14	Input Dataflow
C15	Output Dataflow
C16	Function Logic
C17	Datastore Definition
C18	Function/Business Unit matrix

C19   Function/Entity matrix
C20   Entity/Business Unit matrix
C21   Module/Processing Node matrix (for distributed processing)
C22   Table/Processing Node matrix (for distributed data)
C23   Table/Entity matrix
C24   Table/Module matrix
C25   Module/Function matrix
C26   Module/Column matrix
C27   Function/Attribute matrix
C28   Geographic Location/Processing Node matrix
        (for distributed architecture)
C29   General matrix
C30   Blank form for implementation level.

Matrix Forms

The most important elements used in CASE*Method are shown diagrammatically below, along with their interrelationships. Wherever a double-headed arrow is used it is useful to have a matrix of one element to the other for completeness and consistency checking. (See Forms C18-C29.)

Figure C-1
Important Elements in
CASE*Method and Their
Interrelationshiips

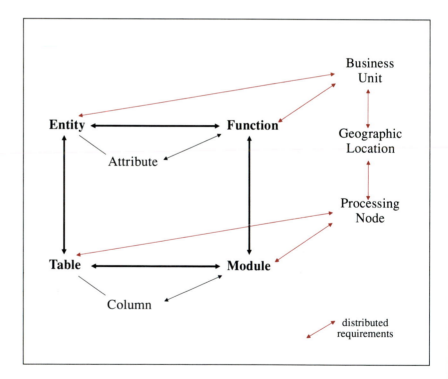

ORACLE®

THE RELATIONAL DATABASE
MANAGEMENT SYSTEM

Reference ....

| Team | Project | Analyst | Date | Sheet .... of .... |
| User | Activity | Checked by | Date | |

Standard Form   C1

ORACLE ® ————— APPLICATION (BUSINESS)

THE RELATIONAL DATABASE MANAGEMENT SYSTEM

Name . . . .   Parent application . . . .

Business description

Business objectives/aims/priorities/constraints/performance indicators

Notes

Team	Project	Analyst	Date	Sheet .... of ....
User	Activity	Checked by	Date	

C2   Standard Form

ORACLE®

THE RELATIONAL DATABASE
MANAGEMENT SYSTEM

DOMAIN DEFINITION
(BUSINESS LEVEL)

Reference ....

Domain Name	....	Subset of domain	....

Description/notes

Format	Max Length	Average	Unit of Measure
....	....	....	....

	User	Access right (C,U,D,A,R,All)	Authority Level
Available to	....	....	....
	....	....	....
	....	....	....
Responsibility of	....	....	....

Validation rule

Normal default value	....
Value for null	....

Normal Derivation

Value	High Value	Abbreviation	Meaning

Team	Project	Analyst	Date	Sheet .... of ....
User	Activity	Checked by	Date	

ORACLE®

THE RELATIONAL DATABASE MANAGEMENT SYSTEM

GEOGRAPHIC LOCATION

Reference ....

Geographic Location Name . . . .

Reference . . . .

Type . . . . e.g. Site

Spatial Reference . . . . e.g. Grid reference

Within Location Name . . . .

Reference . . . .

Type . . . . e.g. Town

Description/constraints

Distances to other geographic locations

Other Location Reference	Name	Absolute Distance	Unit e.g. km	Notes

This form should be used to identify any site, town, city, region, country, etc. at which business location(s) may be found. They would later be refined to sites for nodes on a network.

Team	Project	Analyst	Date	Sheet .... of ....
User	Activity	Checked by	Date	

ORACLE ®
THE RELATIONAL DATABASE MANAGEMENT SYSTEM

BUSINESS UNIT
(Company/Department/Organization unit)

Reference ....

Business Unit Name . . . .

Reference . . . .

Type . . . .   e.g. Department

Subordinate to . . . .

Reference . . . .

Type . . . .   e.g. Company

Address	Purpose of Unit
. . . .	
Post Town/City	
Postal Code	
Country	
Location Ref	

User Group

Name	Description	Named Users (optional)		

Team	Project	Analyst	Date	Sheet .... of ....
User	Activity	Checked by	Date	

ORACLE ® ———— ENTITY DEFINITION ————

Reference ....

THE RELATIONAL DATABASE
MANAGEMENT SYSTEM

Name (plural)	....	Sub-type of ....
Synonyms	....	Initial Vol ....
	....	Average Vol .... Likely Maximum ....
	....	Growth Rate .... % per year

Description: Has significance as

Attributes

Name	Optional	Domain	Format	Max. Length	Notes	See full definition	Unique Identifier

Relationships: Each occurrence of this entity

must / may be	link phrase	one and only one / one or more	entity name	cascade delete	Arc	

Notes/remarks

Please turn over for detailed figures

Team	Project	Analyst	Date	Sheet .... of ....
User	Activity	Checked by	Date	

C6   Standard Form

ORACLE®

THE RELATIONAL DATABASE
MANAGEMENT SYSTEM

ENTITY VOLUMES
(General Volumes)

Reference ....

Entity Name ....

Detailed Volumes (for some entities)

	Volume	or % growth	Notes
Current volumes			
Projected: Period 1			
Period 2			
Period 3			
Period 4			
Period 5			

Retention

	Number	Period	Reason
Archive after			
Destroy after			

n.b. Ensure functions are included for archive and destroy,
with appropriate conditions.

Business Integrity Rules (General)

Condition	Rule

Team
User

Project
Activity

Analyst
Checked by

Date
Date

Sheet .... of ....

ORACLE ® — ENTITY VOLUMES —

THE RELATIONAL DATABASE
MANAGEMENT SYSTEM

(Distributed Requirement)

Entity Name ....

BUSINESS UNIT		From Current	New

Reference ....

Name ....

Initial Vol ....

Average Vol ....   Likely Maximum ....

Growth Rate ....   % per year

Detailed Volumes (for some entities)

	Volume or % growth		Notes
Current volumes			
Projected: Period 1			
Period 2			
Period 3			
Period 4			
Period 5			

Retention

	Number	Period	Reason
Archive after			
Destroy after			

n.b. Ensure functions are included for archive and destroy,
with appropriate conditions.

Special business unit specific Integrity Rules

Condition	Rule

Team	Project	Analyst	Date	Sheet .... of ....
User	Activity	Checked by	Date	

ORACLE® ——— FULL ATTRIBUTE DEFINITION

THE RELATIONAL DATABASE
MANAGEMENT SYSTEM

Name . . . . of entity . . . . in domain . . . .

Description/note

Mandatory/Optional

. . . . % initially   on condition . . . .

. . . . % normally   . . . .

Format	Max. Length	Average Length	Unit of Measure
. . . .	. . . .	. . . .	. . . .

	User	Access right (C,U,D,A,R,All)	Authority/Level
Available to	. . . .	. . . .	. . . .
	. . . .	. . . .	. . . .
	. . . .	. . . .	. . . .
Responsibility of	. . . .	. . . .	. . . .

Validation Rule

Default value . . . .   (only if mandatory)

Value for null . . . .   (only if optional)

Derivation

Value	High Value	Abbreviation	Meaning

Team	Project	Analyst	Date	Sheet .... of ....
User	Activity	Checked by	Date	

ORACLE ® — BUSINESS FUNCTION HIERARCHY

THE RELATIONAL DATABASE
MANAGEMENT SYSTEM

(Process/Operation Hierarchy)

Reference ....

Team	Project	Analyst	Date	Sheet .... of ....
User	Activity	Checked by	Date	

C10   Standard Form

ORACLE ®
THE RELATIONAL DATABASE
MANAGEMENT SYSTEM

ELEMENTARY BUSINESS
FUNCTION DEFINITION
(Process/Operation)

Reference ....

Function Ref .... Name ....

Inferior to Function Ref .... Name ....

Available to .... Authority Level ....

....

Frequency	per	Urgency/Response needed
		see continuation for more detail

Triggered by	Trigger for

Description

Usage of entity (attribute)   Method/action

Notes/remarks

Team	Project	Analyst	Date	Sheet .... of ....
User	Activity	Checked by	Date	

ORACLE®

THE RELATIONAL DATABASE
MANAGEMENT SYSTEM

BUSINESS FUNCTION FREQUENCY
(General Frequencies)

Reference ....

Function Ref .... Name ....

Detailed Frequency (for some functions)

	Frequency or	% growth	Per e.g. day	Urgency	Notes
Current frequencies					
Projected: Period 1					
Period 2					
Period 3					
Period 4					
Period 5					

Available to User Group Name	Authority Level	Named Users (optional)			

Team   Project   Analyst   Date   Sheet .... of ....
User   Activity   Checked by   Date

C12   Standard Form

ORACLE®
THE RELATIONAL DATABASE MANAGEMENT SYSTEM

BUSINESS FUNCTION FREQUENCY
(Distributed Requirement)

Reference ....

Function Ref ....   Name ....

BUSINESS UNIT

Reference ....

Initial Freq .... per ....

Name ....

Average Freq .... per ....

Growth Rate .... % per year

Detailed Frequency (for some functions)

	Frequency or % growth	Per e.g. day	Urgency	Notes
Current frequencies				
Projected: Period 1				
Period 2				
Period 3				
Period 4				
Period 5				

Available to User Group Name	Authority Level	Named Users (optional)		

Team   Project   Analyst   Date   Sheet .... of ....
User   Activity   Checked by   Date

Standard Form   C13

ORACLE ®

THE RELATIONAL DATABASE
MANAGEMENT SYSTEM

ELEMENTARY BUSINESS
FUNCTION DEFINITION
INPUT DATAFLOW

Reference ....

Function Ref .... Name ....

Dataflow Source Type .... Source Name ....

Source Description ....

Dataflow Name .... Dataflow Type .....

Entity	Attribute	Usage
Data Item		

Dataflow Source Type .... Source Name ....

Source Description ....

Dataflow Name .... Dataflow Type .....

Entity	Attribute	Usage
Data Item		

Where: Dataflow Type = Input / Retrieval / Interprocess
   Dataflow Source Type = Datastore / External entity / Function or Process
   Description entered only if function/process or datastore

Team	Project	Analyst	Date	Sheet .... of ....
User	Activity	Checked by	Date	

C14   Standard Form

ORACLE®

THE RELATIONAL DATABASE
MANAGEMENT SYSTEM

ELEMENTARY BUSINESS
FUNCTION DEFINITION
OUTPUT DATAFLOW

Reference ....

Function Ref .... Name ....

Dataflow Destination Type .... Destination Name ....

Destination Description ....

Dataflow Name .... Dataflow Type .....

Entity	Attribute	Usage
Data Item		

Dataflow Destination Type .... Destination Name ....

Destination Description ....

Dataflow Name .... Dataflow Type .....

Entity	Attribute	Usage
Data Item		

Where: Dataflow Type = Input / Retrieval / Interprocess
    Dataflow Destination Type = Datastore / External entity / Function or Process
    Description entered only if function/process or datastore

Team	Project	Analyst	Date	Sheet .... of ....
User	Activity	Checked by	Date	

ORACLE® ──────── FUNCTION LOGIC ────

THE RELATIONAL DATABASE
MANAGEMENT SYSTEM

Function Ref . . . . Name . . . .

On
- date attribute . . . . . . of entity . . . .
- completion of action . . . . . . of function . . . .
- date / time
- external trigger / whim

Step	Action	Action Freq	Attribute changes and other notes

Team   Project   Analyst   Date   Sheet .... of ....
User   Activity   Checked by   Date

C16   Standard Form

ORACLE®
THE RELATIONAL DATABASE MANAGEMENT SYSTEM

DATASTORE DEFINITION

Reference ....

Datastore name . . . .   Reference . . . .

Description . . . .

	Entity	Attributes
Data items		
Input dataflow		from
Output dataflow		to

Team   Project   Analyst   Date   Sheet .... of ....
User   Activity   Checked by   Date

ORACLE ®

THE RELATIONAL DATABASE
MANAGEMENT SYSTEM

ELEMENTARY FUNCTION		BUSINESS UNITS																		
SHORT NAME	REF.																			

Enter the frequency and period of use e.g. 12/YEAR
or just the simple Y/N indication e.g. 100/YEAR

Team	Project	Analyst	Date
User	Activity	Checked by	Date

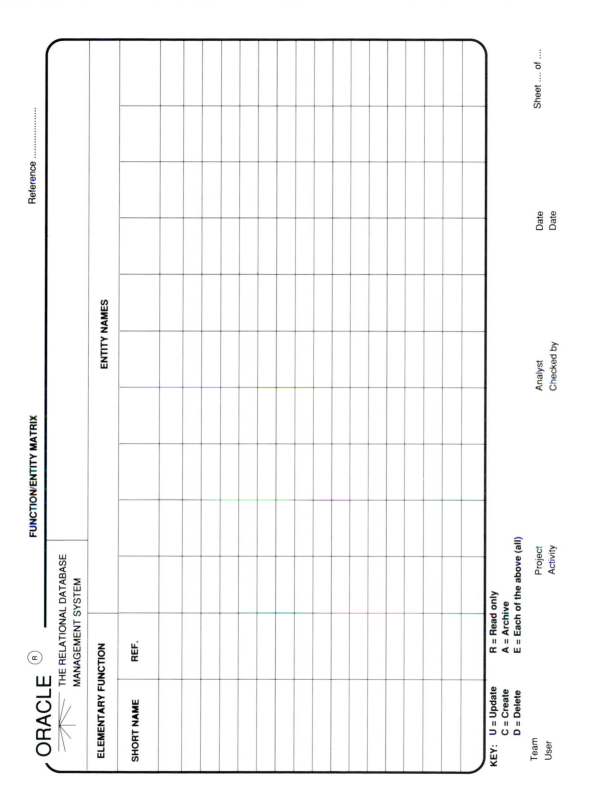

ORACLE ®

THE RELATIONAL DATABASE
MANAGEMENT SYSTEM

FUNCTION/ENTITY MATRIX

Reference ....

ENTITY NAMES

ELEMENTARY FUNCTION

SHORT NAME	REF.

KEY: U = Update   R = Read only
      C = Create   A = Archive
      D = Delete   E = Each of the above (all)

Team   Project   Analyst   Date
User   Activity   Checked by   Date

Sheet .... of ....

Standard Form   C19

ORACLE ®

THE RELATIONAL DATABASE
MANAGEMENT SYSTEM

ENTITY/BUSINESS UNIT MATRIX

Reference ....

Sheet .... of ....

BUSINESS UNIT

ENTITY

SHORT NAME	REF.														

Team

User

Project

Activity

Analyst

Checked by

Date

Date

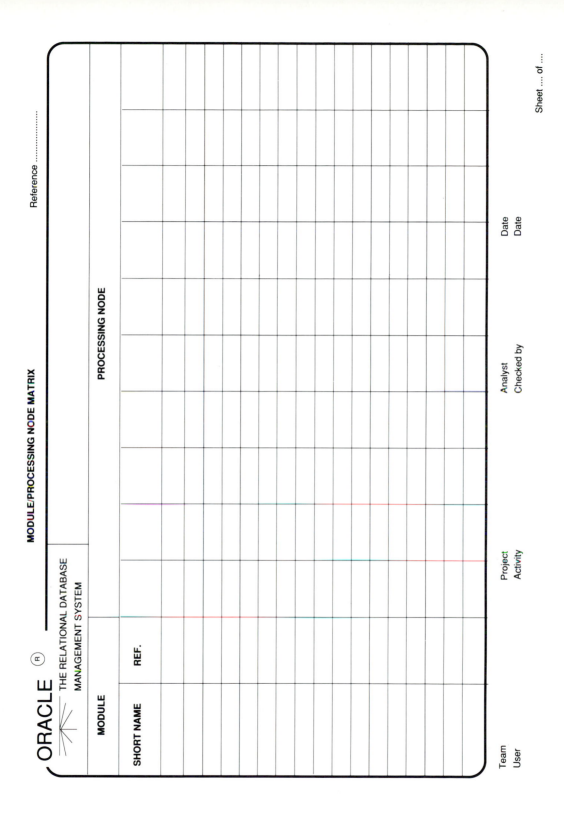

ORACLE ®

THE RELATIONAL DATABASE MANAGEMENT SYSTEM

TABLE/PROCESSING NODE MATRIX

Reference ....

PROCESSING NODE

TABLE												
SHORT NAME	REF.											

Team   Project   Analyst   Date
User   Activity   Checked by   Date

Sheet .... of ....

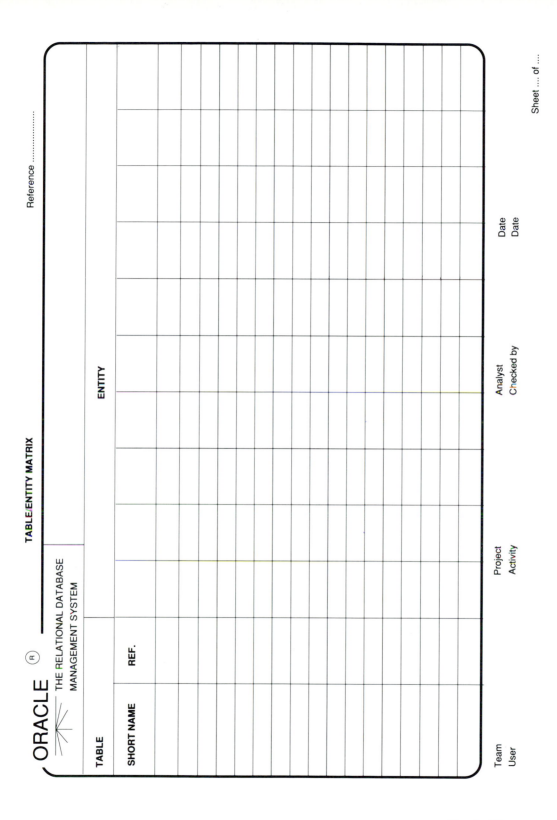

ORACLE ® TABLE/ENTITY MATRIX

THE RELATIONAL DATABASE MANAGEMENT SYSTEM

Reference ....

TABLE

SHORT NAME | **REF.**

ENTITY

Team | Project | Analyst | Date
User | Activity | Checked by | Date

Sheet .... of ....

ORACLE ®

THE RELATIONAL DATABASE
MANAGEMENT SYSTEM

TABLE/MODULE MATRIX

Reference ....

TABLE

SHORT NAME	REF.	MODULE

Team
User

Project
Activity

Analyst
Checked by

Date
Date

Sheet .... of ....

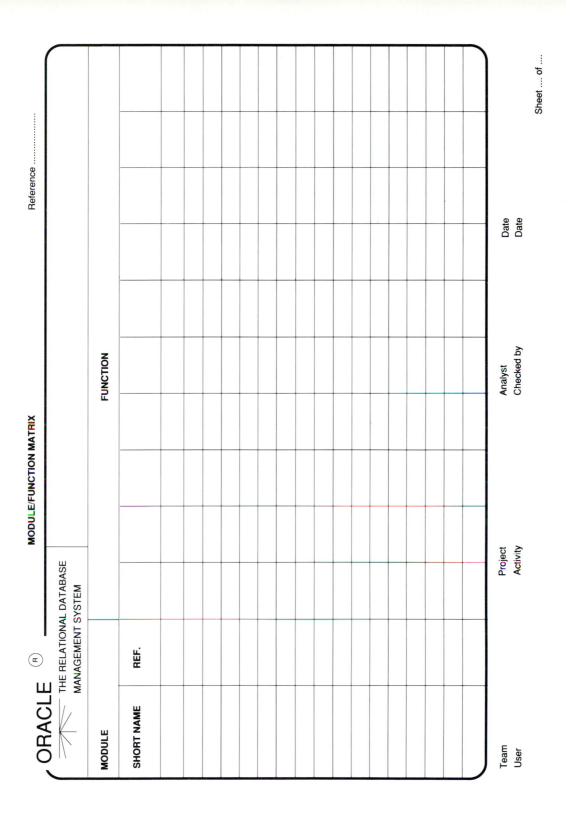

ORACLE ® THE RELATIONAL DATABASE MANAGEMENT SYSTEM

MODULE/FUNCTION MATRIX

Reference ....

Sheet .... of ....

MODULE

SHORT NAME | REF.

FUNCTION

Team
User

Project
Activity

Analyst
Checked by

Date
Date

Standard Form   C25

ORACLE ®

THE RELATIONAL DATABASE
MANAGEMENT SYSTEM

MODULE/COLUMN MATRIX

COLUMN

MODULE

TABLE NAME	COLUMN NAME																

Team
User

Project
Activity

Analyst
Checked by

Date
Date

C26   Standard Form

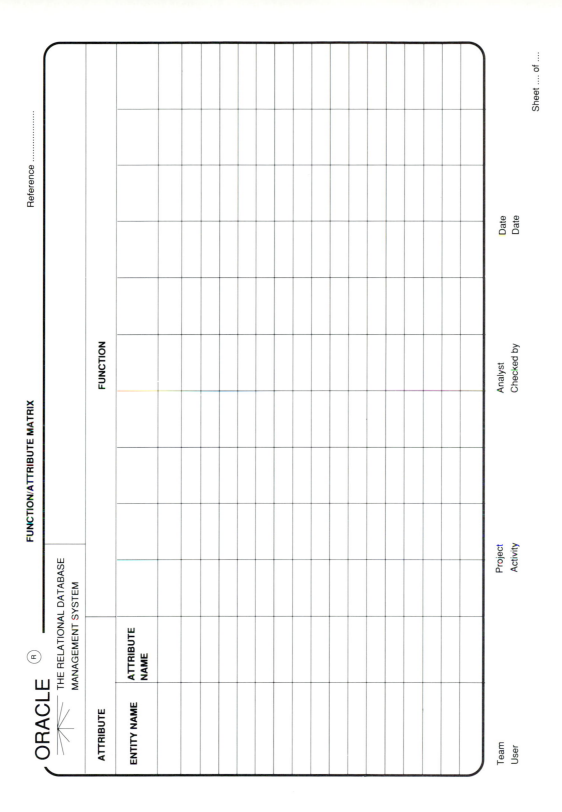

ORACLE ® THE RELATIONAL DATABASE MANAGEMENT SYSTEM

FUNCTION/ATTRIBUTE MATRIX

Reference ....

ATTRIBUTE

FUNCTION

ENTITY NAME | ATTRIBUTE NAME

Team
User

Project
Activity

Analyst
Checked by

Date
Date

Sheet .... of ....

Standard Form   C27

ORACLE ®

THE RELATIONAL DATABASE
MANAGEMENT SYSTEM

GEOGRAPHIC LOCATION/PROCESSING NODE MATRIX

Reference ....

GEOGRAPHIC LOCATION

SHORT NAME	REF.

PROCESSING NODE

Project	Analyst	Date
Activity	Checked by	Date

Team
User

Sheet .... of ....

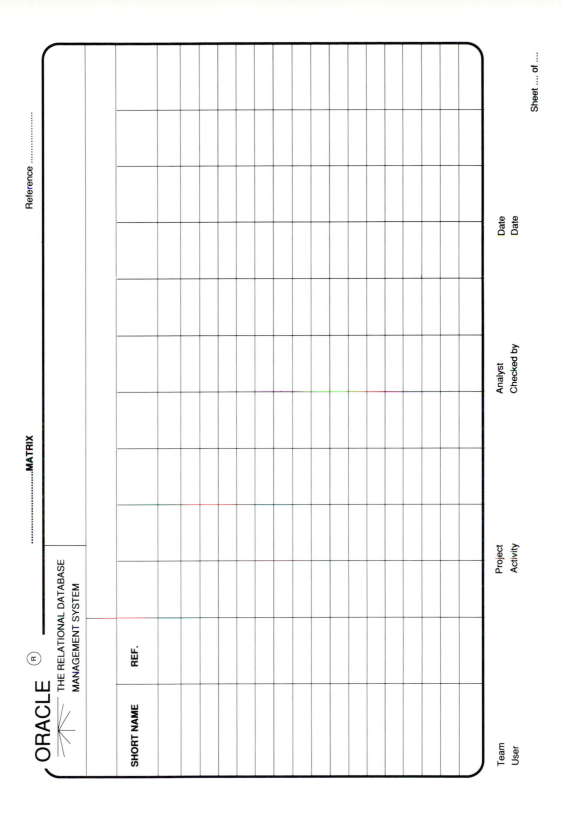

ORACLE ®

THE RELATIONAL DATABASE MANAGEMENT SYSTEM

..................MATRIX

Reference ....

SHORT NAME	REF.															

Team   Project   Analyst   Date

User   Activity   Checked by   Date

Sheet .... of ....

Standard Form   C29

ORACLE®

THE RELATIONAL DATABASE
MANAGEMENT SYSTEM

Team	Project	Analyst	Date	Sheet .... of ....
User	Activity	Checked by	Date	

C30   Standard Form

Appendix

D

USE OF ORACLE CASE TOOLS

The Oracle CASE tools comprise a family of products, all based upon the portable distributed repository CASE*Dictionary. The products support CASE*Method and many of the techniques used by other methods.

CASE*Dictionary

CASE*Dictionary is a multi-user database that acts as a repository for all information relating to an application system under development, and also acts as a database for each of the products described below. It supports all the stages of the Business System Life Cycle using interactive form-fill screens, for maintaining and querying information, thus replacing the need for the paper forms shown in Appendix C. The data is fully cross-referenced and can be examined, checked and communicated to others by a wide range of reports, completeness and consistency checks. In particular, CASE*Dictionary maintains a complete definition of the requirement and the detailed design. It also provides utilities to help application and database design, sizing, and interaction with database management systems and with application generator programs. It is available through a menu-driven forms interface on personal, mini and mainframe computers.

CASE*Designer

CASE*Designer provides a mouse-driven, multi-tasking, window-based, high-resolution graphics interface to the dictionary. This workstation interface allows interactive update to the dictionary database via diagrams and pop-up windows.

Alternative diagrams, providing different views, may be used for update or presentation purposes. Subsequently, these can be plotted or laser printed. Diagram types include Entity Relationship Diagrams, Function Hierarchies, Dataflow Diagrams and sophisticated matrix handlers. CASE*Designer provides a versatile workbench environment on workstations such as SUN, HP, VAX and powerful PCs, which can be networked into a multi-user, distributed dictionary database.

CASE*Generator

CASE*Generator is a family of products, each of which takes the definition of requirement held in the dictionary along with a definition of the target environment and installation preferences, and generates appropriate computer programs. The types of program that may be generated include menus, interactive forms and reports.

CASE*Project

CASE*Project is a multi-user project management system to support CASE*Method. It may be used to estimate and control the tasks and deliverables in an overlapping multi-project environment where key resources may be working on several projects. The system integrates, where appropriate, with elements held in the dictionary, including such objects as diagrams.

CASE*Bridge

CASE*Bridge is a family of products that enable users of the Oracle CASE tools to co-exist with tools from other CASE vendors. Information from one repository may be extracted to a standard repository protocol and then loaded or merged into the CASE*Dictionary or vice versa.

Overviews

To fully use the Oracle CASE*Dictionary and CASE*Designer products you should refer to the appropriate tutorial, reference information or training course. The following diagrams illustrate in overview how these and other CASE products might be used during the Business System Life Cycle, and the rough sequence of events.

CASE SUPPORT
for the
BUSINESS SYSTEM LIFE CYCLE

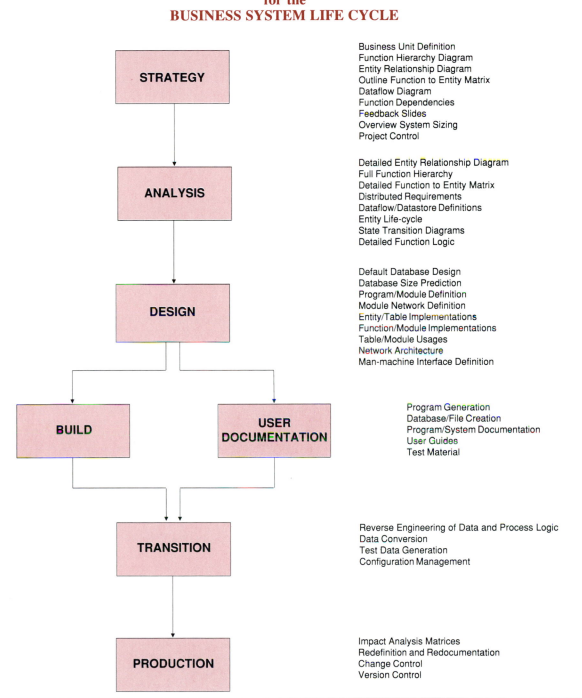

STRATEGY

Business Unit Definition
Function Hierarchy Diagram
Entity Relationship Diagram
Outline Function to Entity Matrix
Dataflow Diagram
Function Dependencies
Feedback Slides
Overview System Sizing
Project Control

ANALYSIS

Detailed Entity Relationship Diagram
Full Function Hierarchy
Detailed Function to Entity Matrix
Distributed Requirements
Dataflow/Datastore Definitions
Entity Life-cycle
State Transition Diagrams
Detailed Function Logic

DESIGN

Default Database Design
Database Size Prediction
Program/Module Definition
Module Network Definition
Entity/Table Implementations
Function/Module Implementations
Table/Module Usages
Network Architecture
Man-machine Interface Definition

BUILD

USER DOCUMENTATION

Program Generation
Database/File Creation
Program/System Documentation
User Guides
Test Material

TRANSITION

Reverse Engineering of Data and Process Logic
Data Conversion
Test Data Generation
Configuration Management

PRODUCTION

Impact Analysis Matrices
Redefinition and Redocumentation
Change Control
Version Control

STRATEGY STAGE

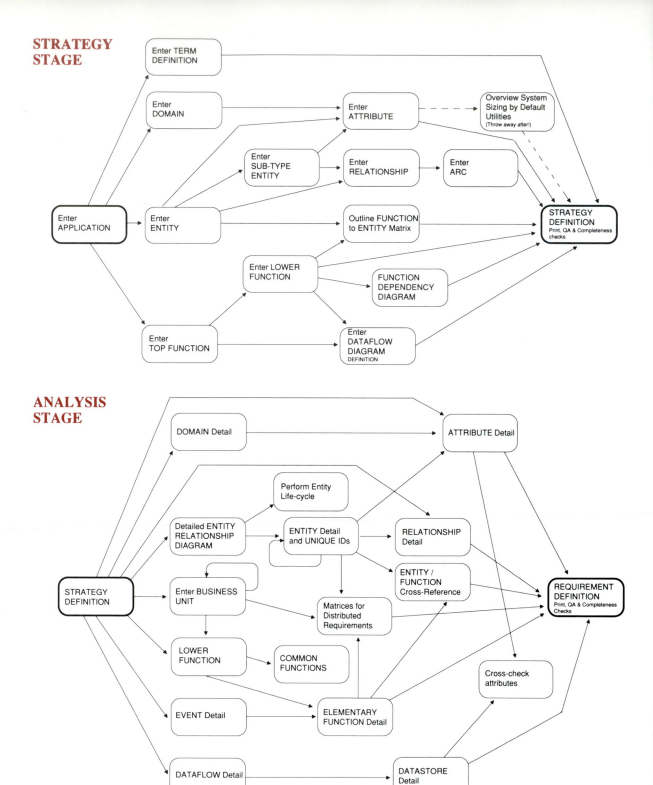

Enter TERM DEFINITION

Enter DOMAIN

Enter ATTRIBUTE

Overview System Sizing by Default Utilities (Throw away after!)

Enter SUB-TYPE ENTITY

Enter RELATIONSHIP

Enter ARC

Enter APPLICATION

Enter ENTITY

Outline FUNCTION to ENTITY Matrix

STRATEGY DEFINITION
Print, QA & Completeness checks

Enter LOWER FUNCTION

FUNCTION DEPENDENCY DIAGRAM

Enter TOP FUNCTION

Enter DATAFLOW DIAGRAM DEFINITION

ANALYSIS STAGE

DOMAIN Detail

ATTRIBUTE Detail

Perform Entity Life-cycle

Detailed ENTITY RELATIONSHIP DIAGRAM

ENTITY Detail and UNIQUE IDs

RELATIONSHIP Detail

ENTITY / FUNCTION Cross-Reference

STRATEGY DEFINITION

Enter BUSINESS UNIT

Matrices for Distributed Requirements

REQUIREMENT DEFINITION
Print, QA & Completeness Checks

LOWER FUNCTION

COMMON FUNCTIONS

EVENT Detail

ELEMENTARY FUNCTION Detail

Cross-check attributes

DATAFLOW Detail

DATASTORE Detail

D-4   Tasks and Deliverables

DESIGN STAGE

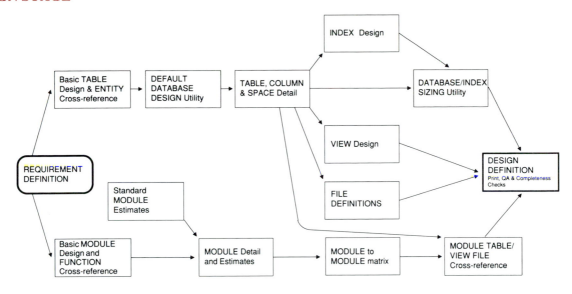

IMPLEMENTATION STAGE

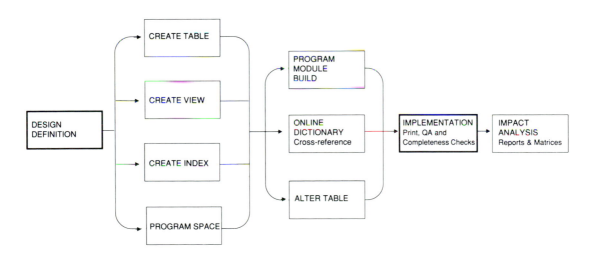

Screenshots of Diagrammers

The following screenshots from the Oracle CASE*Designer product illustrate some of the advantages of using computer-aided tools rather than paper-based systems for system development. The pictures show the use of a function hierarchy, entity relationship, dataflow and matrix diagrammer. These represent the primary diagrammatic techniques used in the strategy and analysis stages to encompass the information and functional needs of a business, in this case a hypothetical airline.

Each of the windows has a set of buttons and devices to carry out actions such as:

- make a window fill the entire screen
- resize the window to a chosen size and aspect ratio
- where several overlapping windows are being used, 'stack' the windows so those required are to the front or back as appropriate
- iconize the window so that it may be temporarily represented by a small icon or symbol until needed again.

Diagrams can be any practical size required. A subset of a diagram can be seen and manipulated using further devices, which include:

- scroll bars to pan the visible window (or diagram drawing surface) horizontally or vertically across the diagram
- buttons to zoom in or out by degrees or to preset magnification levels
- buttons to select objects on the diagram and then both menu options and further buttons to manipulate the object in some way; for example, delete, edit or run a report.

Further menu options and buttons are used to re-define preferences on how to use the facility, request tutorial hints or help messages, run utilities, load/save diagrams, invoke other tools, system windows, output options and so on.

All these facilities are available in a similar manner under different workstation configurations, using different window management systems; however, the appearance or precise manner of use will vary with the different environments.

Function Hierarchy Diagrammer

This diagrammer is used to define **what** functions occur in a business and to group the functions into sensible sets for consistency and completeness checking. Facilities exist to add and delete functions and to reconfigure the structure of the hierarchy in various ways; for example, give a function a new parent function.

The analyst in this case has chosen preferences to lay out the diagram in a classic organization structure format and has deliberately used a medium-sized box for each function, which doubles the number of functions that can be viewed and manipulated on the drawing surface. Note that this box size truncates the function descriptions, but these can be accessed in full by scrolling or resizing the box.

Any changes to this or any other diagram interactively update the contents of the CASE*Dictionary and are automatically subject to management facilities such as back-up, recovery, version control and multi-user access to the diagram and underlying objects.

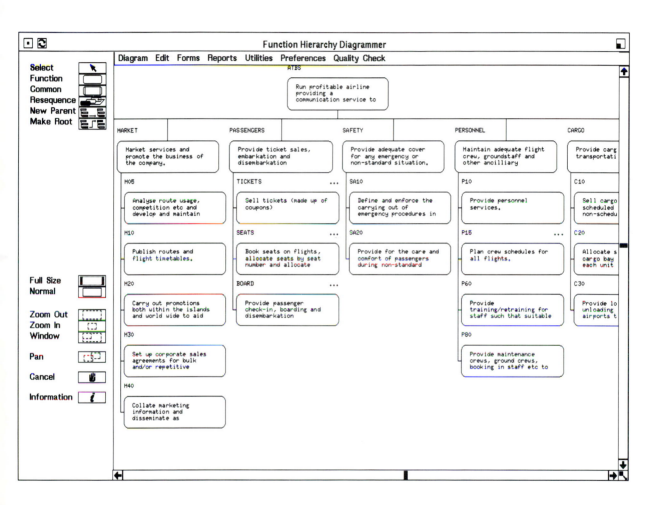

**Entity Relationship
Diagrammer**

The entity relationship diagrammer enables the analyst to define the information needs of the business in terms of the things of significance about which information needs to be known or held (the entities, which are shown by the boxes) and the significant business relationships (the lines between the boxes). In this case the lines include symbols to denote properties such as the relationship name, degree, optionality and whether there is any mutual exclusivity with other relationships.

Boxes within boxes represent types of things, where inner boxes are entity sub-types, which inherit all the properties of their outer super-type entity.

It is common practice to have many subset entity relationship diagrams of an application to aid communication with different users and build up a complex model in digestible chunks. It is interesting to note that each such subset diagram can be used to update the dictionary in a multi-user team environment.

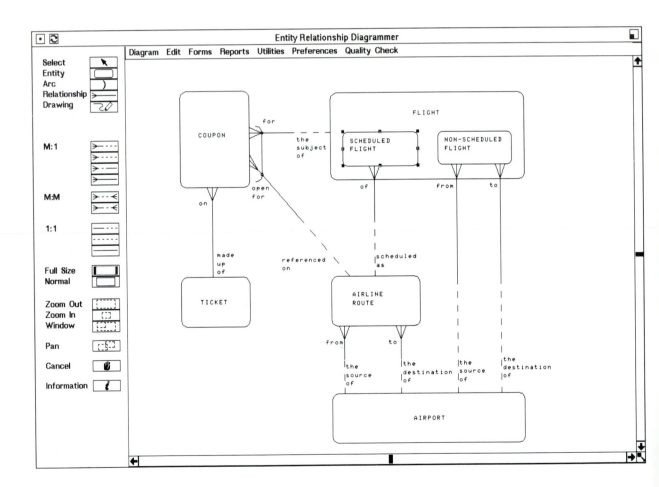

In this second picture of the entity relationship diagram, a pop-up window is shown for the entity SCHEDULED FLIGHT. This entity had been selected on the previous screenshot, shown by the highlighting around its box. The pop-up window was invoked by selecting an option from a pull-down menu system, available under the heading 'Forms' at the top of the picture. This window now enables the analyst to add more detail about the entity in the form of its attributes, their optionality, format, length and so on. Notice that the implied attributes of 'latest revised departure date' and 'latest revised arrival time' are automatically inherited from the super-type entity FLIGHT, shown on the diagram as the outer box. This is a good example of how the dictionary enables you to record things only once and then cross-relate them or imply them from other related areas.

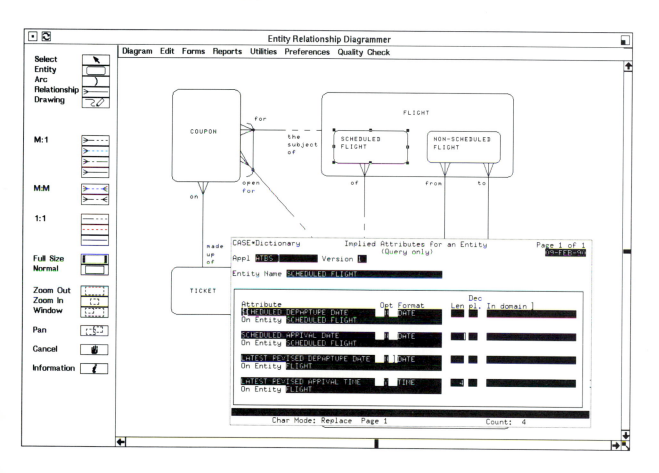

It is interesting to note that the pop-up window is one of the interactive form-fill screens supplied by CASE*Dictionary. The same form could be used from a character or block-mode terminal thus enabling team members to share the dictionary from whichever type of terminal they may have.

Dataflow Diagrammer

The dataflow diagrammer is used to show the flow of information between different functions. The functions are shown by the larger boxes, and are a subset of the same functions shown on the function hierarchy diagram. A two-level function decomposition is shown by the large function box encompassing four of its child functions. Dataflows are shown by the arrows and a datastore by the open-ended box in the centre. Boxes around the outside can represent source or destination external functions or entities.

This form of diagram covers the complex interrelationships between the business functionality and the corresponding information needs. Notice that useful quality checks are provided to ensure completeness and consistency.

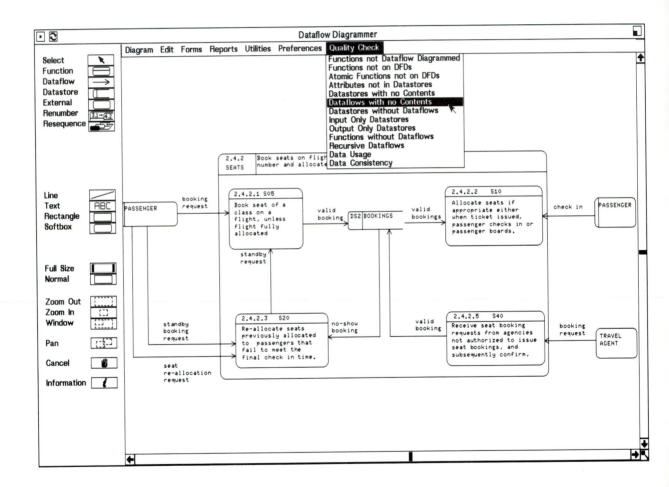

Matrix Diagrammer

The matrix diagrammer is a general purpose tool that may be used to show the interrelationship between different objects held in the dictionary. In this case the business functions are arranged across the columns and their associated entities (with their average volumes) are shown down the rows. Where the rows and columns intersect, data can be displayed to indicate more detail about any association.

Here the analyst is checking a function for which the description starts 'Hold details of normal aircraft' against the entity AIRCRAFT. This association was initially created by a lexical analysis utility, which scans the function description for the names (or synonyms) of entities already known to the dictionary – a useful, time-saving utility. Now the analyst has qualified the information by recording the fact that the function may retrieve and update information about AIRCRAFT.

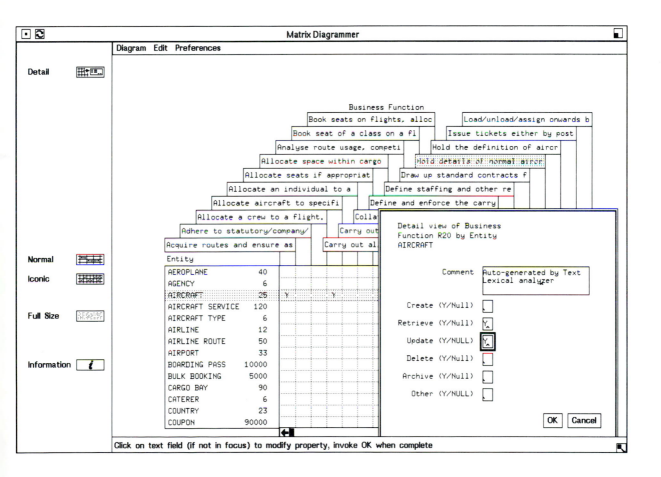

This diagrammer is a very flexible input/output device, and is particularly useful for fast input, quality and completeness checking. The data may be sorted in many ways for either or both axes, enabling the user to view and check the information from many alternative perspectives.

The same diagram can be used for many other purposes, such as manipulating:

- critical success factors to business functions
- program modules to tables
- business units/location to entities
- processing nodes to program modules.

Complex Screenshot

This final illustration shows three windows being used simultaneously, with a report for the entity COUPON being displayed on the front window. Notice how the diagrammatic notation for the relationship lines on the entity relationship diagram has been translated into an unambiguous English equivalent on the detailed entity definition report.

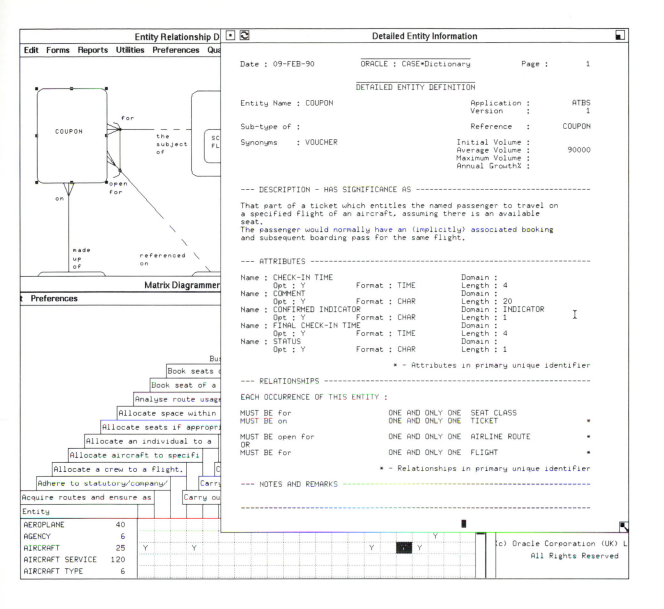

Workstation Use

The workstation interfaces enable the system engineers to gain access to each of the CASE tools, along with other tools or facilities available on their computer network. Multi-tasking capability aids productivity, along with the ability to switch between different and complementary views of related information. Productivity gains of fifteen to twenty percent are often claimed by workstation users, even without such software productivity tools.

Team Orientation

This type of CASE tool has caused some interesting changes in the way that development teams are set up and conduct their day-to-day work.

The central dictionary or repository enables all the members of a team to work on their application system at the same time, thus speeding up communications and minimizing duplication of effort. Multiple teams can share overlapping definitions, under the control of the dictionary management system, and version control enables a controlled evolution of the systems being engineered.

In the past, analysts and designers have used template-drawn diagrams and whiteboards. Now their efforts are focused on the shared database, CASE*Dictionary, and the user interfaces enable them to share their work with their colleagues in real time.

Appendix

E

PROTOTYPING IN THE BUSINESS SYSTEM LIFE CYCLE

Use of Prototyping Techniques

Prototyping is a very useful technique when used in the right place for the correct purpose. Uncontrolled prototyping can be positively bad for the health of a system and the credibility of the Information System department. Frequent problems found with its misuse include duplication of data and function, no common look and feel, no documentation and generally incoherent systems. Prototyping is often thought of as simply the rapid production of screen-based computer programs. The concept is really one of producing a mock-up of some intended design to enable its intended users to gauge acceptability. It can also mean a benchmark to check performance or some other design critical component.

During the strategy stage there are various prototyping techniques that may be deployed. These include the use of entity relationship diagrams, function and dataflow diagrams, mock-ups of new 'paper' forms, use of 'what-if' examples of new ways of running the business, financial modelling and a variety of ways of feeding back understanding of what the business may need to be doing in the future. The models may be used to accurately reflect what happens now or, of more use, to enable the decision makers to perceive what might happen in the future. Used by top strategists, prototyping of this type can provide large-scale benefits and competitive advantage to a business, based simply on the insight gained and catalytically helping the executives who drive the business to work together with a common considered focus.

During analysis, prototyping of forms, screens, reports and system storyboards is a powerful technique for checking requirements for completeness, continuity, usage by different roles in the business and to gain commitment. Often it is beneficial to check out alternative styles of work and usability issues as they relate to different user roles. But beware. At this stage it is important not to get attached to the prototypes, which are only being used for this checking process.

Design sees another use of prototyping. It can often be difficult to assess whether or not a particular design idea or solution is feasible, would perform adequately or could otherwise satisfy the requirement. An example might be to mock up a coherent subset of a system, without all its complex controls and processing, just to test out the feasibility of using a chosen implementation technique or tool. With complex systems this may be extended to cover the interrelationship between techniques, helping you resolve issues such as will the chosen database management system, transaction processing monitor, network protocol, hardware, programming languages, terminals and other devices actually work together?

Figure E-1
Using Prototyping at Different
Stages of the Life Cycle

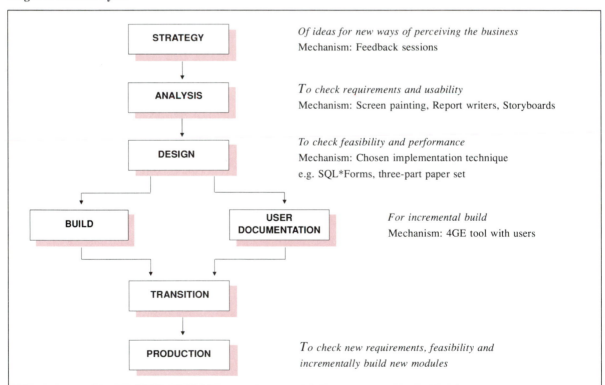

Thus in simple terms, prototypes can be used effectively during both the analysis and design stages to answer questions about the proposed system, such as:

Requirements   "Is this what is needed?"
Feasibility   "Can these tools be used?"
Performance   "Can this approach work fast enough?"
Usability   "Will the end users accept this?"

This broad classification of the use of prototypes is shown in the diagram below.

Figure E-2
Classification of the Use of Prototypes

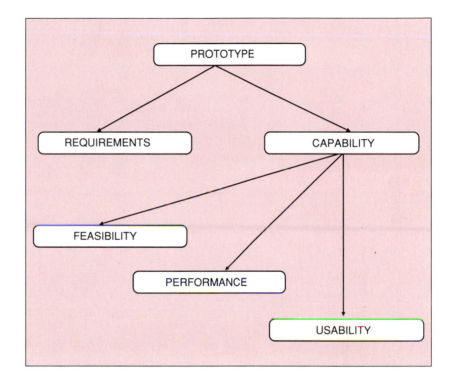

By this definition, prototypes are aids to analysis and design. The iterative techniques of prototyping can, however, be extended into the construction of systems as illustrated in Figure E-3. We have, therefore, distinguished between prototypes that essentially are disposable and those which go towards the incremental development of parts of a production system.

During the build stage prototyping tools may be used to help incrementally build a system, when the tools can actually produce operational quality capability. In other cases prototypes may be used as part of the specification and then be totally rebuilt using other tools more likely to give suitable operational capability.

Figure E-3
Prototyping During the
Build Phase

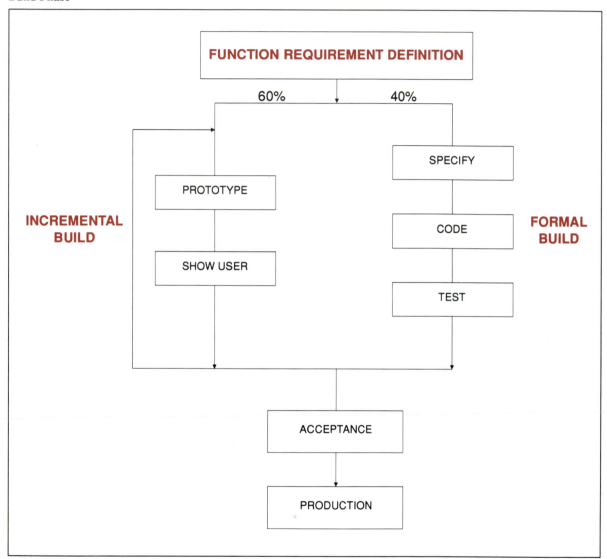

The diagram gives a likely percentage of programs that could be expected to be built using prototyping techniques when using tools such as relational database management systems, fourth-generation languages and application generators, and other CASE tools. But these numbers will vary and must be gauged by assessing the requirements against the chosen implementation tools and the skill set of the implementors.

While it is impossible to exclude any area of a project's scope from prototyping, for each class of prototype one expects a focus on particular aspects of the task in hand. These are illustrated in the table below.

PROTOTYPE CLASS	LIKELY TRIGGER FOR PROTOTYPING	EXAMPLES
Performance	High-volume data High-frequency function Time-critical response	Insurance company monthly direct debit run Telephone order entry
Usability	New technology Wide user base Critical user base	Adopting 4GE application generator Query system for the president
Feasibility	New technology New application software	New business venture
Requirements	Ambiguous or conflicting statements of requirement New application need	Merger of business units
Incremental Build	Reference data maintenance screens Most reports Query-by-example screens Menus Simple to medium complexity data capture screens Set-up and conversion procedures	Supplier data Orders outstanding for more than 30 days Main customer file take-on

A Word of Warning   Whilst prototyping is a very useful technique, it must always be remembered that it is only a means not an end. The final modules that are put into production must be engineered sufficiently well for the users and the functions for which they were built.

Appendix

F

FEEDBACK STRUCTURE

**Preparing for a
Feedback Session**

The essence of CASE*Method is an iterative process of information gathering, checking, divergent and then convergent modelling, followed by the essential process of feeding back the ideas, concepts and understanding to users, peers or anyone who can help get it right. This feedback process may then be followed by further fact gathering, modelling and feedback until an adequate understanding is gained to enable the final deliverables to be prepared.

During the strategy stage this vital task will be conducted with key executives and opinion leaders, to ensure that the understanding and intended strategic direction is correct. During analysis it is conducted with users to ensure that the requirement is complete, and during design it will be with peers to ensure that an optimum design has been produced within the constraints applied.

Feedback, as a technique, can be used in these and many other situations. The same guidelines apply: making the session relevant; setting clear and achievable objectives; using appropriate examples to illustrate points being made; scheduling 'high spots' to keep interest going; knowing when to bring in refreshments to revive flagging spirits; listening to what other people actually say.

In the strategy stage a complete task is devoted to preparation for the feedback of the work to date. The suggested structure given overleaf is designed with this major session in mind but the principles apply in general.

Figure F-1
Presentation Timetable

INTRODUCTION	OVERVIEW	BUSINESS DIRECTION	SUBJECT 1	SUBJECT 2	SUBJECT 3
State the project: objectives timescales etc.	Briefly describe the work to date	State: business objectives priorities performance indicators critical success factors and so on ↑ **high spot**	Present core model using entity build-up slides with examples and relevant business functions	The first evolution outwards from the core	Need to keep interest going as lunchtime approaches ↑ **high spot**

LUNCH   "Make the day relevant"

SUBJECT 4	SUBJECT 5	SUBJECT 6	SUBJECT 7	MANAGEMENT ENTITIES and FUNCTIONS	CONCLUSION
"To cater for after-lunch apathy" ↑ **high spot**		"Even the least interesting subject needs handling somewhere!" ↓	↑ **high spot**	To cater for their: business objectives performance indicators etc. ↑ **high spot**	Tentative plans for the future and next steps ↑ **high spot**

A day-long presentation like this needs careful preparation. It is sensible to involve two or three presenters, rotating them around different roles such as presenter and note taker. Keys to success include relevance, interest, careful use of humour and keeping everyone involved. Whilst one person is presenting a second should be unobtrusively managing the group. This may be because the recipients do not appear to follow the thrust of the discussion; perhaps the presenter has not noticed that a question has gone unanswered; or perhaps the sequence of material needs to be changed to help understanding. These are important events that can often move thinking forward, gain consensus and contribute greatly to quality. But they are also opportunities to demonstrate incompetence in public – so prepare well!!

Appendix

G

CHECKLISTS

This appendix covers some checklists for the system as a whole, and the strategy, analysis, design and build stages.

The lists should not be considered comprehensive since every project is different. Rather, the thinking techniques shown in Chapter 10 on project management should be used to help construct project-specific lists. In particular, the design and build checklists are focused on only some of the areas of concern, and at a general level as technology is continually changing and such lists rapidly become out of date.

Other books in this series cover techniques such as entity relationship modelling and contain even more detailed checklists as applicable.

Remember, if your system passes all the following checklists, it merely proves that it has passed the checklists.

Completed checklists should not be taken as the sole evidence that you have a good system. They are rather like intelligence tests – these tend to show how good you are at passing intelligence tests, not how intelligent you really are! At the end of the day your users will tell you if the system is any good.

The System as a Whole

System Overview

- Is the purpose of the system clearly described?
- Are the system's objectives, aims and critical success factors clear?
- Is the boundary of the system clearly defined?
- Are interfaces to other systems defined?
- Are the different user groups clearly identified?
- Is there a complete list of functions to be implemented?
- Is there a description of the system architecture?
- Are the client's acceptance criteria for the system as a whole known and documented?
- Do we know the cost, benefit, timescale and scope?

Business Model

Entity Relationship Model:

- Is there adequate and accurate documentation of all the entities, attributes and relationships that are relevant to an understanding of the application?
  - what is the volume information for each entity? By location if necessary?
  - datetype, format and validation rules for each attribute
  - consistent sample data with typical attribute values
  - expected changes when considered over a period of time.

Function Definitions:

- Is there a function hierarchy in which the functions to be implemented are broken down to elementary business functions?
- Is there adequate, accurate and unambiguous documentation of all the elementary business functions to be implemented?
  - what triggers each function?
  - how often does each function occur? By location if necessary?
  - what does the function consist of in terms of detailed function logic?
  - what entities and attributes are accessed, and how?
  - what functions are triggered?
  - do dataflow, function dependency, state transition or other diagrams exist where relevant?
- Has the correctness of the model been confirmed by user representatives?

- Have automated consistency checks been run against the business model?
- What changes are expected when considered over a period of time?

Business Direction

- Is it clear what the business is that the system is going to support?
- Are there clearly-defined business objectives, aims, priorities, constraints, critical success factors, problems and issues that may be wholly or partially addressed by the system?
- Is it clear which business functions correspond to these business directions? Similarly, does the entity relationship model cover the data required to predict and monitor against any quantifiable business indicators?

Fact Gathering

- During the strategy and analysis phase, was fact collecting done correctly?

Check:

- interview coverage (does it include key people on the organization chart?)
- interview depth (should show thorough investigation)
- user attitude shows commitment and good input (all dragons should be slain!)
- all other information sources were explored, including forms, files and existing system definitions
- all material was put to good use (documented, indexed and referenced well).

Verifying Business Correctness and Scope

Check:

- material has been tested in some way with users, peers and industry experts
- no obvious bits of interview material have been left out of models
- no parts of the models look odd, feel wrong or are inconsistent
- user conflicts or business problems have been raised as issues, and handled
- team members are good analysts
- team now know the business well.

Feedback and Rapport with the Organization

User commitment and involvement is a key to successful system development. Check:

- the 'top man' was high enough in the organization
- user and team have confidence in the benefits of the work and the approach taken
- feedbacks and reviews were well received and constructive ("no comment" is a worrying reaction)
- reaction to the recommendations (by users/IS) was acceptable.

System Development Plan

Check:

- what is expected (detail, presentation method)
- what is appropriate (the need versus level of certainty)
- whether timescales, costs and resources are reasonably accurate
- whether timescales, costs and resources are acceptable
- whether assumptions are documented and percentage accuracy is stated
- whether the control structure is clear, and user involvement is specified
- whether contingency and risk are addressed
- who has to approve the plan
- regularity of update and change control procedures
- who is responsible for each aspect of the plan.

System Structure

- Is the database design a 1:1 match with the entity model? If not, have the design decisions been recorded?
- Is there adequate and accurate documentation to explain the structure and purpose of each table or file?
  - table abbreviations for use as synonyms
  - column definitions and descriptions
  - keys and indexes identified
  - the significance of each column and each data item made clear
  - examples of data.
- Is there accurate documentation to show which tables are accessed by each processing module and how they are accessed?
- Is there evidence of a carefully-thought-out approach to the locking of tables and other potential performance throughput bottlenecks?
- Is there accurate documentation to show which modules implement each function and how modules call one another/fit together?

- Have modules been designed to handle each function to be implemented?
- Has sufficient thought been given to the security of the system?
  - does the system allow different types of access to different types of user?
  - how easy will it be to change the type of access for a user?
- Are there back-up procedures? Have they been tested?
- Has a trial shown that data and function integrity are not at risk?
- Have calculations been done to estimate the processor power required for peak loading?
- Will the system cater for the maximum connectivity of devices and users?
- Have calculations been done to estimate the final size of the database?
- Is the proposed hardware adequate for the type of system that has been specified? And projected use of the next few years?
- If it is necessary to enhance the proposed system, what will the limiting factors be?
  - e.g. communications to user terminals, raw processor power, memory, disk access.
- Is there a sensible plan for implementing the system in phases?
  - does each phase deliver significant functionality to at least one group of users?
  - do budgets and timescales allow for the additional user training, support and software maintenance?
  - is the plan in line with the expectations of the different user groups?
- Is there documentation to show which modules are required for each implementation phase?
- Have the clerical procedures been defined and cross-referenced to the business functions and computerized modules?

Project Organization

- Are there adequate standards defined for use on the project?
- Are all team members familiar with the project standards?
- Are there plans for the production, validation and reviewing of work, and are team members aware of their responsibilities with respect to these plans?
  - is there adequate change control of documentation and code?
  - is the status of every version of each component easy to ascertain?
  - do developers have access to the latest approved version?
  - do developers have authorization to work to a given version?
  - where a change is necessary during the current development phase, is there a formal procedure for informing all affected people?
  - are there procedures to avoid confusion between different versions?

Strategy Study Checklist

Terms of Reference

Check:

- objectives are brief (with well-chosen words), measurable, achievable, apt
- key issues are spelt out where it is difficult to judge the range of options involved
- scope is as explicit as possible
- acceptance criteria clearly express how the strategy will be judged
- project success factors include everything 'contentious' the team would need to know
- constraints are comprehensive and reasonable
- approach is sufficiently clear so that everyone understands what will be done and what is expected of them
- deliverables are sufficient to document strategy, obtain agreement and provide a starting point for the next stage.

Entities

- Does each entity have a meaningful name that is unique within the application? Is the name a singular noun?
- Does each entity have a short name that is unique within the application?
- Does each entity have a concise, meaningful description?
- Does each entity have a unique identifier?
- Does each entity have at least two significant attributes?
- Do the sets of data specified by sub-type entities make up the total set of data represented by the super-type entity?
- Are examples quoted to ensure clarity of understanding?

Attributes

- Does each attribute have a name that reflects its purpose, and that is unique within its entity?
- Do any attributes really imply a missing relationship?
- Does each attribute have a concise and meaningful description?
- Is the optionality of each attribute specified?
- If any attribute forms part of the unique identifier of an entity is this recorded?

Relationships

- Is each end of the relationship named?
- Is the optionality and degree of each end specified?
- If any relationship forms part of the unique identifier of an entity, is this recorded?
- Are there any missing relationships, which might be implied by attribute names; for example, the attribute department-code on the entity EMPLOYEE?
- Is the relationship valid?
- Can the relationship be read out unambiguously to a user to aid checking?

Functions

- Do any functions refer to a mechanism?
- Does each function have a concise and meaningful description that starts with a verb?
- Is the sum of the functionality of the child functions equal to the functionality of the parent node?
- Are there any parent nodes with excessive numbers of children (say ten or more) that could be further split?
- Do any functions refer to objects that are not entities, synonyms of entities, attributes or business views?

Diagrams

- Are crossing lines reduced to the minimum possible? Is it cluttered?
- Does the diagram have a label indicating the name of the drawing, version number and author?
- Is the diagram clear and unambiguous?
- Are the conventions on how to interpret the diagram clear?

Business Direction

- Is each objective measurable?
- Could someone determine if a business aim had been met?
- Are the critical success factors agreed and really critical?
- Do the entity relationship and function models relate to the business direction?
- Were identified priorities agreed by the appropriate level of management?
- Is it clear how any recommended system might go towards helping the business?

System Boundary

- Is the boundary of any proposed system clear?
- Are any cross-system interfaces clear?

Glossary of Terms

- Has a system glossary, containing an explanation of terms used, been produced?

Strategy Report

- Is the strategy report slim, with back-up appendices?
- Has it been checked out with key users and management before issuing it widely?
- Does it contain a clear and approved phased development plan?
- Does it contain a potential system architecture that is viable with current or expected technologies?
- Does it reflect the contents list in Appendix B, modified as required by this project?
- Is it clear what issues are not yet resolved?
- Has the resourced development plan been approved?

Recommendations

Are there recommendations to cover the following?

- the way ahead plus alternatives
- methods and techniques to be used
- hardware and software to be selected or criteria for selection
- development roles and organization
- training and education
- changes to business practice.

Analysis Checklist

Entities

Each entity must have:

- a concise and meaningful description
- all attributes fully defined
- all relationships fully defined
- a name that is a singular noun and unique
- synonyms, if present, that are unique within the context
- a unique identifier defined
- minimum and maximum volumes defined, possibly by location
- volumetric information by sub-types
- examples to clarify understanding
- a function for its creation, update, deletion, archiving and other forms of use.

Attributes and Domains

Each attribute or domain must have:

- a meaningful name
- a concise and meaningful description
- a format
- optionality (null/not null)

and may have:

- reasons for optionality
- ranges or allowed values specified
- explanations of code values and meanings
- a derivation.

Relationships

Each relationship must have:

- entities specified at each end of the relationship
- a name, degree and optionality at each end
- a profile of degree if complex.

Arcs (exclusive relationships)

Each arc must:

- pass through more than one relationship
- be between relationships of the same optionality
- span relationships to the same entity only.

Unique Identifiers

- Each unique identifier should be made up of a mandatory attribute or relationship or a combination of both.

- Is the data that makes up the unique identifiers available to the functions that create instances of the entity?

Functions

Each function should:

- have a concise meaningful description, that starts with a verb
- have a unique function reference within the context
- have a set of children whose functions perform all the functions of the parent, apart from bottom-level functions
- have frequencies specified, if the function is a bottom-level function
- as far as possible appear only once, or common functions should be defined
- not refer to a mechanism unless the mechanism is recognized as compulsory within the business
- refer only to entities that are in the scope
- refer to entity names in the description
- have leaf functions that are elementary business functions
- have function logic specified if it is a complex elementary business function
- have entity, attribute and relationship usage, and mode of usage specified
- have triggering events defined
- have dependent functions and dependencies defined
- have user-required response and deadlines defined.

Do some of the functions cover the following?

- audit requirements
- back-up
- recovery
- security and access control
- privacy enforcement
- monitoring
- manual procedures
- set-up, transition or coexistence.

Transition

- If data is to be derived from existing systems then specify:
  - the sources of data
  - the procedure for export from the old system
  - data conversion procedures
  - procedures for import of data into the new system
  - timescales and resources needed.

- If not, have default values, derivation rules or sources of value been defined?

- Has all old data either been catered for or has it been agreed that it is no longer required?

- If existing systems overlap the new system then specify:
  - replacement functionality
  - changes to procedures
  - the removal of redundant processes in the existing system.

- Are acceptable periods for transition defined?

- Are transition plans viable and agreed?

Dataflows

Each dataflow must be:

- named
- between two functions or
- between a function and a datastore or
- between a function and an external entity or function
- made up of known attributes of entities or data items whose destination or source is clear.

Datastores

Each datastore must be:

- named
- made up of known attributes of entities or data items whose destination or source is clear
- capable of construction from its input dataflows
- capable of acting as a source for any output dataflows.

Users   Each user role should be defined along with:

- the acceptable or relevant style of working
- the type of working environment and potential working constraints (e.g. no desk for a terminal)
- cross-reference to functions carried out
- ownership of data
- access rights and levels of working.

Analysis Report   The analysis report should contain as a minimum:

- system scope
- hardware and software environment
- back-up and recovery procedures
- archiving rules
- security and audit procedures
- systems testing criteria and acceptance criteria
- sign-off criteria
- preliminary sizing
- revised development plan
- timescales
- resources (physical and human)
- development environment
- transition plan
- outline of manual procedures
- details of any project-specific problems
- user expectations
- constraints and assumptions
- identification of users for future roles
- cross-reference to a full functional requirement definition, possibly held in a CASE dictionary
- definition of user working style requirements
- agreed approach to subsequent stages.

Design Checklist

This section is targeted at a relational database implementation only, but reflects the sort of list that would be needed for any aspect of design.

System Architecture

- Is it clear what databases, processing and communications nodes will exist and their geographic location?
- Are the major components of the system defined, along with their interrelationships?
- Is the intended application of vendor and in-house technologies clear?

Table Design

- Is it clear which entity or entities it is an implementation of?
- Are foreign keys identified?
- Does the table name relate to the source entity?
- Are data volumes specified?
- Does it conform to normalization rules or are reasons for de-normalization listed?
- Does every table have a prime key?
- Does every table have a description, which should include design considerations, decision trees for sub-type implementation, and so on?
- For each column are the following given?
  - format
  - datatype
  - size
  - percentage null
  - null/not null
  - description
  - domain checks
- Are full referential integrity constraints defined?

Index Design

- Is there a unique index on the primary key for each table?
- If the primary key is on a single column, is this column not null?
- Concatenated keys should be on not null columns? If they are not, is this correct?
- Is the order of fields in a concatenated key correct?

- Are all foreign keys indexed with a non-unique index?
- Are common query paths indexed?
- Are there sufficient indexes to use all parts of a concatenated index?
- Are small tables (250 rows) indexed?
- Are any non-compressed indexes used? If so, why?

Program Modules

- Is each module cross-referenced to the function(s) it supports?
- Does the module definition or specification have the following?
  - a header
  - a user overview
  - a technical overview
  - process logic and insertion/change/deletion rules
  - tables (and columns used), and mode of usage
  - the vehicle for implementation
  - the degree of complexity
  - assumptions
  - limit and exception handling.
- Are the weighting factors for programming specified?
- Are they realistic, given the experience of development staff?
- Does the user interface match the user working style?

Database Design

- Are the physical partitions, areas or other subdivisions on the disks defined?
- Do we know how big the database will be initially and in the future?
- Is the operating system file usage documented?
- Have the distributed database aspects been fully covered?
- Is there a clear differentiation between the logical and physical schemas?
- Has clustering been used in an appropriate manner?
- Is a shadow database mechanism required for resilience?

Views

- Does each view have a name that indicates its purpose?
- Is the derivation of each view documented?
- Does each view have a description?
- Have view-specific referential integrity checks been defined?

Host Environment

- Are the access rights correct?
- Has sufficient hardware been specified for both development and production? This should include:
  - terminals
  - printers
  - communications
  - special needs.
- Are procedures specified for registering uses?
- Are the work classes and modules to be accessed specified?
- Have development and production logging and recovery mechanisms been designed?

Design Report

The design report should include:

- system architecture
- program module architecture for key programs
- specification of manual procedures
- system network definition overview
- system test plans
- cross-reference to full design documentation, possibly in a CASE dictionary
- physical database design overview
- tables and space usage
- indexes and space usage
- sizing
- transition strategy
- the development environment specification
- draft operations documentation
- major assumptions
- key issues
- a revised development plan.

Build Checklist

It would be nearly impossible to create a checklist for every type of implementation technique, therefore this list reflects some general aspects used on interactive forms and reports.

Interactive Forms Checklist

- Does the form do what the business function requires?
- Is the screen usable and pleasing to use?
- Does each screen page have the correct header?
- Are individual zones on the screen clearly defined?
- Are the screen labels clear, unambiguous and in the correct format?
- Does related data on the screen change in a synchronized manner?
- Are the fields on the screen laid out in a useful and pleasing manner?
- Has entered text been forced into upper case? If not, is this intentional?
- Are the field-level attributes correct?
- Does each field have an informative help message?
- Are primary key fields non-updatable?
- Is the use of derived fields fully annotated?
- Do foreign key values have a list of values, or a help screen set up?
- Is the validation consistent across the system?
- Has the locking strategy for updating forms been followed?
- Have the performance, integrity or other acceptance criteria been met?
- Does the form make sensible use of the device upon which it is run?
- Is the look and feel across all screens consistent and usable?
- Is the use of any transaction processing system sensible?
- Is the form only accessible to authorized users?

Reports Checklist

- Does the report work on the correct subset of data and produce the correct result?
- Does the report have a header and titles in the correct format?
- Has indentation been used to improve legibility?
- Does any data manipulation statement prevent the use of indexes, whether or not the tables being used are currently indexed?

- Are unnecessary complex conditional clauses used?
- Is there any unnecessary procedural logic?
- Is it clear for whom the report is intended?

Hardware

- Is it safe to use?
- Have full installation checks been completed?
- Have all interconnections been tested?
- Are maintenance contracts in place?
- Is the performance of the system on different sets of hardware known? Is it scaleable in case of an increase in demand?
- Will response be adequate initially and when subsequent systems are added?
- Are terminals, disks and other devices physically secure to the level required?

Ease of Maintenance

- Are complex modules provided with an overview and some form of structure diagram?
- Are error/warning messages which are intended for action by the user meaningful and helpful?
- Are error/warning messages which are intended for reporting to the system manager meaningful and identified uniquely?
- Are comments used liberally and maintained as the code is changed?
- Is all installation-specific code commented in detail?
  - e.g. host operating system commands.
- Could **you** use it to perform change in a sensible, controlled manner?
- Is the system documentation complete and clear? Is it held in a CASE dictionary or repository?

GLOSSARY OF TERMS

This glossary contains a list of terms used in the CASE*Method references and associated documents. Some of the words may not appear in this particular document, but they are included here for completeness and understanding.

Activity   Anything that needs to be done to complete a task. See **Task**.

Aim   See **Business Aim**.

Application System   A name given to a collection of business functions, entities, programs and tables, which can be further described by system documentation of various forms.

Arc   A means of identifying two or more mutually exclusive relationships. See **Exclusive Arc**.

Attribute   Any detail that serves to qualify, identify, classify, quantify or express the state of an entity.
or
Any description of 'a thing of significance'.

Note that each entity occurrence may only have one value of any attribute at one time.

Business   An enterprise, in either the private or public sector, concerned with providing products and/or services to satisfy customer requirements; for example, car manufacturer, refuse collection, provision of legal advice, provision of health care.

Business Aim   A statement of business intent that may be measured subjectively; for example, to move up-market or to develop a sustainable level of growth. See also **Business Objective**.

Business Constraint   Any external, management or other factor that may confine the business or development in terms of resource availability, dependencies or timescales.

Business Function   What a business does or needs to do, irrespective of how it does it. See **Elementary Business Function**.

Business Location   A uniquely identifiable geographic location, from which one or more business units may be wholly or partially operating.

Business Model   See **Entity Relationship Diagram** and **Function Hierarchy**.

Business Objective   A statement of business intent that may be measured quantifiably.

Aims and objectives are similar concepts but the achievement of an objective is measurable in some specific manner; for example, to increase profit by 1% during the next financial year.

Business Performance Indicator　Any measure that may be used to quantify the success or failure of a business objective.

Business Priority　A statement of important business need or requirement within an ordered list.

Business System Life Cycle　The structured approach used in CASE*Method for the task of developing a business system. The seven major stages are strategy, analysis, design, build, documentation, transition and production. (Also called the development life-cycle.)

Business Unit　Part of an organization which is treated for any purpose as a separate formation within the parent organization; for example, a department.

CASE　Computer-Aided Systems Engineering is the combination of graphical, dictionary, generator, project management and other software tools to assist computer development staff in engineering and maintaining high-quality systems for their end users, within the framework of a structured method. (See also Appendix D "Use of Oracle CASE tools".)

CASE*Method　CASE*Method is a structured approach to engineering systems in a data processing environment. It consists of a set of stages, tasks, deliverables and techniques, which lead you through all steps in the life-cycle of a system.

It is delivered to you via training courses, books and consultancy support, and can be automated by a wide range of CASE tools from both Oracle and other companies.

Character　A single location on the computer system capable of holding one alphabetic character or numeric digit. One or more characters are held in a field. One or more fields make up a record, and one or more records may be held in a file.
or
The format of an attribute, which may contain alphabetic characters or numeric digits.

Column　A means of implementing an item of data within a table. It can be in character, date or number format, and be optional or mandatory.
or
An implementation of an attribute or relationship.

Common Function　During analysis the objective is to eliminate identical functions wherever possible by overlapping, making them more generic or recognizing that they were not identical in the first place. When this is not practical, one or more common functions may be created, each of which is a slave to (copy of) a master function. Only the master function may then be further described, whilst the slave functions can appear in different parts of the function hierarchy, as required.

Constraint　See **Business Constraint**.

Copy Function　An alternative word for a common or slave function. It is a copy of the master.

Critical Success Factor　Any business event, dependency, deliverable or other factor which, if not attained, would seriously impair the likelihood of achieving a business objective.

Database　An arbitrary collection of tables or files under the control of a database management system.

Data Dictionary　A database for holding definitions of tables, columns and views, and so on.

In the context of CASE tools, it is used by the development staff to record all significant results from the strategy, analysis, design and implementation stages of the system development.

Dataflow　A named flow of data between business functions, datastores and external entities. See **Business Function**, **Datastore** and **External Entity**.

Dataflow Diagram　A diagram representing the use of data by business functions. See **Dataflow**, **Dataflow Diagrammer**, **Datastore**, **External Entity** and **Process**.

Dataflow Diagrammer　A CASE tool that enables you to interactively draw and change dataflow diagrams, allowing updating of the CASE dictionary itself via the diagram.

Data Item　In some systems the definition of a logical data item is equivalent to an attribute at the business level. When used with other file management systems, a data item is a means of implementing an item of data within a file.

The term data item is sometimes used as an equivalent to column. See **Attribute** or **Column.**

Datastore   A temporary or permanent storage concept for logical data items/attributes, as used by specified business functions/processes.

DBMS   A database management system, normally encompassing computerized management facilities that are used to structure and manipulate data, and to ensure privacy, recovery and integrity in a multi-user environment.

Delivery Vehicle   A term that describes the mechanism for producing or implementing something; for example, SQL*Forms is a means by which a computer program may be produced.

Derived Data Item   A value that is derived by some algorithm from the values of other data items; for example, profit, which is the difference between income and costs.

Development Life-cycle   See **Business System Life Cycle**.

Distributed Database   A database that is physically located on more than one computer processor, connected via some form of communications network. An essential feature of a true distributed database is that the user and/or program work as if they had access to the whole database locally. All processing to give this impression is carried out by the database management system.

Distributed Processing   The ability to have several computers working together in a distributed network, where each processor can be used to run different activities for a user, as required.

Domain   A set of business validation rules, format constraints and other properties that apply to a group of attributes. For example:

- a list of values
- a range
- a qualified list or range
- any combination of these.

Note that attributes and columns in the same domain are subject to a common set of validation checks.

Elementary Business Function   A business function which, if started, must be completed. It cannot exist in an intermediate stage. Elementary business functions are at the lowest level of a function hierarchy

and cannot be further decomposed. See **Function Hierarchy**.

Entity   A thing of significance, whether real or imagined, about which information needs to be known or held. See **Attribute**.

Entity Relationship Diagram   Part of the business model produced in the strategy stage of the Business System Life Cycle. The diagram pictorially represents entities, the vital business relationships between them and the attributes used to describe them. See **Entity, Attribute**, **Relationship** and **Entity Relationship Diagrammer**.

The process of creating this diagram is called entity modelling. The terms entity model, entity relationship model and entity/relationship model are all synonyms for Entity Relationship Diagram.

Entity Relationship Diagrammer   A CASE tool that enables you to interactively draw and change complete (or subset) Entity Relationship Diagrams; it should be possible to produce and amend diagrams and to update the CASE dictionary itself via the diagrams within the context of a specific version of an application system.

Event   There are three types of event, all of which may act as triggers to one or more business functions.

> **External or Change Event** – any point in the life of the enterprise when, under specified conditions, data is created or changed in such a manner as to act as a trigger for some business function(s). It may be identified when an entity is created or deleted, the value of an attribute is changed, or a relationship is connected or disconnected.

> **Realtime Event** – any point in the life of an enterprise when, under specified conditions, real time reaches a predetermined date and time.

> **System Event** – any point in the life of an enterprise when one or more functions have been completed, which event acts as a trigger to initiate further functions.

Exclusive Arc   Two or more relationships are diagrammatically shown to be mutually exclusive by means of an exclusive arc. See **Arc**.

External Business Function A business function, outside the scope of the application system, that acts as a source or recipient of dataflows into or out of the system.

External Entity A thing of significance, outside the scope of the application system, that acts as a source or recipient of dataflows into or out of the system.

Field A means of implementing an item of data within a file. It can be in character, date, number or other format, and be optional or mandatory.

File A method of implementing part or all of a database.

Foreign Key One or more columns in a table that implement a many to one relationship that the table in question has with another table. This concept allows the two tables to be joined together.

Format The type of data that an attribute or column may represent; for example, character, date, number.

Function See **Business Function** and **Elementary Business Function.**

Function Decomposition Any business function may be decomposed into lower levels of detail that are business functions themselves, and so on, until reaching the business functions that are elementary. This function decomposition gives rise to functions arranged in groups/hierarchies known as a business function hierarchy.

Function Dependency Diagram A visual means of recording interdependencies between business functions, and showing events that cause functions to be triggered.

Function Hierarchy A simple grouping of functions in a strict hierarchy, representing all the functions in an area of a business. This forms part of the business model produced in the strategy stage of the Business System Life Cycle. See **Business Function** and **Function Hierarchy Diagrammer**.

Function Hierarchy Diagrammer A CASE tool that enables you to create and change complete (or subset) function hierarchies interactively within the context of a version of an application system.

Function Logic Language An English-like pseudo-code for defining in detail the actions that make up an elementary business function. Sometimes the term action diagram is used.

Fuzzy Model A modelling diagram that conveys understanding without being rigorous or definitive.

Glossary A compilation of terms with their meanings; it shows a tendency to grow exponentially.

Incremental Development A technique for producing all or part of a production system from an outline definition of the need. The technique involves iterations of a cycle of build/refine/review so that the correct solution gradually emerges. This technique can be difficult to control, but nonetheless is very useful when properly used. Also called quick build and iterative development.

Index A means of accessing one or more rows in a table with particular performance characteristics, implemented by a B-tree structure on ORACLE. An index may quote one or more columns and be a means of enforcing uniqueness on their values.

Information Systems That part of an organization responsible for the development, operation and maintenance of computer-based systems. Also known as Information Technology, Information Systems Technology or Data Processing.

Iterative Development See **Incremental Development**.

Key Any set of columns that is frequently used for retrieval of rows from a table. See also **Unique Identifier** and **Column**.

Location See **Business Location**.

Matrix Diagrammer A CASE tool that enables you to create and change complete (or subset) matrices interactively. Matrices covered include:

- Function: Entity
- Function: Business Unit
- Function: Module
- Entity: Business Unit
- Entity: Table
- Module: Table.

Mechanism   A particular technique or method of implementing a function.

Module   A program or procedure that implements one or more business functions, or parts of business functions, within a computer system.

Module Network   Modules (or program modules) may be arranged in a network in the sense that:

- A module may be broken down into sub-modules.
- A module may be used as a sub-module of several others (e.g. a common sub-routine).

By this means a network of modules may be created.

Network   This may be used to mean:

- Module network (see definition).
- An interconnected network of computers as referred to in distributed processing.

Normalization   A step-by-step process that produces either entity or table definitions that have:

- no repeating groups
- the same kind of values assigned to attributes or columns
- a distinct name
- distinct and uniquely-identifiable rows.

Operation   In other methodologies the term operation has the same meaning as business function or elementary business function when used in a business context. See **Business Function** and **Elementary Business Function**.

ORACLE RDBMS   The relational database management system from Oracle Corporation, available on most hardware environments worldwide.

Phase   In the context of CASE*Method, phase refers to a part of the business that is being taken through the stages of analysis to production.

Primary Index   An index used to improve performance on the combination of columns most frequently used to access rows in a table.

Primary Key   The set of mandatory columns within a table that is used to enforce uniqueness of rows, and that is normally the most frequent means by which rows are accessed.

Priority   See **Business Priority**.

Process   In other methodologies the term process has the same meaning as business function or elementary business function when used in a business context. See **Business Function** and **Elementary Business Function**.

Program   A set of computer instructions, which can enter, change or query database items, and provide many useful computer functions.

Prototyping   A technique for demonstrating a concept rapidly, to gain acceptance and check feasibility.

Within CASE*Method use of a prototype is recommended during:

- Analysis – to check requirements and then be discarded.
- Design – to check feasibility of alternative options and to agree style (optionally discarding it).
- Build – to incrementally construct modules that need close user involvement.

Quick Build   See **Incremental Development**.

RDBMS   Relational database management system.

Record   In a non-relational database system, a record is an entry in a file, consisting of individual elements of information, which together provide full details about an aspect of the information needed by the system. The individual elements are held in fields, and all records are held in files. An example of a record might be an employee. Every detail of the employee (e.g. date of birth, department code, full names) will be found in a number of fields.

In a relational system record is an alternative word for row. See **Row**.

Record Type   A predetermined set of fields within a file.

Relation   A relation is a term that embraces the concepts of both table and view. See **Table** and **View**.

Relationship   What one thing has to do with another.
or
Any significant way in which two things of the same or different type may be associated.

Note that it is important to name relationships.

Row   An entry in a table, consisting of values for each relevant column.

Schema   A collection of table definitions.

Secondary Index   An optimization technique used on a set of columns (optional or mandatory) that improves the performance of access to rows.

Stage   One of the seven major parts of the CASE*Method Business System Life Cycle.

State Transition Diagram   A visual means of modelling an object, the states through which it might go during its life-cycle, events that affect it and interrelationships to other objects and states. Such diagrams may be used to model objects such as an entity, a system, a process/function, a program. These diagrams are particularly useful to model realtime situations.

Storyboard   A technique, borrowed from the film industry, for describing screen dialogues. A storyboard consists of an ordered series of pictures, illustrating stages of the dialogue. The pictures are annotated with notes about logic and user input.

Sub-entity   Synonymous with sub-type. See **Sub-type.**

Sub-schema   A subset of a schema. In relational terms, a view is often a more applicable concept.

Sub-type   A type of entity. An entity may be split into two or more sub-types, each of which has common attributes and/or relationships. These are defined explicitly once only at the higher level. Sub-types may have attributes and/or relationships in their own right. A sub-type may be further sub-typed to lower levels.

Success Unit   This term is normally used to mean that component of work carried out by a computer program which takes the database from one state of consistency to another.

Super-type   A means of classifying an entity that has sub-types.

System   A defined and interacting collection of real world facts, procedures and processes, along with the organized deployment of people, machines and other resources that carry out those procedures and processes.

In a good system the real world facts, procedures and processes are used to achieve their defined business purposes within acceptable tolerances. Also see **Application System**.

Table   A tabular view of data, which may be used on a relational database management system to hold one or more columns of data. It is often an implementation of an entity. Tables are the logical and perceived data structure, not the physical data structure, in a relational system.

Task   A task is the first sub-division of a stage. See **Stage.**

Trigger   Any device that activates some other mechanism. An event that precipitates another event or series of events.

Tuple   A set of values for an attribute, synonymous with row. See **Row**.

Unique Identifier   Any combination of attributes and/or relationships that serves, in all cases, to uniquely identify an occurrence of an entity.
or
One or more columns that will always supply a single row from a table.

Version control   A mechanism to help system engineers handle the problem of a system going into a production (live) state and then moving on to a second or subsequent development state. Version control is a facility that includes the capability of changing the state of a version of an application, archiving a version, creating new versions, and so on.

View   A means of accessing a subset of the database as if it were a table. The view may:

- be restricted to named columns
- be restricted to specific rows
- change column names
- derive new columns
- give access to a combination of related tables and/or views.

Working Style Requirement   A definition of a manner of working which may apply to different roles of user when performing business functions; for example, use of a few simple easy-to-use buttons for shop-floor working; use of sophisticated workstations for designers.

INDEX

You may find it useful to look up your job role, such as **analyst**. The index contains page references for a definition of the job role, tasks applicable to you and other information about your role in the project. The index similarly contains page references for various tools and techniques, such as entity relationship diagramming, to help you identify the tasks where they may be used.

Where there is a long list of references, primary references are highlighted in bold. If facing pages would be read together, the index only references one of them. Where an index entry is referenced by a single number, refer to the entire chapter.

A

Acceptance **4-20**, 5-2
  criteria 4-2, 4-10
  test 8-2, 8-12, 8-14, 8-22
Action 3-17
Activity 2-9, **Gl-1**
Agency 8-17
Agenda 3-16
Agreement 3-4
Aims **3-1, 3-12**, 3-14, 3-18, 3-20, 3-32, **4-1, 5-1, 6-1, 7-1, 8-1, 9-1, B-2, Gl-1**
Alternative 3-24, 5-3
Analysis 1-3, **4**, 10-16, A-1, E-2
  checklist G-10, G-11, G-12, G-13
  deliverables 5-6, 6-6
  detailed 4-8
  process 4-4
  report G-13
  stage **4**, D-3, D-4
  stage, deliverables 4-7 et seq.
  stage, tasks 4-6 et seq.
Analyst **2-4**, 2-7, 3-9, 3-11, 3-13, 3-15, 3-17, 3-19, 3-21, 3-23, 3-29, 3-31, 4-3, 4-7, 4-9, 4-11, 4-13, 4-19, 4-21, 4-23, 4-25, 4-27, 4-29, 4-31, 5-3, 5-7, 5-23, 5-25, 5-29, 5-33, 5-35, 6-4, 6-7, 6-11, 6-13, 6-15, 6-17, 7-7, 7-9, 8-9, 8-11, 8-13, 8-15, 8-17, 8-21, 8-23, 8-25, 8-27
  programmer 2-4
  senior 2-4
  systems 2-4
  technical 2-4
Annual report 3-11
Application 2-8, 5-8, 5-10
  area 3-24
  control 4-22
  design 2-8, 5-8, 5-10
  designer 4-27
  system 3-27, C-2, **Gl-1**
  system definition 3-11

Approach **3-3, 4-3**, 4-8, 4-16, 4-30, **5-3, 6-3, 7-2, 8-2, 9-2**
Aptitude 4-20, 8-4
Arc   G-10, **Gl-1, Gl-3**
Archiving 4-10, 4-25
Assessment 9-13
Assumption 3-27, **4-2**, 4-9, 4-11, 4-27, 5-10, B-4
Attribute 3-15, 3-22, 4-2, **4-18**, 5-15, **Gl-1**
   checklist G-7, G-10
   definition 3-13, 3-23, 4-13, 4-19, C-9
   documentation 4-18
   usage 5-10
Audit **2-5**, 4-2, 4-4, **4-22**, 5-2, 5-4, 5-14, **5-18**, 5-22, 5-25, 7-6, 8-16, 9-2, 9-13, 11-9
   requirement 4-10, 4-22, 4-28
Auditor **2-5**, 3-6, 4-6, 4-22, 4-28, 5-6, 5-8, 5-32, 6-6, 8-8, 8-16, 8-28
Authority level C-12, C-13
Authorization 4-12, 4-30
Automation 4-18, 5-1
Availability 4-20, 8-4

B

Back-up 4-2, 4-24, 5-2, 5-17, **5-20**, 5-22
Batch procedure 5-8
Benchmark 5-14, 8-21
Benefits 3-25, **3-32**, 4-3, B-2
Bottlenecks 5-33, 6-2
Brainstorm 10-8
Briefing 3-12
Brochures 3-11
Budget 3-9, 3-11
Bugs 6-14, 6-16, 8-26, 9-8
Build 1-3, **6**, A-2, E-2
   checklist G-17, G-18
   database 5-12, 5-14
   stage 4-17, 4-28, **6**, E-3
   stage, deliverables 6-7 et seq.
   stage, tasks 6-6 et seq.
Builder 2-5
Business **Gl-1**
   aims 3-14, **3-32**, 8-11, 9-12, B-3, C-2, **Gl-1**
   analysis 3-32
   analyst 2-4, 3-27, 3-33, 3-35, 9-13
   constraints 3-2, 3-14, 3-32, B-3, C-2, **Gl-1**
   control 4-22
   critical success factors 1-5, 3-2, 3-14
   direction 3-2, B-3, G-3, G-8
   function 3-4, 4, B-3, **Gl-1**

issues 3-16, 3-31, 3-32, 4-9
location 3-14, **Gl-1**
model 3-2, 3-12, 3-14, 3-22, 9-12, B-2, B-3, G-2, **Gl-1**
needs 1-1, 3-24
objectives 1-5, 3-2, 3-5, 3-14, 3-16, **3-32**, 4-8, 8-11, 9-12, B-3, C-2, **Gl-1**
performance indicators 3-14, 9-12, C-2, **Gl-2**
plans 3-11
priorities 1-5, 3-2, 3-14, **3-24**, C-2, **Gl-2**
system life cycle **1-3, Gl-2**
unit 3-14, 4-2, 4-12, 4-15, C-5, **Gl-2**

C

Capacity requirements 9-10
CASE 2-7, **D, Gl-2**
   tools 2-7, 3, 4, 5, 6, 7, 8, 9, 9-2, C-0, **D**
CASE*Bridge D-2
CASE*Designer B-1, D-1
CASE*Dictionary B-1, D-1
CASE*Generator D-2
CASE*Method **1, Gl-2**
   task list 3-11, 4-7, 4-9, 4-31, 5-7, 5-35, 6-7, 7-7, 8-9
CASE*Project D-2
Central requirements 4-13, 4-18, 5-22
Change 1-1, 1-6, 8-26
   request 5-24, 9-10
Change control 2-1, 3-7, 4-7, 5-6, 5-33, 6-6, 6-15, 7-7, 8-8, **8-13**, 9-2, 9-7, 9-8
   log 4-7, 5-7, 8-9, 8-27, 8-29, 9-2, 9-7, 9-8
Character **Gl-2**
Checklist 2-1, 3-7, 3-12, 4-7, 5-7, 5-33, 6-7, 8-25, 8-29, B-1, **G**
Checkpoint 2-9, 2-10, 4-9, 4-17, 4-28, 5-30, 6-16, 8-22
Cluster analysis 3-15, **10-9**
Code 6-10, 6-12
Coexistence 8-4
Colour 5-11
Column **Gl-2**
Comments 3, 4, 5, 6, 7, 8, 9
Communication 1-2, 6-14, 10-14
   architecture 5-2
   design 5-16, 5-22
   requirement B-4
Company culture 3-8
Competitive edge 1-1
Completeness 3-23

Complexity 5-10
Computer
    program 5-11
    screen 4-14
Conditions 4-18
Configuration management 5-25, 6-9, 7-6, 8-17,
    9-7
Consensus 3-2, 3-17, 3-19, 3-21, 3-31, 3-33
Consistency 3-23, 3-26
Consolidate 3-13, 3-20
Constraints 3-2, 3-8, 3-14, 3-27, 4-2, 4-3, 4-10,
    Gl-2
Consumables 8-18
Control 1-2, 2-9, 4-2, **4-22**, 5-1, **5-18**, 5-22,
    8-23, 8-25
    copy 3-30, 3-33
    information 3, 4, 5, 6, 7, 8, 9
    requirement 4-23, 4-28
    source code 8-13
Control information 3, 4, 5, 6, 7, 8, 9
Conversion 8-4, 8-17
    window 5-30, 8-22
Corporate direction 3-4
Costs 3-25, 3-32, 4-30, 5-34, 11-2, 11-5, B-2,
    B-5
Costings 3-28
Criteria
    assessment 9-12
    audit 5-25, 9-11
Critical factors 4-20
Critical success factors 1-5, 3-2, **3-3**, 3-14,
    3-27, **4-2, 5-2, 6-2, 7-2, 8-2, 9-2**, B-3, **Gl-2**
Cross-checking 1-4
Cut-over 2-6, 4-20, 4-28, 5-2, 8-12, **8-22, 8-24**

D

Data
    administration 7-6
    administrator **2-5**, 3-6, 3-27, 4-6, 4-21, 4-22,
        4-28, 5-6, 5-32, 6-6, 8-8, 8-28
    analysis 4-3
    analyst 2-8
    clean-up 4-21
    converted 8-2
    converting 5-8
    design 5-10
    dictionary **Gl-2**
    item **Gl-2**
    item, derived **Gl-3**

normalization 5-15
    retention 4-24, 5-20
    structure 4-26
    take-on 4-20, 5-2, **8-16**, 8-22
    usage 4-2
Database 2-7, 4-25, 4-26, 4-32, 5-12, 5-14, 6-2,
    D-1, **Gl-2**
    administration 7-6
    administrator **2-6**, 2-8, 2-9, 3-6, 4-6, 4-21,
        4-22, 4-28, 5-6, 5-8, 5-21, 5-32, 5-34, 6-6,
        8-8, 8-12, 8-28
    design 2-8, 3-27, 5-2, 5-12, 5-14, 5-16, 5-22,
        G-15
    designer 2-8, 4-26, 5-15
    distributed **Gl-3**
    first-cut design 5-14
    hierarchic 5-13
    management system 4-10
    network 5-13
    relational 5-13
    sizing 3-27, 4-11, 4-26
    training 8-10
    views 6-8
Dataflow 3-15, C-0, G-12, **Gl-2**
    diagram 1-5, 3-31, 4-12, 4-14, 5-9, **Gl-2**
    diagrammer 3-31, 4-15, 4-19, D-10, **Gl-2**
    input C-14
    output C-15
Datastore C-17, G-12, **Gl-3**
DBMS **Gl-3**
Deadline 2-11, 4-12, 8-4, 8-22
Deliverables 1-4, 2-1, 2-9, 3-2, 3-34
    Analysis 4
    Build 6
    Design 5
    Production 9
    Strategy 3
    Transition 8
    User Documentation 7
Delivery vehicle 5-35, 6-9, **Gl-3**
Denormalization 5-15
Dependencies 2-9, 3-24, 3-27, 3-28, 4-2, 4-18,
    5-7, 5-30, 8-5, 8-5, B-4
Design 1-3, 4-27, **5**, A-2, E-2
    application 5-8, 5-10
    aspects 5-4
    assumptions 4-26, 5-8, 5-10
    checklist G-14, G-15, G-16
    database 5-12, 5-14
    decisions 5-8, 5-10
    issues 4-10, 4-13

Design continued
  report G-16
  stage 4-15, 4-17, 4-20, **5**, D-3, D-5
  stage deliverables 5-7 et seq.
  stage tasks 5-6 et seq.
Designer **2-4**, 2-7, 4-11, 4-12, 4-21, 4-29, 5-3,
    5-7, 5-9, 5-10, 5-19, 5-21, 5-23, 5-25,
    5-33, 5-35, 6-9
  systems 2-4
Desktop publishing 3-35, 7-9, 8-11
Detailed analysis 4-8, 4-28
Detailed requirement 4-12, 4-14, 5-1
Development
  life-cycle **Gl-3**
  manager 2-3
  plan 3-2, 3-28, 3-30, 3-32,
    also see System development plan
Diagrammer 2-7, 3-17, 3-31, 3-35, 4-29, 6-11,
    7-9, also see under specific diagrams or
    diagrammers
Diagramming 4-19, 4-23, 5-33, G-8
Dictionary 2-6, 2-7, 2-8, 3-10, 3-12, 3-14, 3-20,
    3-22, 3-30, 8-11, D-1
Distributed
  database **Gl-3**
  dictionary database 2-7, D-1
  processing **Gl-3**
  requirement 4-12, 4-18, 5-22
Document 2-12
Documentation 3-7, 3-22, 4-3, 4-10, 4-29, 4-30,
    4-32, 5-11, **7**, 8-25, 9-7, 9-9
  hand-over 7-2, 7-10
  online 7-9
  operations 5-19, 5-20, 7-2
  project 8-24
  system 5-11, 6-18, 8-24
  test 5-24
  user 5-11, **7**, 7-8
Domain 3-12, 3-15, G-10, **Gl-3**
  definition 3-13, C-3
Demonstration 8-11
DP manager 2-3
Dragon 3-13

E

Education 8-2, 8-10, 10-14
Enhancements 8-27, 9-8
Entity 3-12, 3-18, 3-24, 4-18, 5-14, C-0, **Gl-3**
  checklist G-7, G-10

  definition 3-13, 4-13, 4-19, C-6
  description 4-18
  external **Gl-4**
  life-cycle diagram 4-12, 5-9
  life history 1-5
  model 1-5, 3-14, 3-32, 4-19, B-5
  reports 3-23
  sub- **Gl-6**
  usage 5-10, 5-15
  volume 4-27, C-7, C-8
Entity relationship
  diagram 3-2, 3-12, **3-14**, 3-17, 3-18, 3-20,
    4-2, 4-12, 5-10, 5-12, 5-15, **Gl-3**
  diagrammer 3-13, 3-15, 3-17, 3-21, 3-23,
    4-15, D-8, **Gl-3**
  model 5-2
Environment 6-5, 8-22, 8-26, G-16
  development 6-8
  test 6-14
Error 6-14, 6-17
  handling 4-22
  log 8-13
  messages 7-2
Estimates 3, 4, 5, 6, 7, 8, 9, 3-9, 3-29, 4-11,
    4-30, 6-8, 6-10, 6-13, B-5
Estimating 3-7, 4-7, 4-13, 4-25, 5-7, 5-29, 6-7,
    6-9, 9-9, 10-3
Event 1-5, 4-18, 5-9, **Gl-3**
  modelling 3-15
Examples 3-13, 3-18
  business 3-16
Exceptions 6-2

F

Fall-back 4-25, 5-30, 8-22
Fault 8-14
  diagnosis 9-7
  log 8-2, 9-6
Feasibility 4-1, 4-18, 5-10, E-2, E-3, E-5
  study 3-24, 3-27
Feedback 3-3, 3-30, 4-8, 4-14, 8-28, E-1, **F**
  agenda 3-17, 3-19
  objective 3-16
  post-implementation 8-28
  session 3-3, 3-4, 3-8, 3-12, **3-16**, **3-18**, **3-20**,
    3-32, E-2
  structure F
Fiche 4-23
Field **Gl-4**

File   2-8, 5-12, 5-14, 5-24, **Gl-4**
   design   5-2, 5-14, 5-16, 5-22
Financial transactions   4-22
Finite capacity   3-29
First-cut   5-9, 5-14
Font   5-11
Format   **Gl-4**
Form
   checklist   G-17
   standard   C-0
Framework   3-2
Fraud   4-22
Frequency   3-24, 4-2, 4-12, 4-14, 4-26, 5-15
Function   3-4, 3-24, **4**, 4-2, 4-14, 4-18, 5-10,
   6-9, 7-8, C-0, **Gl-4**
   analysis   4-3
   business   **Gl-1**
   checklist   G-8, G-11
   common   **Gl-2**
   copy   **Gl-32**
   decomposition   3-15, 3-17, **Gl-4**
   definition   4-13, 4-19, C-11
   dependency   3-15, 4-2, 4-12, 4-14, 4-18, 5-9
   dependency diagramming   3-31, 4-13, 4-19,
     4-15, **Gl-4**
   description   4-12, 4-14, 7-2
   detail   4-2, 4-15, 4-18, 4-20, 5-9
   documentation   4-14, 4-18
   elementary business   4-12, 4-18, 5-8, 5-11,
     Gl-3
   external business   **Gl-4**
   frequencies   4-27, C-12, C-13
   model   3-14, 3-24
   reports   3-17, 3-23
   usage   4-12, 5-2, 5-15
Function hierarchy   1-5, 2-7, **3-2**, 3-12, **3-14**,
   3-16, 3-18, 3-21, 3-32, 3-35, 4-10, 4-12,
   B-6, C-10, **Gl-7**
   definition   3-13
   diagrammer   3-13, 3-15, 3-17, 3-21, 3-23,
     4-15, D-6, **Gl-4**
Function logic   1-5, 3-15, 4-13, 4-14, 4-18, 4-27,
   5-9, 6-13, C-16
   language   **Gl-4**
Fuzzy model   3-32, B-1, **Gl-4**

G

Generator   5-9, 5-25, D-2
Generic modelling   1-5, 3-15

Geographic location   3-14, 4-12, 5-16, C-4
Glossary   3-15, G-9, **Gl-4**
Graphics   D-1
Group interview   3-19
Growth   3-26

H

Hardware   3-24, 4-10, 4-20, 5-2, 5-9, **6-9, 8-18,**
   B-4, G-18
   environment   1-6, 8-10
Help desk   8-2, **8-12**, 8-15, 8-17, 8-22, 8-26, 9-6

I

Ideas   3-3
Impact analysis   4-19, 5-9, 5-15, 6-17, 9-7, 9-9,
   9-13
Implementation stage   D-5
Implementor   2-5
Incident log   8-26
Incremental build   6-2, E-2, E-3, E-4
Incremental development   5-22, 6-8, 6-10, **6-12**,
   Gl-4
Index   5-14, **Gl-4**
   design   G-14
   primary   **Gl-5**
   secondary   **Gl-6**
   utilities   3-27
Industry specialist   3-10, 3-15, 3-27
Information
   gathering   3-12
   requirements   3-4
   storage   4-22, 4-24
Information systems   **Gl-4**
   architecture   3-24, 3-26
   director   2-3
   management   **2-2**, 3-8, 3-10, 4-8, 4-16, 4-30,
     5-34
   personnel   4-12, 4-21, 4-22, 4-24, 5-26, 8-29
   strategy   B-2
Inputs   3, 4, 5, 6, 7, 8, 9
Installation   3-29, 4-20, 5-2, **8-18**, 8-22
   hardware   8-2
   plan   4-20, 8-19
   software   8-2
   standards   5-9, 5-10

Integrity 4-11, 5-24, 8-4
   constraints 4-15
   controls 4-22
   rules C-7, C-8
Interface 3-32, 4-18, 5-11, 8-15
   definitions 4-19
Interview 3-3, 3-7, 3-8, 3-10, **3-12**, 4-3, 4-8,
    4-12, 8-28, 9-13
   environment 3-2, 3-12
   notes 3-15
Interviewee 3-9, 3-10, 3-12, 4-8
Interviewing 3-13, 4-13, 8-29, 9-13, 10-7
Investment 3-29
Irritant 8-26, 9-3
Issues 3-2, 3-18, 3-25, 3-27, 3-31, 3-32, 3-35,
    4-2, 4-7, 4-9, 5-7, 6-7, 6-11, 7-7, 8-8, B-2
Iteration 4-18, 5-9
Iterative development **Gl-4**

J

Jargon 3-12, 3-23
Job
   control language 5-24
   types 2-2

K

Key
   deliverables 3-2, 4-2, 5-2, 6-2, 7-2, 8-2, 9-2
   foreign **Gl-4**
   primary **Gl-5**

L

Language 5-11
Layout 5-10
Lecturing 8-11
Legal
   requirement 4-22, 5-24
   test 4-22
Lexical analyzer 3-23
Life-cycle 1-2, 2-7
Limit 6-2
Location **Gl-4**
Log
   change control 4-7, 5-7, 6-7, 8-9, 8-27, 8-29,
    9-2, 9-7, 9-8

   fault 8-27
   faults 9-6
   incident 8-25, 8-27, 8-29
   operations 9-7
   operations fault 8-2, 8-27, 8-29
Logos 5-11

M

Machine availability 8-22
Maintenance G-18
Man management 3-7, 4-7, 5-7
Management 3-30, 3-32, 8-2
   decision 1-1, 3-31
   style 1-2
Manager 9-13
Manual procedure 4-2, 4-18, 5-2, 5-8, 5-22,
    5-24, 9-6
Matrix 3-14, 4-2, 4-9, 4-12, 5-8, 5-10, 5-14,
    5-16, 6-13, 10-11, B-5, C-0, D-1
   diagrammer 5-15, 9-7, D-11, **Gl-4**
   modelling 3-15
Mechanism **Gl-85**
Meeting 3-6, 3-9, 4-6, 5-6, 6-6, 7-8, 8-8, 8-19
   minutes 3-7, 4-7, 5-7, 6-7, 7-7, 8-9, 9-7
Menu 5-11, D-1
   structure 5-8
Message
   error 7-8
   help 7-8
Methods 3-11
Metrics 6-9
Milestone 2-9, 3-32, 6-10
Mind map 2-11
Minutes 3-7, 4-7, 5-7, 6-7, 7-7, 8-9, 9-7
Model 3-4, 3-14
Modelling 1-5, 3-13, 3-21, 4-13, 9-13
Models, generic 1-5
Module 4-15, 5-2, 5-8, **5-10**, 5-22, C-21, **Gl-5**
   definition 5-9, 6-7, G-15
   design 5-2, 5-9, 5-22
   designer 5-14
   linkages 5-2
   network **Gl-5**
   specification 5-10, 5-19, 5-20, 5-22
   structure 4-26
Monitor progress 3-8, 4-6, 5-6, 6-6, 7-6, 8-8
Monitoring 5-16, 9-11, 9-13
Motivation 2-9

N

Naming conventions 4-10
Network 6-14, **Gl-5**
   administrator 2-6
   analyst 2-6
   architecture 5-16, 8-19
   control procedure 8-19
   controller 2-6
   design 5-16, 5-22
   designer 5-17
   diagram 2-9, 3-5, 4-5, 5-5, 6-5, 7-5, 8-5, 9-5
Node 5-16
Normalization 5-15, **Gl-5**
Notes 3, 4, 5, 6, 7, 8, 9

O

Objectives 1-1, 1-5, **3-1**, 3-12, 3-18, 3-20, 3-32,
   4-1, 5-1, 6-1, 7-1, 8-1, 9-1, B-2
Operating system environment 1-6
Operation **Gl-5**
   hierarchy C-10
Operational requirement 5-30
Operations
   fault log 8-27, 8-29
   manager 2-3
   staff **2-6**, 3-6, 4-6, 4-21, 4-25, 4-28, 5-6,
     5-19, 5-21, 5-30, 5-32, 6-6, 7-2, 7-4, 7-6,
     7-11, 7-12, 8-2, 8-5, 8-8, 8-12, 8-27, 8-28,
     9-2, 9-7, 9-11
Operator 2-6
ORACLE
   CASE tools D
   RDBMS **Gl-5**
Organization 4-10, 4-15, 4-28, 5-32, 8-4, G-4,
   G-6
   chart 3-9, 3-11
   structure 4-12
Outcomes 3, 4, 5, 6, 7, 8, 9
   other 3, 4, 5, 6, 7, 8, 9

P

Packages 3-25, 5-14, 10-18
Paper, weight of 5-11
Parallel run 4-20, 8-21
Peer group 3-14, 3-26
People 1-2, 1-4, 2-12

Performance 2-6, 3-25, 3-26, **4-26**, 5-11, 5-14,
   5-16, 5-24, 6-2, 6-15, 8-2, **9-10**, E-2, E-3,
   E-5
   benchmark 8-21
   expectations 4-2, 4-10, 4-26
   indicators 3-14, 3-27
   measures 3-18, 3-20
   measuring 9-11
   predictions 4-11
Phase 3-15, 3-28, **Gl-95**
Phasing B-4
Picture 5-11
Plan 2-4, 2-9, 3-2, 3-6, **3-10**, 3-27, 4-6, 4-16,
   5-6, 6-6, 6-18, 8-8
   capacity 5-15, 5-17
   cut-over 4-20, 4-30, 5-29, 5-30, 6-18, 8-23,
     8-24
   data take-on 4-20, 4-30, 5-29, 6-18, 8-17
   delivery and acceptance 4-20, 4-30, 5-29,
     6-18, 8-12, 8-15
   development B-4
   exception test 5-24
   installation 4-20, 4-30, 5-16, 5-29, 5-30,
     6-18, 8-19
   quality 2-12, 3-11, **11**
   strategy study 3-10
   system development 3-2, **3-28**, 4-2, 4-7, 4-9,
     4-11, 4-17, 4-31, 5-2, 5-7, 5-35, 6-7, 6-9,
     7-7, 7-13, 8-9
   system test 5-2, 5-19, 5-21, 5-24, 5-26, 6-15
   test 6-11, 6-12
   training 4-20, 4-30, 5-29, 6-18, 8-10
Planning 2-1, 4-9, 4-21, 4-31, 5-29, 5-35, 9-9,
   10-1, 10-2
   disaster 5-21
   matrix 10-11
Policy 1-5
Politics 2-11
Presentation 3-32, 10-12
   agenda 3-33
   material 3-35
   structuring 3-17, 3-31
   techniques 3-19, 3-31
Priorities 1-5, 3-14, 3-27, **Gl-5**
Problems 3-25
Procedures
   back-up 5-10
   change control 5-34
   control 5-10
   exception 5-10
   reconciliation 5-10

Procedures continued
 recovery 5-10
 special 5-10
 terminal sign-on/sign off 5-10
 update 5-10
 validation 5-10
Process **Gl-95**
 hierarchy C-10
Processing 4-12, 5-10
 cycles 4-13
 distributed **Gl-3**
 requirement 4-18
Processor 5-16
Production 1-3, **9**, A-2, D-3, E-2
 stage deliverables 9-7 et seq.
 stage tasks 9-6 et seq.
Program 2-5, 2-9, 6-4, 6-10, **6-12**, G-15, **Gl-5**
 conversion 8-16
 design 6-2, 6-11, 6-13
 specification 2-4, 4-30, 5-1, 5-2, **5-22**, 6-8, 6-11, 6-13
Programmer **2-5**, 2-8, 5-7, 5-23, 5-25, 5-33, 5-35, 6-3, 6-4, 6-7, 6-9, **6-11**, 6-13, 6-15, 7-7, 8-9, 8-17, 8-19, 8-21, 8-23, 8-25, 8-27
 analyst 2-4, 2-5
 chief 2-4
 senior 2-4, 2-5, 6-11
Progress
 meeting 3-6, 4-6, 5-6, 6-6, 7-6, 8-8
 reporting 3-7, 4-7, 5-7, 6-7, 7-7, 8-9
Project **2**, 2-1, 2-9, 2-11, 2-12, 3-34, 4-8, 4-10, 4-28, **10**
 administration 3-6, 4-6, 5-6, 6-6, 7-6, 8-8
 book 3-11
 constraints 3-8
 control 2-1, 2-4, 3-7, 3-11, 3-29, 4-7, 4-31, 5-7, 5-29, 5-35, 6-7, 6-9, 7-7, 8-9, **10**
 control documentation 8-25
 deliverables 3-8
 leader **2-4**, 3-7, 3-9, 3-11, 3-12, 3-14, 3-16, 3-18, 3-21, 3-22, 3-26, 3-29, 3-31, 3-33, 3-35, 4-7, 4-9, 4-11, 4-17, 4-19, 4-21, 4-23, 4-25, 4-29, 4-31, 5-7, 5-29, 5-33, 5-35, 6-7, 6-9, 6-17, 6-19, 7-7, 7-9, 7-11, 7-13, 8-9, 8-13, 8-23, 8-25, 8-26, 8-29, 9-13, 10-17
 management 3-6, 3-8, 4-6, 5-6, 6-6, 7-6, 8-8, **10**
 manager 2-3, 2-4, 2-12
 objectives 3-8, 10-1, 10-2
 pilot 10-17

plan 2-12, 3-36
planning 2-4, 3-11, 3-29, 4-9, 10-1, 10-2
quality 3-29
size 3-9, 10-13, 10-15
starting point 10-17
team 2-4, 8-13, 8-15, 8-16, 8-28
Protocols 5-16
Prototyping 3-19, 4-14, 4-18, 5-2, **5-9**, 5-11, 5-15, 5-22, 5-33, 6-2, 10-17, **E**, **Gl-5**

Q

Quality 11-1, 11-2
 approach 11-3
 assurance 3, 4, 5, 6, 7, 8, 9, **2-12**, 3-6, 3-10, 3-23, 4-6, 4-8, 4-29, 5-6, 6-6, 7-6, 8-8, 8-29, **11**
 assurance report 4-28
 assurance results 3-6, 4-6, 4-28, 5-7, 5-33, 6-7
 checks 2-12
 control 2-11, 3-11, 3-28
 plan 2-12, 11-4, 11-7, 11-8
Query
 screen 5-19, 6-17, 8-27, 9-7
 -only database 8-3
Questionnaire 3-26, 8-11
Quick build 6-1, **Gl-5**

R

RDBMS **Gl-5**
Recommendation 3-2, 3-18, **3-24**, **3-26**, 3-29, 3-32, 8-28, 9-12, B-2, G-9
Reconciliation total 4-22
Record **Gl-5**
 type **Gl-5**
Recovery 5-2, **5-20**, 5-22, 5-24
 need 4-2, 5-20
 requirement 4-24, 5-17
Referential integrity 5-18
Regression 5-24, 8-21, 9-7
Relation **Gl-5**
Relationship 3-22, 4-18, 5-15, G-8, G-10, **Gl-6**
Reliability 9-10

Report   3-22, 3-31, **3-32, 3-34**, 4-17, 4-18, 4-23, 4-29, 5-2, 5-23, 6-17, 7-9, 7-11, 8-27, 9-7, G-17
  analysis   G-13
  design   G-16
  fault   9-2, 9-7
  post-implementation review   8-2, 8-29
  stage-end   4-31, 5-35
  strategy study   B, G-9
  verbal   3-30, 3-34
  writers   E-2
  writing   3-35, 4-31, 5-35, 8-29
Reporting   3-6, 4-6, 5-6, 6-6, 7-6, 8-8
Repository   2-6, 2-7, D-1
Requirement   1-2, 4-3, 4-4, 5-3, 9-2, E-2, E-3, E-5
Resources   2-1, 3-28, 3, 4, 5, 6, 7, 8, 9
  financial   2-11
  human   2-11
  management   10-19
  physical   2-11
  statement   3-2
  utilization   4-2
Response   C-11
Reverse engineering   4-13, 4-15
Review, post-implementation   8-28, 11-9
Risk
  analysis   2-13
  containment   10-4
  control   2-11
Role   2-2, 2-3, 2-4, 2-5, 2-6, F-2
Row   **Gl-16**
Rules of thumb   4-27, 10-3

S

S.W.O.T.   3-27
Schedule   3-28
Scheduling   2-9, 3-29
Schema   **Gl-6**
  logical   5-2, 5-15
  physical   5-2, 5-15
  sub-   **Gl-6**
Scope   **3-8**, 3-28, 4-8, 4-18, 4-28, 4-30
Screen   4-18, 5-2, 5-23
  dialogue   5-8
  painting   E-2
Screen painter   5-9, 6-11
Script   5-24
Secretary   3-7, 3-35, 4-7, 5-7

Security   2-5, 4-10, 5-18, 8-22
  requirement   4-22
Sequence   4-18
Service   9-2
  levels   4-15, 5-1, 9-2, 9-6, 9-10
  operational   9-6
Sign-off   2-12, 4-8
Simulation   8-21
Sizing   3-26, 4-2, **4-26**, 4-28, 5-14
Software   3-24, 6-14, 8-10, B-4
  monitoring   9-11
  package   10-18
  system   6-9, 8-18
Solution   3-32, 4-28, 8-8
Specification   **4-18**, 4-25, 5-2, 5-8, 5-10
Spelling   3-23
Spreadsheet   5-17
Staff
  operation – see Operations
  performance   3-6, 4-6, 5-6, 6-6, 7-6, 8-8
  roles   5-28
  support   9-2, 9-7, 9-9
  technical   **2-6**, 4-25, 4-28, 5-6, 5-8, 5-32, 6-6, 6-9, 8-19, 8-21, 8-23, 8-25, 8-27, 9-11
Stage   1-3, 2-9, **Gl-6**
  Analysis   4
  Build   6
  Design   5
  Production   9
  Strategy   3
  Transition   8
  User Documentation   7
Standard
  deliverables   1-4
  forms   C
  layout   5-22
  strategy report   B
  style   5-22
Standards   1-4, 2-12, 3-23, 3-29, **4-10**, 5-9, 6-10, 7-6, 7-9, 7-11, 7-13, 8-28
  audit   5-19
  documentation   7-7
  installation   4-22, 5-18, 5-20
  legal   5-19
  look and feel   4-18, 4-28, 6-4, 6-8, 7-9
  programmimg   6-8
  security   5-19
State analysis   1-5
State transition
  diagram   4-2, 4-13, 4-14, 5-9, **Gl-6**
  diagramming   4-15, 4-19

Statistics 5-17
  performance 9-2, 9-10
  system 9-13
Steering group 2-1, 3-6, 4-6, 5-6, 6-6, 7-7, 8-8
Storage 5-14
Storyboard 4-18, 5-8, E-2, **Gl-6**
Strategy 1-3, **3**, 3-5, 3-30, 3-32, 10-16, A-1,
    E-1, E-2, F-1
  objective 3-2
  recommendations 3-15
  report 3-27, 3-30, 3-32, 3-35, 4-9, 4-11, **B**,
    G-9
  stage 2-9, **3**, D-3, D-4
  stage, deliverables 3-7 et seq.
  stage, tasks 3-6 et seq.
  study 3-18, 9-12
  study checklist G-7, G-8, G-9
  transition 4-30, **5-28, 5-30**, 5-34, 6-2
Style 4-2, 4-10, 4-14, 5-8, 8-4
Sub-type **Gl-6**
Subject area 3-16, 3-32
Success unit 5-11, **Gl-6**
Super-type **Gl-61**
Supplier 3-6, 4-6, 4-28, 5-6, 5-32, 8-19
Support
  manager 2-3
  facilities 8-13, 8-15, 8-17, 8-27
Synonym 3-12, 3-14, 3-23
System **1-1**, 4-28, **Gl-6**
  architect 2-8, 3-27
  architecture 3-2, **3-24**, 3-26, 3-29, 3-30,
    3-32, 4-32, 5-2, 5-8, G-14
  audit 9-2, 9-12
  boundary 3-2, 3-24, 3-27, 4-13, G-9
  checklist G-2, G-3, G-4, G-5, G-6
  controls 4-15
  deliverables 3, 4, 5, 6, 7, 8, 9
  development 1-1, 3-35
  development plan 3-28, 4-2, 4-7, 4-9, 4-11,
    4-17, 4-31, 5-2, 5-7, 5-35, 6-7, 6-9, 7-7,
    7-13, 8-9, G-4
  documentation 3-27, 6-18, 8-2, 8-11, 8-25,
    9-9
  needs 3-4, 3-25
  objectives 3-25
  operational 8-21, 8-23, 8-25
  overview G-2
  requirement 5-32
  sizing 3-27
  software 4-21
  structure G-4

support 8-27
test 6-2, 6-14
test plan 5-2
Systems
  analyst 2-3, 2-7
  existing 3-4, 3-25, 5-8
  manager 2-3

T

Table 2-8, 5-18, C-22, **Gl-6**
  design G-14
Tasks 1-3, 2-9, 2-12, **Gl-6**
  Analysis 4
  Build 6
  Design 5
  list of 3-5, 4-5, 5-5, 6-5, 7-4, 8-5, 9-4
  prevention 11-5
  Production 9
  safeguarding 11-6
  Strategy 3
  summary of A
  Transition 8
  User Documentation 7
Team 2-9, 2-12, 8-5, 8-16
  briefing 3-11
  meeting 4-6, 5-6, 6-6, 8-9
  member 3-7, 7-11
  orientation D-14
Technical
  staff – see Staff
  services manager 2-3
  writing 7-9, 7-11
Techniques 2-2, 3, 4, 5, 6, 7, 8, 9
Technology 1-1, 1-2, 3-4, 3-24, 4-10
Terminal 8-11
  characteristics 5-17
Terminology 3-15
  definition 3-13, 3-21
Terms of reference 3-6, **3-8,** 3-24, 3-27, 3-28,
    3-30, 4-2, 4-7, 4-12, **4-16, 4-28**, 5-7, 5-32,
    6-7, 7-7, 8-9, 8-25, B-1, G-7
Test
  acceptance 4-20, 8-2, 8-4, 8-12, **8-14**
  batch 6-14
  harness 5-25, 6-13
  link 6-12
  notes 4-19, 5-24
  regression 9-6, 9-8
  results 6-16

Test continued
  results log 8-13
  script 6-14
  system 5-24, 6-14
  unit 6-10, 6-12
  user acceptance 8-12
Testing 5-24, 5-26, 8-13, 8-19
  acceptance 8-12
  disaster 8-21
  performance 8-12
  recovery 8-21
  regression 8-21, 9-7
  software 5-25
  volume 8-12
Textual attributes 4-26
Time scheduling 3-29
Timescales 3-9, 4-2, 10-3
Timesheet 3-7, 4-7, 5-7, 6-7, 7-7, 8-9
Timings 8-22, 9-11
Tools 2-7, 3, 4, 5, 6, 7, 8, 9
Top-down 1-4, 3-3
Trainer 8-11
Training 1-2, 1-6, 2-2, 3-27, 4-20, 5-2, **5-28**, 8-2, **8-10**, 8-29, 9-8, 10-14
  schedule 8-10
Transaction 4-18
  processing monitor 4-10
Transition 1-3, 3-32, 4-2, 4-3, 4-10, 6-18, **8**, A-2, G-12
  incremental approach 8-6
  issues 3-24, 4-12, 4-14
  stage **8**, D-3
  stage deliverables 8-9 et seq.
  stage tasks 8-8 et seq.
  strategy 4-20, 4-28, 4-31, 4-32, 5-2, **5-28**
Trials 8-20
Trigger 5-9, **Gl-6**
Tuning 5-15, 6-10, 9-11
Tuple **Gl-6**
Tutorial 7-2, 8-11, 7-9
Typists 3-23

U

Unique identifier G-11, **Gl-6**
Usability 5-10, E-3, E-5
User **2-3**, 3-9, 3-13, 3-16, 3-18, 3-24, 3-33, 3-36, 4-3, 4-7, 4-8, 4-11, 4-19, 4-21, 4-25, 4-30, 5-7, 5-9, 5-11, 5-19, 5-21, 5-25, 5-29, 5-31, 5-33, 5-35, 6-4, 6-7, 6-13, 6-15, 6-19, 7-2, 7-6, 7-9, 7-12, 8-2, 8-4, 8-8, 8-11, 8-12, 8-15, 8-17, 8-19, 8-23, 8-25, 8-27, 8-28, 9-6, 9-8, 9-13, G-13
  approval 8-17
  class 5-8, 5-11
  group 3-6, 4-6, 5-6, 6-6, 8-8
  group name C-12, C-13
  interface 5-8
  management 2-3, 9-13
  manual 4-15, 5-2, 5-9, 5-11, 7-9, 8-11, 8-15
  request 9-8
  sponsoring **2-3**, 3-9, 3-10, 3-12, 3-30, 4-7, 4-9, 4-11, 4-16, 4-29, 4-31, 5-29, 5-33, 5-35, 6-11, 6-17, 6-19, 7-13, 8-13, 8-23, 8-25
User Documentation 1-3, 4-15, **7**, 9-9, A-2
  stage **7**, D-3
  stage deliverables 7-7 et seq.
  stage tasks 7-6 et seq.
Utilities 3-27, 4-27, 5-15

V

Values 4-15
Vendor 3-27
Verbal presentation 3-30
Version 5-26, 7-6, 8-21
  control **Gl-6**
Video equipment 8-11
View 5-14, 7-9, G-15, **Gl-7**
Visual aids 3-17, 3-19, 3-20, 3-31, 3-33, 8-11
Volumes 3-24, 4-2, 4-12, 4-15, 4-26, 5-15, 8-16, 9-10
Volumetrics 3-24, 3-26, 4-2

W

Walkthrough 7-13
  structured 5-8, 6-11
Windows 8-5, 8-8
Word processor 7-9
Work
  breakdown 10-2
  load 9-10
Workbench 3-15
Working pattern 5-11
Working style requirement 4-2, 4-13, 5-9, **Gl-7**
Workstation 2-7, D-1, D-14